MW01097985

The Gnostic

A Journal of Gnosticism, Western Esotericism and Spirituality

Issue 5

Copyright Page and Acknowledgments

The Gnostic 5, Late 2011.

Photographs of Nick Cave are by David Shankbone, licensed under Creative Commons. Visit David's blog at http://blog.shankbone.org

Opinions expressed are those of the contributors and not necessarily those of the publisher.

Editor: Andrew Phillip Smith

Published by Bardic Press
71 Kenilworth Park
Dublin 6W
Ireland.

ISBN: 978-1-906834-15-9

Thanks to the contributors and all others who have made this possible, including but not limited to: Tessa Finn, David Shankbone

The Gnostic

A Journal of Gnosticism, Western Esotericism and Spirituality

Issue 5

Stevan Davies, Gary Lachmann, Patrick
Harpur, Nicholas Baker-Brian, Scott
Finch, Miguel Conner, Sean Martin,
Sorita D'Este, Jeffrey Kupperman, Dean
Wilson, Jordan Bloom, et al

Edited by Andrew Phillip Smith

Bardic Press
Dublin 2011

Contents

Editorial

From the Mouth of the Demiurge

Well, here it is. Months in the making, years in the delaying, I proudly present to you the latest issue of *The Gnostic*, latest in more ways than one. Why didn't this issue come out six months ago? A host of unprecedented and unpredictable obstacles prevented publication. Life changes and loss leaders, one stumbling block after another, making me a laughingstock among men. I'd blame the archons if I believed in them. Especially the archons of procrastination that lead us to wait for the perfect circumstances to complete something.

We have the usual smorgasbord of articles, interviews, reviews and other material. This issue is particularly well-served with a variety of interviews: Miguel Conner interviewed Gary Lachman on Hermes Trismegistus and I had the pleasure of interviewing scholar Nicholas Baker-Brian on the intricacies of Manichaeism and Patrick Harpur, currently one of my very favourite authors, on the elusive world of the soul.

Scott Finch returns with another superb cover and an excerpt from his graphic novel A Little World Cunningly Made, which offers the best version of the Gnostic myth since the fourth century.

The variety continues with Jordan Bloom's brilliant look at the influence of Christianity on the work of Nick Cave, Sorita d'Este's investigation into the roots of the Wiccan Great Rite and Jeffrey Kupperman's examination of Marsilio Ficino.

Previous contributor Dean Wilson now has his own publishing company and is the author of *Enochian Magic In Theory*. His article here looks at the spooky similarities between Gnosticism and the Enochian material communicated to John Dee. Sean Martin takes a look at *A Voyage to Arcurus* and promises us further insight into the world of David Lindsay.

Meanwhile there are those pesky pieces by yours truly that have contributed so much to the delay in the publication of this issue. Somehow Darwin pops up in three places. What's going on there?

However, pride of place must be given to Stevan Davies' article on the Odes of Solomon and its implications for the origins of Christianity. This is a brilliant and controversial piece, the culmination of ideas that Steve has been developing for years.

Jeremy Puma wasn't able to put together a column for this issue, but he has a good excuse. He is the proud father of a baby daughter. Congratulations also to Miguel Conner, who also has a daughter, a second to add to his collection. By the time this issue goes to press, I believe each of them will be finishing university.

I still plan to put out issue 6 but, realistically, don't expect to see it till 2013. (I won't even bother to include the obligatory "if we survive 2012 that is.")

Comments or proposed contributions are, as always, welcome. Please email them to andrew@bardic-press.com or post them to

Andrew Phillip Smith/The Gnostic

71 Kenilworth Park

Dublin 6W

Ireland.

Miguel Conner

An Interview with Gary Lachman

MC: You are known primarily as a scholar of occultism in modern times. What exactly inspired you to write a book on such an ancient figure?

GL: I had written a book called *Politics and the Occult.* Part of that book dealt with understanding some of the political implications of a school of contemporary esoteric or spiritual thought called the Traditionalists—René Guenon and Frithjof Schuon and Julius Evola and some other figures. The theme uniting these different writers and thinkers is that there was some sort of primordial tradition, some primordial knowledge or wisdom or ancient teaching that was revealed to mankind in the dim, dark past. This primordial tradition, which became known as the perennial philosophy or the pristine theology, was this initial primary revelation of the truth, and then in time it later got filtered down and separated into all the different religions that we know: Christianity, Judaism, Buddhism, Hinduism, Islam and so on. But uniting all of them was the idea that there was some sort of ancient teaching which was the central one from which they all came. This idea seems to have originated with the figure called Hermes Trismegistus, Thrice-Greatest Hermes. Hermes Great-Great-Great. (Tony the Tiger used to say that about Frosties Flakes when I was a kid.)

So I just became very interested in this character and this whole idea. Anyone who is interested in the occult and esotericism and the inner tradition of the West and all these teachings, they know who Hermes Trismegistus is. He's the character who is supposed to be one of the great creators of magic and writing and thinking and civilization and so on. I became interested in who this character was, because when you look into it you realise that for a great many centuries he was a revered figure. At certain times he was considered to be an actual real person, at other times a God, at other times a half-human god, a magician, and so on and so on. But in the early 1600s it was found out that actually there was no figure like this at all, he was more like an invention of certain spiritual groups and devotees in the first and second centuries following Christ, who invented this character. So you can see in the history of ideas suddenly he loses credibility and the Hermetic teachings and the Hermetic philosophy and the character of Hermes Trismegistus himself suddenly drops down to be seen as mere superstition. And the whole school of Hermeticism, that for many years has been considered prestigious and up there with Plato and Jesus and Moses and all of the other big hitters of western civilization at the time, he becomes a kind of charlatan figure, this fool, in some ways. His followers are seen to be mere followers of superstition, and that's where the whole esoteric tradition goes underground. So I just became fascinated with the whole shift in our thought. It's almost as if someone like Einstein, let's say, or Stephen Hawking, the smartest man in the world, who can say important things about everything, it's as if 200 years from now people figure out they were completely wrong. Or even decided they didn't exist and suddenly their street cred collapses down to nothing. I just was fascinated with that whole shift because in may ways our modern world, our modern times, begins at the same time that this Hermetic teaching and this figure of Hermes Trismegistus goes into eclipse.

MC: As your book points out, Hermes was respected and at least accepted in early Christendom, in the Byzantine Empire, in medieval times. How exactly does this pagan figure become so much a part of the pantheon with the other luminaries in the Christian dispensation? How did he get away with it?

GL: Well, there were various different thinkers and philosophers and theologians in the Christian tradition, going back to Clement of Alexandria, of the early church father, going up into the Renaissance, people like Marsilio Ficino and Pico della Mirandola and other who wanted to somehow find a place for the Hermetic philosophy within Christianity, within Christian philosophical thinking, and they all wanted to find a place for Plato. So they basically wanted to find a place for the Greek philosophers and what were known at the time as pagan philosophers. When the church, or the church up into the Renaissance, refers to pagans, it's not talking about people here in England who go out into the forest

MC: [laughter]

GL: I'm not in any way dismissing them, but it's not that kind of wicker man paganism, it's not nature mysticism, it's the Greek neoplatonic philosophy, that they considered pagan. And there were many within the church who were very intelligent thinkers, who realised there was much of value in that. People like Plato were seen to be precursors of Christianity. There was no doubt that Christianity and Christ were the culmination, the final product of dialectic, let's say. But earlier than that you have these pagan thinkers who, in abstract terms or logical terms, seem to be saying the same thing. So you find thinkers in this period seeing some of the parallels between the Hermetic, platonic philosophies and some of the things in Christianity. And even at times during the Renaissance when there were Christian thinkers advocating the inclusion of figures like Hermes Trismegistus within the canon as being one of

the prophets, let's say, of Christ. So this is to suggest how important this figure of Hermes Trismegistus was, and also how at a certain time in the west, in Christianity, there was a possibility when what we today see as the strange, woo-woo, weird world of the occult, and mysticism and esotericism was actually being promoted as something that could be an active living part of the whole western consciousness.

MC: Yeah, and he even survived the barbed words of Augustine, didn't he?

GL: Yeah, well, Augustine took argument with the Hermetic philosophy and Hermes Trismegistus. He wasn't aware of the Corpus Hermeticum, but he did know of a book called the Asclepius, one of the longer Hermetic books. What Augustine didn't like is that in the Asclepius there's instructions on how to animate statues, this notion of bringing the god down, the god-force down, and fusing it into these figures that were made, and these become animated. This was something that Augustine thought was something that I guess we would consider something like Satanic or black magic. At the same time he also recognised, even by arguing against, he recognised the importance of this character Hermes Trismegistus, so again you have people like Augustine, Clement of Alexandria and other in the Church recognising how important this figure is, and then in the early 1600s it becomes clear that actually he's not what everybody thought he was. It would be the equivalent today, let's say somebody figured out the sort of thing that goes on with the *Da Vinci Code*, this whole idea that what we thought the case turned out not to be, and the effect this has on western consciousness in general.

MC: In your research, Gary, and obviously most conservative scholars would say that Hermeticism began around the second century after Christ. What do you think are the historical origins for Hermeticism?

GL: I think that term, Hermeticism, starts up around then or a little bit earlier. In that sense I think that's a correct assessment. But the ideas, the knowledge, the wisdom that is being transmitted in Hermeticism, as you say, probably goes back earlier. One of the things I try to do in the book is answer my own question: What is this Egyptian wisdom? You hear stories of Plato going to school in Egypt, and Pythagoras beforehand, and the whole idea that for everybody back then it had to be part of their curriculum vitae that they went to Egypt and sat at the foot of the priests there and learned something, much like today people go backpacking off into some third world country in search of the indigenous shamans or whatever, or in the 60s or 70s going out to India to meet the gurus there. So there may have been something like that going on then, and it got me thinking: well, what is this Egyptian wisdom you hear so much about in books about magic and the occult and esotericism and so on? And I speculate on a few different things, on what it might be. I draw on the work of a very brilliant writer names Jeremy Naydler who has this notion of Egyptian shamanism in the ancient Egyptian time, the priests performed rituals or participated in ceremonies that are very much like what we understand shamanistic practices to be, and the central theme around this is that the Egyptians had a very complex notion of the soul, of the human being—its eight parts—and there's something particular that relates to this. It's something called the *akh* and the *akh* is this kind of immortal, immaterial, spiritual undying essence that one can come to awareness of oneself through certain rituals and practices. Naydler presents the idea that the *Egyptian Book of the Dead*, which most mainstream Egyptologists

see as basically a funerary text, something to be read over the dead body of the mummy. And Naydler says, yes, it was used like that but it was also equally used as a kind of instruction book, a kind of Rough Guide to experiencing the underworld, what the Egyptians called the *Duat*, while still alive, without having to physically die. This, Naydler argues, is an idea that gets picked up by Plato, or appears in Plato, the whole notion that Socrates argues in the *Phaedo* and also the *Apologia*, the notion that philosophy is a kind of discipline in which you practise dying. You learn how to die to the physical, external world while still alive in order to awaken what the Hermeticists call Nous, Mind, this kind of immortal, immaterial, universal mind that we all participate in. So looking at some of the things that Naydler talks about, also looking at some of the work of René Schwaller de Lubicz, his ideas about what he called *symbolique*, which was what he thought was happening with Egyptian hieroglyphics, in the sense that the kind of figures that the hieroglyphics are composed of, they serve two purposes: they denoted things, they pointed to things as language does, this particular figure meant that sort of thing, but they also evoked, they triggered this broader consciousness that de Lubicz called the intelligence of the heart, where you have intuitive, participatory experience of what Egyptians called the *neters*. So looking at that, comparing those sorts of ideas with those things that are in the Corpus Hermeticum, this collection of Hermetic writings that more than likely were written in the first few centuries after Christ and later resurfaced a thousand years or so later, in the Renaissance, looking at some of the things that are talked about in there, I see some parallels. So the reason I'm getting into this is to suggest that, yes, even though these texts were written in the first, second, third century after Christ, they seem to look back to or to be informed by metaphysical, psychological, esoteric ideas that go much further back and seem to have an Egyptian origin.

MC: Very interesting Gary, because it was Valentinus who called Gnosis "the knowledge of the heart" and you mentioned that the Egyptians called it the intelligence of the heart. You also call Hermeticism the religion of the mind. You're basically saying that to the Hermetics, who are maybe the closest bridge we have to the really alien consciousness of the Egyptians, which we will probably never be able to understand—and the Greeks wanted to understand—but as a way of completely gaining the access of our lower and higher mind and expanding our consciousness to its extremes, right?

GL: Well, yes, the central idea in Hermeticism is the notion of Gnosis. We know Gnosis is shared with another philosophical-spiritual school of the time called the Gnostics and Gnosticism, but they both were very much centred on this idea, and it's the Greek word for knowledge. For the Hermeticists this Gnosis was the experience of the Nous, the experience of the universal mind, that is the fundamental really real thing in existence is this mind and we participate in it, it's all around us. The Hermeticists have this notion they call the One or the All, which when you think about it makes a lot of sense, because the only one that we could conceive of in the world that we live in would have to be the entire world itself. Within that collection of things, basically everything, there's multiplicity, there's diversity, there's all different sorts of things. So for us to in any way comprehend the one it would have to at the same time mean comprehending the All and for the Hermeticists this is the basic kind of movement or direction for their spiritual practices and for their meditative work. In the

book I try to relate it to this notion that starts up in the early twentieth century called cosmic consciousness. Now we know in the sixties this phrase, cosmic consciousness, got picked up and used for anything that was groovy. In the early 1900s, 1901 I think, a fellow named Richard Maurice Bucke, who was a psychiatrist, a psychologist, in Canada, he wrote a book called *Cosmic Consciousness* in which he argues that the human race was evolving into this wider, deeper, more profound, more expanded form of consciousness, and he traces throughout history different examples of that: Buddha, Christ, lots of other sorts of people that are in there. And he himself talks about an experience he had. Now what struck me about this was the way Bucke described his own experience of cosmic consciousness and the descriptions of it with others, especially people who read Bucke's book, one was William James, who experimented with nitrous oxide and had other mystical experiences, and another was P.D. Ouspensky who is best known for being Gurdjieff's brightest student but was a very important insightful thinker in his own right. He, having read Bucke and also having read William James' *The Variety of Religious Experience*, he too experimented with nitrous oxide and had very similar experiences. And this cosmic consciousness, the way they all describe it, suddenly they become aware of everything going on around them in very minute and vivid detail. They all describe it as this flood of information. In some ways there's nothing very mystical about it, it's not this kind of supernatural thing, it's not a visitation by Christ or Buddha or Krishna or anything like that, it's basically becoming aware of a huge amount of facts, of knowledge—too much actually for any of them to handle at any one time. I was struck by the way William James and Ouspensky described their experiences and how it seemed to relate and parallel the way Gnosis is described in the Hermetic books. That was exciting for me because it made me feel that because these guys back in the second, third century talking about their experiences and then you have these modern accounts of the same sort of thing. So I'm always very thrilled when

I find parallels and similar accounts about our inner world and our inner experiences coming from different sources because that reaffirms my notion that we're talking about something real. These are from different times in history, different cultures, totally different backgrounds, but the experience is very similar. Again, as you say, it has to do with this notion of the sense of mind.

MC: You give plenty of really great examples. For examples, Herman Hesse and Aldous Huxley. It seems the point is, whatever you need to do to get to that state of consciousness, go ahead and do it. We really don't know what the rituals were of the ancient Hermetics, do we?

GL: No. There's some speculation. It's probably easier for us now, because we can go and get ayahuasca or mescaline. Aldous Huxley took mescaline. Herman Hesse's experience is different in that he's describing the experiences of his character Harry Holler in his novel *Steppenwolf*. Steppenwolf is this middle-aged intellectual who has basically given up on life and the novel is basically

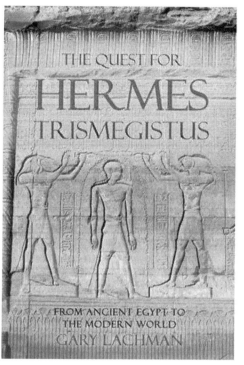

him avoiding going home, because if he goes home he's going to slit his throat. So he tries to keep himself away from the razor. But he does have these moments when suddenly this tension that he's living under and this excruciating boredom relaxes and he has experience of being somehow vividly aware of other times in his life. The same sort of thing happens in *Remembrance of Things Past*, the huge novel by Marcel Proust. Famously the character in the novel tastes a bit of biscuit or cake dipped in this tea and it suddenly reminds him of his childhood, and he's thrown back into this other time, and it's not as if he knows, oh yes, I'm here in this place when I was ten years old, it's as if he's there again, it's living, it's alive. It's 3D as, sadly, most movies are today. This relates too to this Hermetic notion of becoming God. To me, one of the most tremendously thrilling passages in the Hermetic books is one in which—usually it's either Nous talking to Hermes, or it's Hermes talking to his disciples, his students—this is one of the early forms of the teacher student, guru-chela structure. He's saying that if you want to experience Gnosis, if you want to know God, if you want to become like God, and that means to exist in all points of your life, at the same time be the foetus in the womb, be rotting in the grave, be the young man, be the mature man, but also be everything else. There's this tremendous sense of participating in everything, hence this notion of cosmic consciousness. And it's something that Hesse's character Harry Haller and Proust's character in his novel, it's something that they both experience and again it's interesting for me because neither Hesse nor Proust are making any ostensible references to the Hermetic teaching, but the phenomenology of the experience they're describing is similar, if not exactly the same as the kind of thing that the Hermetic books are advising the students to participate. Again, it's a religion of the mind. It is a kind of religion in that there's a belief in a spiritual reality beyond the material, but it doesn't depend on any particular kind of rites or hierarchy or structure or ritual or whatever. It's basically coming to understand your own mind, the potentials of your own consciousness. This is what excites me about the Hermetic school. And it's one of the differences between the Gnostics and the Hermeticists who were around at the same time. They knew of each other. We know some Hermetic texts were found among the Gnostic texts that were discovered at Nag Hammadi in the 1940s and we know that at least the Gnostics were reading some of the Hermetic stuff as well. The difference between the two is that for the Gnostics there is this kind of paranoia consciousness, there's this kind of conspiracy consciousness, the whole notion of the archons, the whole notion that we live in this false world, we're trapped in this world of matter and space and time that's been created by this idiot demiurge God who in the Bible is Yahweh, and William Blake referred to him as Nobodaddy, and all of this, a dark Phillip K Dick sense that there are others out there who are controlling everything, like *The Matrix* or something, we have to escape from it. But the Hermeticists don't have that sort of paranoid sensibility about the cosmos. They say, yes, we are sunk into matter. What we have to do is actualize our own full self, our own full being, our own full consciousness in order to master the world of matter and space and time and reality, and to take our rightful place within it, which is that of the caretaker, this whole notion that's discussed in more than one of the Hermetic books, that's man's place as the cosmic caretaker. We're here to help take care of things, similarly to a notion in Kabbalah of *tikkun*, the whole idea that humanity's job is to repair the mistakes in creation. When God or whoever created the everything, he actually did a sloppy job, and things broke, and things spilled, and so our job was to clean up the mess, and this was something that the Hermeticists shared with the later kabbalist thinkers. There isn't this wanting to escape the cosmos that you get with the Gnostics. The Gnostics are closer to the existentialists, or even to some more modern esoteric schools like Gurdjieff and the Fourth Way, this notion that we're trapped in a prison and we have somehow to find a way to burrow our way out. It's very different with the Hermeticists.

MC: You do mention, Gary, the Goldilocks effect, in which we have to have one foot in the spiritual world and one foot in the material world. And what I also liked, and I often have arguments between people on the difference between Gnosis and mysticism, and you put it very well when you say that part of Gnosis is having that valve, is to be able to control archetypal energies that flow through us, or else we can't go to our jobs. We've got to keep it in control.

GL: Well, yeah, it's great to have these powerful mystical experiences either produced through spiritual practices or taking some psychoactive substance. But Aldous Huxley said, when he was under the influence of mescaline, yes, if everyone took mescaline there would be no wars, but there would be no civilization either. Huxley talked about looking over at a sinkful of dirty dishes—which gives us some idea of how Huxley lived—and thinking, well, they are beautiful. Why would you want to go over and wash them? Thankfully, Huxley was a fairly responsible psychedelic imbiber, but I'm sure we all know from experience that many agreed with him, why go wash those dishes? So in a very practical, simple way, the idea isn't completely to be immersed in this cosmic consciousness all the time, but to draw from the experiences that we do get the knowledge that the universe is much more fascinating and more interesting living place than we generally take it for. We have to get on in the world and Huxley talks about how mind at large has to be siphoned out to a kind of tiny trickle, but it's just the amount of consciousness we need in the trickle to deal with things. We seem to have two forms of consciousness: one is to deal with things, which we all do, and the other is to appreciate things. Our problem in the modern world is that we're very successful at dealing with things, which is why we're very successful and the most dominant species on the planet and so on and so on, and why we're able to focus our consciousness and our attention onto minute specifics and actually do things that, as far as we can tell, most other living creatures can't do. But the downside of that, that funnelling of our attention, is that we lost awareness and consciousness of the rich meaning that saturates the world around us. And this is when Huxley takes mescaline, as he tells us in *The Doors of Perception*, that's more or less what happens, that part of his consciousness, that kind of consciousness that's focussed on dealing with the world, was put out of commission, and suddenly the richness, the meaning that's soaking in things became available to him, and he could see it. But, as I said, he had absolutely no inclination to do anything. William James, talking about his experiences with nitrous oxide, when he had this deep conviction of this metaphysical profundity that he perceived, also came to the realisation that, after spending some time in this absolute oneness of things, the complete total relation of everything to everything, where everything made sense, there was a sense of indifference, because if everything was one, why do one thing rather than another? Why do this rather than that? So he came, like Huxley, to the conclusion that our consciousness seems to be limited and filtered through necessarily, in order for us to go on. One of the things I propose in the book is this notion that, well, even though most of us tend to enjoy the other form of consciousness, which is why we drink wine or take other sorts of things, to relax or dealing with consciousness in order to sink into the other mode, that we need to find some balance, to open up this reducing valve, and after that we don't think, with so much of modern culture, that so much of life is meaningless and pointless. There isn't anything out there. It's just atoms floating about meaninglessly. But not too much so that we are able to actually function in the world. The point that I make in the book, getting back to this notion of Gnosis, I think our job is to translate those insights that one gets in those moments of cosmic consciousness into this other form of knowledge which we use another Greek word for, *episteme*, which is the knowledge we can house in books and libraries, on computers, and so on and so on, and it's a knowledge you can pass on to others. I might have this incredibly ecstatic cosmic experience, but if all I can say

to somebody is, "Oh wow!" they're not going to get a heck of a lot out of it. But if like Huxley and others, who are able to write clearly and logically about their mystical experiences I can do that, and pass that on, that's how knowledge in the broader, larger sense grows. To me this is one of the important realisations I came to, that the whole idea isn't to go plunging into cosmic consciousness and mystical consciousness and oneness and stay there. It's to dip your head in for a bit and then come back and tell us all about it.

MC: And the other thing about the Gnosis of the Hermetics, and this is probably attractive to many of the medieval thinkers and the renaissance thinkers is the fact that part of it is really maximising your own mind so that you understand the world. It seems the culmination of this would probably be Giordano Bruno and the way he was drawn to the Hermetic ethos and created these amazing memory techniques. That story of being in front of the pope in that seven year trial and being able to quote the Bible backwards and forwards. So isn't that part of the Hermetic Gnosis—I'm quoting Giordano Bruno, "Be all you can be"—be as smart as you can be?

GL: Well yes, absolutely, at the side of it there are people like Giordano Bruno and others, Pico della Mirandola was another one, who had tremendous powers of memory, something that we rely on memory sticks to do now, or hard drives. They seem to be able to not only house a lot of information but somehow to create this inner space, this inner architecture, that knowledge somehow existed in this form of encompassing the whole universe, and this goes back to the Hermetic notion of as above, so below, the idea that humankind, we are all microcosms of the macrocosm. Within us the entire universe exists, in the sense that it exists outside of us. This is part of this fantastic notion of what being human was, or meant to these Renaissance thinkers. They had come out of a period that we call the middle ages or medieval times, and human beings were pretty much considered these abject creatures, riddled with sin, corrupt, who live in this corrupt world and basically our life is a kind of test and trial to see how we are going to spend eternity. You know the picture when a leaf falls from a tree: why did God do that? What does it mean? Did the devil really do it? And so you get this sense starting with Marsilio Ficino—I mean, the whole reason we're talking about this is because Ficino, this young Italian scholar of the Greek philosophers, Plato, was in the employ of Cosimo de Medici,

enough of an incredible discovery at the time to have, and he'd been lost for many centuries, but then to have him made second best, he played second fiddle to Hermes Trismegistus, that's how high a street cred Hermes Trismegistus had then. And then these books are translated. Ficino passes this on to Pico della Mirandola who wrote the *Oration On the Dignity of Man* and argued his case in front of the pope and other church officials. He's basically arguing this

the great Florentine powerbroker in the Renaissance and he was translating Plato from Greek into Latin for Cosimo to read,, and Cosimo was a big reader, and he had book scouts, out all over the world of the time, and one of them had found this collection of texts in Macedonia and brought it back to Florence, and it turned out to be the Corpus Hermeticum, these books that had been written 100-200AD but had been lost until then. Cosimo is excited about this discovery and he tells Ficino, put Plato on the back burner, give Plato a break, forget that, translate these first. Now Plato was

Hermetic view, this whole new vision of man that is no longer a medieval vision of us being these abject sinners, but suddenly this notion of being human as being something absolutely unique. Pico says that unlike all the creatures in the universe we have no set place. We are even higher than the angels in the sense that even though they're transcendent, they are a superior, superabundant being above ours, that they have a particular place in the cosmic scheme and they have to stay in it, whereas we can do anything. Man can soar to the heights and sink to the depths. This is unheard of. This is absolutely unheard of before, and humanism comes out of it. Now strangely if you follow the historical path, humanism is something that is actually anti this point of view. "Curb your enthusiasms" becomes its sensibility. But still, this early humanism, this kind of superhumanism in the way I speak of it in the book, is something that's completely informed by these Hermetic ideas, and it has to do with our own mental capacities, and what is called the art of memory becomes developed then, whereas these Renaissance thinkers were able to create in their own minds these vast cathedrals of space, these imaginary spaces they would walk through, and the idea was that when they orated, when they gave speeches like Pico's *Oration On the Dignity of Man*, in order to remember everything, and to remember the different parts of the speech, and so on, they created this mnemonic system where they would create this inner theatre, with stage sets and so on, and different symbols that they would visualise would be the triggers for different parts of this speech. So when they were giving a speech, when they were talking, inwardly when they were walking within this inner cathedral of ideas. It just boggles our very tiny minds nowadays as to how they could possibly do this. It's this notion of the macrocosm and the microcosm. We can house the entire universe within our own consciousness. And we're the only beings in creation, outside, I guess, God, who can do that. Sadly, that's something that we don't really think about much these days.

MC: No, not at all, unfortunately. What I found interesting about your book, Gary, I don't know if you caught this, but you write about how you've got Asclepius and he's in a very relaxed state, a trance, maybe his chakras are open, maybe his channels of communication are open, and there comes Hermes and begins to teach him. Then suddenly you're going through history and you're looking at these figures who were influenced by the Hermetic spirit, like Paracelsus or Giordano Bruno and you're going, man, these guys really had some big egos, how did they get relaxed? Did that cross your mind at all?

GL: I guess the whole idea of that is that in our little universes we are supposed to be godlike in order to know God. I guess that could go to many people's heads, and that's something that's a bit of an occupational hazard.

MC: It made a lot of bigheads.

GL: No, you're absolutely right and they were two rather belligerent characters. Paracelsus was famous for getting into tussles with his critics and he was notorious for the kind of language he would use, and he was able to curse people in ways they didn't even know were possible. Giordano Bruno locked horns with papal characters who were equally convinced that they were right and knew everything. So, yeah, you do have that sort of thing. Perhaps there is a dissonance at times between those who know what to do and how things work, and those who are actually able to do it and know it as well, the ones who can actually sink into these mystical states might not be the same ones who can write about them lucidly and clearly. You talked about Hermes Trismegistus and when Nous comes to him he's in this very relaxed calm state, and again this is something that was the same in the later figures, people I talked about before like William James and Ouspensky and R.M. Bucke. Again that suggests to me that we could possible do that too. We can learn ways in which to relax the tension over everyday consciousness which we have. Most of us aren't aware of this, but I think pretty much all of us exist in a state of hypertension. We have to deal with so many things. We're talking about people who live in 200-300 and the Renaissance, but I think the world we live in today is probably much more hectic than anything they lived in. So we probably live in a state of hypertension where we don't even know it. We just accept it as how things are in order to deal with it. The idea that there's so many different schools and approaches to relaxing or meditating or whatever, going within, now, suggests that there's a whole plethora of variety of different techniques to somehow learn to relax and open up, and all the different ways we talk about it. But you're absolutely right about characters like

Paracelsus, Bruno and Pico della Mirandola. But again, because they did that back then, we can learn from them. We don't need to blow our horns quite as loudly as Paracelsus may have, or Pico did. Because they did that we can learn from what they did and build on it. I myself, I'm thrilled by the vision of humanity that people like Paracelsus and Bruno and Pico had, but I'm not going to start trumpeting it. Nowadays the whole idea of celebrating your humanity, celebrating being human, is politically incorrect. We're supposed to feel mea culpa, we're supposed to feel guilt.

MC: We've gone full circle.

GL: We're supposed to feel how bad we are because we've ruined the environment and we've screwed up the planet and so on and so on, and we've done all these bad things. And rightly so, all these problems exist and we have to deal with them. For myself, I feel we would have more of a chance of dealing with them successfully if we had something more of the sense of confidence that these Renaissance magi had.

MC: The Hermetics have always been associated with alchemy and this grand Egyptian magic. For some reason I'm picturing the cover of an Iron Maiden album or something like that. But there really isn't anything of that in there, is there?

GL: Well, alchemy doesn't turn up in the collection we call the Corpus Hermeticum, or in the Asclepius which is the one Hermetic text that was available during the long stretch of time when the Corpus Hermeticum wasn't. Asclepius was the text that kept Hermes Trismegistus' name alive. The early alchemist Zosimos from Alexandria talks about the Hermetic texts and you can tell from his writings that he must have been aware of them. If there's one text that people associate with Hermes Trismegistus it's what is known as the Emerald Tablet, the Emerald Tablet of Hermes Trismegistus. But there's no mention of that in the Corpus Hermeticum, there's no mention of it in the texts that Ficino translated from Greek into Latin. There's no mention of it in any other of the Hermetic texts

that came to light, those discovered with the Nag Hammadi Gnostic texts. As far as we know it doesn't appear until an Arabic version of it in the works of Jabir, who in the west we know as Geber. The word gibberish is said to come from him. The alchemical writings were so obtuse and nobody could make any sense of it so when people got a piece of writings they couldn't understand, they basically said, well you write like Jabir. This was more than a few centuries later than when the Corpus Hermeticum was written. It's interesting the connection between the two. More than likely there was alchemy going on in Alexandria at the time the Hermetic texts were being written and the two groups probably knew of each other, maybe even knew each other, but it isn't something that's part of the Hermetic teaching until later on. And one of the things I do in the book is devote one chapter to alchemy. But I make a point of saying, well, actually when you look at it, alchemy isn't a part of these early Hermetic texts. The macrocosm-microcosm notion as above, so below, which is the Hermetic or alchemical aphorism that most people know, is part of the Emerald Tablet, but that's the focus really off the Corpus Hermeticum. It's much more this cosmic consciousness focus, this notion of expanding your mind so that you can encompass the All within your mind. So that's the focus rather than the hands-on alchemical work of transmuting the elements. Part of the whole esoteric tradition is this ambiguity that's involved with so many different esoteric writings. More than likely, the authors of the Hermetic texts, whoever they were—we don't know their names, we have no names that have come down to us of these Alexandrian hermeticists. We have the names of some of the Gnostics from the time, but we don't have the names of any hermeticists. But more than likely they had already heard of Hermes Trismegistus, this notion of the Thrice-Greatest Hermes starts up a bit earlier than that, and we know that the Greek God Hermes was associated with the Egyptian God Thoth and the blend of the two created this figure, Thrice-Greatest Hermes. So the people writing the Hermetic texts used that name for a few different reasons. One was probably to get people to pay attention to them, and if somebody said, oh, here's a piece of writing by Aleister Crowley, you'd read it, just because you knew the name, or if it was by the Buddha or someone. But also in a sign of respect, they're writing not about their own minds, not their own personal ideas. This is the wisdom of the mind, the universal mind, so they use the name of one of the most revered thinkers they could think of as the author. So likewise, whether Jabir, Geber, this alchemist, came up with the emerald tablet or he found some text. There's supposed to be a Greek original but it's never come to light. Whoever wrote it, they too used the name of Hermes Trismegistus, so by that time somebody decided, yeah, we should use Hermes to give alchemy some more street cred because it's a very renowned name, and he's a very revered figure, and we're talking about the highest things here, the transmutation of matter into spirit, and so on, yeah why not, why shouldn't we associate Hermes with this?

MC: And it should be mentioned too, Gary, because you do spend a chapter on it, but Hermes was even popular in the Islamic world.

GL: Yeah, that's one of the things I loved about doing this book, was discovering these things, or rediscovering or understanding more deeply. Certainly, we know a great deal about Hermetic philosophy because when the Arabic Islamic invaders came to Alexandria and that part of the world, they absorbed their philosophers, their thinkers, their mystics, their esotericists. They absorbed the whole Hermetic philosophy and kept it alive during time when in the west Christianity, which it would again do later on, a thousand years or so down the line, was trying to wipe it out. Alexandria was a remarkable place, a Greek city in Egypt, that developed this really unique atmosphere, this milieu of philosophical, scientific, spiritual and esoteric study and knowledge and blending. It's very much what we'd like things to be like today, a multicultural, multi-faith combination of things, and that was going on then. Over time as history progressed, Christianity rose to power and it became more and more the dominant force in Alexandria

until finally it was completely in power and, as it did in other places, it started to wipe out its rivals or its predecessors. And it did that to Hermeticism and the pagan philosophies. And it was later when the Arabic powers invaded and conquered Egypt and Alexandria that the Hermetic thought was transmitted into the wider world. One of the places it went to was this remarkable place called Harran in northern Turkey that actually was a Hermetic city for a time. Hermes Trismegistus and Hermetic books were more or less the official religion, or official sacred book of the city. This is one of the things I found fascinating when I was doing this book, which was to see the collision between the spiritual energy of these texts and writings and thoughts and ideas of the different people who carry the ideas on, with historical forces, mostly of conquest and war. Much like today you have refugees from different areas, and in that part of the world, having to flee different cities and different countries because of the wars and conquests going on. Among the other things that were transported during these chaotic times were the fragile pages of the Corpus Hermeticum. This is very encouraging to me. You have these tremendous forces, these historical forces, at work—wars, fire, burning, destruction—and these tiny fragile leaves of whatever these things were written on managed to survive. They sunk, they went out of view, they went underground, but they surfaced again. And it's very encouraging to recognise that the mind can survive in these very difficult times. They moved from Harran to Baghdad, Baghdad to Constantinople, and then Constantinople to Macedonia and Macedonia to Florence. From there they re-entered the mainstream of western culture. So certainly Arab Islamic thinkers of the time kept the whole Hermetic philosophy alive, and we have to thank them very much for that.

MC: Well, I was going to end by asking you how the Hermetic sensibility can help our modern days, Gary, but you've given a lot of hints and your whole book is full of gems about how Hermes can help us get back on track, especially in this era which has become the realised eschatology of Jean Baudrillard or Marshall McLuhan, where we're just in this cul-de-sac or this desert of the real, and we are stormed by social media and technology and everything, but I'm presuming the answer could be as simple as the Blake attitude of "A universe in a grain of sand and heaven in a wild flower." and "My business is to create." Is that the attitude you think we need to get back to?

GL: Well yes, I think more or less something along those lines. There's quite a few things we can learn from the Hermetic books. I mentioned earlier this notion of us being caretakers of the cosmos. Certainly we are animals, but we're not only animals. We're animals-plus which sounds like a vitamin of some kind, but it's actually I think a very important thing to recognise. To recognise that isn't to pat ourselves on the back and trumpet our superiority. It is to accept and embrace the obligations and responsibilities we have for doing that. We're the only creatures on the planet who can be concerned about the environment. We're the only ones who can worry about nature and how it's being upset, and all that. And the reason we can do that is that we're something more than the environment, more than nature. There's a part of us that stands above it, and that's the mind. Whatever you want to call it, you want to call it the spirit, the soul, whatever, the Hermeticists called it Nous, they called it the mind. I think you're absolutely right, it behooves us to try and understand and experience and live and make a practical application of this notion that you said of Blake, that infinity is in the palm of our hand and eternity in an hour, whatever. We have the capacity to do that. I give different examples in the book of that, and one is directly related to the Hermetic teaching, from the Hermetic books itself, others as I said from people like William James, Ouspensky and R.M. Bucke and later on examples that turn up in literature that ostensibly may not have anything to do with Hermeticism, but describe the kinds of consciousness that are associated with it. And to me I think are much more available to us than we realise. I think one of the things that confronts many people who get interested in different spiritual and esoteric disciplines and practices, this idea that it's an incredibly hard, difficult sort of thing and you have to sacrifice everything for it. And yes, of course you have to commit and, yes, of course one shouldn't be complacent, yet at the same time think we experience more of these things than we actually realise. One of the things I try to do in the book is point to some of these experiences that we have and also to suggest that there might be a new way to look at things and the world and the chaotic mess we seem to exist in right now, not so much from wanting to retreat from it into some earlier primal, more certain form of thought, which I think both the traditionalist school that I mentioned earlier and forms of fundamentalism, whether Christian or Islamic or whatever, do, or throw ourselves into some strange future world of transhuman, or somehow blending with machines, or something like that. But it's to understand more fully what our humanness is, and I think that's what the Hermetic books are about. You mentioned earlier that they were at the core or beginning of humanism and that humanism somehow turned into something smaller than what it started out as, and that's why you talk about a kind of superhumanism. I just use that as a way to look at it, because I'm not thinking of any kind of ubermensch elite character, but really just becoming more and more fully human, and I think that's really what the Hermetic things are about. If we can do that I think it would if not solve, it would certainly throw a lot of light on many problems today.

MC: I think that's all the time we have. Gary, I'd like to thank you very much for coming on Aeon Byte and giving us a very stimulating and edifying conversation based on your book *The Quest for Hermes Trismegistus from Ancient Egypt to the Modern World.*

GL: Well, as I said it's absolutely my pleasure, and thank you very much for having me.

Jordan Bloom

A Beauty Impossible to Define
The Theology of Nick Cave

Christ was forgiving, merciful, and loving, but he was after all the Son of the Old Testament God and his father's blood still boiled in his veins. In creating his Son, God the Father had evolved, he had moved on…Christ came to right the wrongs of his father…Christ is the imagination, at times terrible, irrational, incendiary, and beautiful; in short, Godlike.

Nick Cave

In 1997, Nick Cave released *The Boatman's Call*, a tender collection of songs, with somber, minimalist piano tones feeling delicate and personal in comparison to the snarling, wrathful character of his earlier oeuvre, its sonic content being augmented on every song by lyrical meditations on love. Just the year prior, the album *Murder Ballads* featured a relentless sideshow of grotesque characters within songs that were universally about murder. *Murder Ballads* concluded with a cynical rendition of Bob Dylan's "Death is Not the End," small consolation after the brutalities of "Stagger Lee," "Henry Lee," and all the other pseudo-Americana characters on the album. The transition in tone between *Murder Ballads* and *The Boatman's Call* is as stark as from Malachi to Matthew, and speaks to a personal epiphany. A review in Allmusic was receptive to the shift, noting, "*Murder Ballads* brought Nick Cave's morbidity to near-parodic levels, which makes the disarmingly frank and introspective songs of *The Boatman's Call* all the more startling." A song cycle equally inspired by Cave's failed romantic affairs and religious doubts, *The Boatman's Call* captures him at his most honest and despairing."

In order to explore Cave's peculiar understanding of Christianity — and his significant shift in tone from 1996 to 1997 — it is necessary to explore the history of his own relationship with religion, which began at the Anglican Church in Warracknabeal, Victoria, where he attended services twice a week between the ages of 8 and 12. In a BBC lecture, he describes his days as a choirboy: "The God I heard preached about there seemed remote, and alien, and uncertain. So I sat in the stalls, in my crimson cassock, while rogue thoughts oozed beneath the bolted door of my imagination." But, "back then, I had no idea that those dark mutterings were coming from God."

Nick Cave's older albums are informed by a focus on the Old Testament, which he understands to express "a pitiful humanity suffering beneath a despotic God." His transition in understanding from Anglicanism to apostasy to his own unique creativist theology in many respects parallels other modern Christian thinkers, but is unique in others. Based on that narrative of his childhood, the subsequent heroin-riddled apostasy of his young adulthood and his later reconciliation with Christianity can be understood as a reaction to the Anglican dogmatism of his upbringing. Indeed, the very first line of the very Christian *Boatman's Call* reads, *"I don't believe in an interventionist God."* It explores how he redefines his theology as he returns to the Christian faith.

So how, then, does Cave understand Christ? In his "The Flesh Made Word" lecture, he offers a compelling reading of John 8: 6-8, the story of Jesus defending the adulterous woman. He makes rhetorical hay out of the oft-neglected depiction of Christ stooping to the ground, before saying, "He who is without sin, cast the first stone." Cave writes, "Christ did not answer straightaway, but rather stooped down and with his finger wrote on the ground, as though he didn't here them... For me, this seemingly distracted gesture, the stooping down and the writing on the ground, is Christ accessing the God in himself. Christ then delivers the line that disempowers his opponents — and what an extraordinary remark it is — then stoops again to re-commune with God." That explanation offers a dramatically mystical reinterpretation of the way that verse is traditionally preached. To be sure, Cave's interpretation still contains the admonition against zealotry, but he argues the stooping action speaks of communion with Christ's own creative spirit in a uniquely realized form, which allows him to concisely deliver a considered, original but uncompromising thought to the crowd.

METAPHORS FROM *THE BOATMAN'S CALL*

The Boatman's Call is best described as a set of love songs with heavy theological undertones. On the album, the love song is the creative form by which he describes the world — it is the canvas on which his philosophy is written. The woman in each love song is often analogous to the creative force, which he understands to have a companion-like relationship with the individual; *"The imagination desires an alternate and through the writing of the love song, one sits and dines with loss and longing, madness and melancholy ecstasy, magic, joy, and love with equal measures of respect and gratitude."*

The titular boatman appears in the song "I Do Love Her So (Lime Tree Arbour)" during the first verse as God, calling to him and a woman — analogous to Christ, the imagination. When the boatman disappears midway through the song, he despairs that *"There will always be suffering/ It flows through life like water,"* but *"Through every word I speak/ and every word I know/ There is a hand that protects me/ and I do love her so."* The use of naturalistic metaphors and a universal presence of the spirit, *"everywhere I go,"* already suggests a departure from buttoned-down Anglican ecclesiasticism.

The third track of *The Boatman's Call,* "People They Ain't No Good," Cave lays out his own theodicy of sorts. He denies the doctrine of original sin as an explanation for human behavior by singing, *"It ain't in their hearts they're bad/ They'd stick by you if they could/ But that's just bullshit/ People just ain't no good."* Though some *"Nurse you when you're ill of health,"* they're mostly no good. The gulf between human aspiration and human depravity gapes wide in Cave's universe. Like in "Lime Tree Arbour," he is singing to a mysterious woman in an intimate setting, looking out at a frightening, uncertain world, whose *"Winter slammed us like a fist."* The woman with whom he communes is, again, Christ as the creative spirit, protected from the world in the intimacy of creative endeavor.

A feminine portrayal of Jesus might seem unusual, but it's not without precedent, even within Protestantism. Aaron Fogleman, historian of radical religious movements in America, wrote a book in 2007 called *Jesus is Female*, which explored the impact of Moravian theology that feminized Jesus on the other German-speaking, predominantly Lutheran communities in early British North America. Turns out, mainstream Protestants at the time weren't too pleased to hear about hymns that compared Christ's spear wound to vaginas. This one, written in the first half of the 18th century by the son of the Moravian Church's founder, contains the words, *"Seiten-holgen/ du bist meinen seelgen/ doch das liebste platzlein;/ Seiten-schrein!/ leib und seel fahrt in dich nein."* [*"Little side hole/ thou art my little soul/ yes the dearest little place;/ Side shrine/ body and soul passes into thee."*]

Cave is acting within a rock tradition that borrows from the blues, with its references to floods and other divine acts; the older cosmological language is probably better explained by the fact that he probably listened to a lot of records and thought the Old Testament sounded cool.

After we're told about the irredeemable no-goodness of humanity, "Brompton Oratory" follows, a pastoral song about Cave's reconversion, complexly set within a metaphorical church service. It isn't friendly to the established church, referencing Luke 24

explicitly, the chapter wherein Christ appears to his followers on the road to Emmaus but they fail to recognize him. Cave muses that he wished he could make himself like the *"stone apostles"* outside the church building, so he wouldn't have to see the *"Beauty impossible to endure/ The blood imparted in little sips."* The apostles, emblematic of the church, are numb to the true nature of Christ as Cave sees him — made of stone. He sees the disconnect between himself, a 'true believer,' and the established church as in the spirit of Christ himself, who Cave argues saw the jurisprudential Pharisees as "enemies of the imagination, who actively blocked the spiritual flight of the people, and kept them bogged down with theological nitpicking, intellectualism, and law." Instead, in the song Cave hails the revelations of the natural world, and its *Pentecostal morn.*

"Fifteen Feet of Pure White Snow," from the later album *No More Shall We Part*, expresses a similar antagonism to the established church, so it bears mentioning in relation to "Brompton Oratory." He makes apocalyptic predictions for overzealous Puritanism, depicting a buried town and a narrator that's been *"paralyzed by a lack of feeling/ I can't even find anything that's worth stealing/ under 15 feet of pure white snow."*

It would be a mistake to make too stark of a foreground/background reading of *The Boatman's Call*. On "Are You the One I've Been Waiting For?" Cave makes the lover-Christ analogy explicitly:

There's a man who spoke wonders though I've never met him
He said, "He who seeks finds and who knocks will be let in"
I think of you in motion and just how close you are getting
And how every little thing anticipates you
All down my veins my heart-strings call
Are you the one that I've been waiting for?

Within previous songs, wherein Cave would simply describe a metaphorical relationship with the creative imagination, this one speaks of a relationship with another human being that embodies divine love. God, then, is to be found between human beings, and Christ is its mediator. This is very similar to 20th-century Christian philosophies that emphasize ethics above supernaturalism and ritual. Likewise, on the final track of the album, Cave expresses doubts about his own salvation, singing, *"If it were but a matter of faith/ measured in petitions and prayer/ she would materialize, all fleshed out/ But it is not, nor do I care."* They are lines that echo Tillich's concept of 'estrangement' from God, a condition that he sees in the entire world.

Cave's depictions of the world at large in *The Boatman's Call* are of an unfriendly, desolate place. "Where Do We Go Now but Nowhere" is a grotesque meditation on modernity, with all its unfamiliar creations. He describes a kitten *"with the paw of a bear,"* and a crazed girl *"gnawing her knuckles in the chemical light."* The despairing verses are punctuated by a mantra-like chorus that simply pleads, *"wake up, my love, my lover wake up."* The chorus is an appeal to Christ crucified and resurrected in humanity as the creative spirit. The *"fresh, clean, antiseptic air"* is the modern world from which Cave desires deliverance.

However, the question of his belief in salvation or even an afterlife is deliberately left uncertain. In "Idiot Prayer," a man facing his fate asks, *"Will I be seeing you soon?/ If what they say around here is true/ then we'll meet again/ me and you."* The same song also speaks to a lack of human knowledge of the machinations of divine justice: *"If you're in hell, then what can I say/ you probably deserved it anyway,"* but ends with the line *"We each get what we deserve."* Either by the wages of sin or fate, death is universal, says the dying man in the song.

"Crises of love and faith make for more resonant songs than does senseless bloodletting, and Cave seems to be in the process of uncovering the roots of his macabre obsessions and revealing more of himself along the way. His language is as packed with biblical imagery as ever, but it seems more honest than his earlier intoxicating jaunts through the valley of the shadow of death," so said a review of *The Boatman's Call* in *Salon.* The album represented the first fully articulated version of Cave's return to the Christian tradition. Over successive albums, he continued to flesh out the concepts initially explored on *The Boatman's Call.*

"PEOPLE THEY AIN'T NO GOOD": NICK CAVE'S ETHICS

In place of faith, Cave seems to endorse a humble uncertainty about divine affairs. Because God has been relocated to the relationships between people, enabled by a creative force symbolized by Christ, divine command ethics are impossible, as is certainty about eternal life. The richly illustrative "Oh My Lord," from *No More Shall We Part*, embodies his new vision well: *"The ladders of life that we scale merrily/ move mysteriously around/ so that when you think you're climbing up, man/ in fact you're climbing down."* It's a paradox that finds humanity anxious and uncertain, facing important questions about how one might rightly live.

On the gospel-inflected "There She Goes, My Beautiful World," from 2004's *Abattoir Blues/ The Lyre of Orpheus*, Cave takes on the character of a writer experiencing writer's block (*"Me, I'm lying here, with nothing in my ears."*). Pleading, he sends up the final verse:

> I will be your slave
> I will peel you grapes
> Up on your pedestal
> With your ivory and apes
> With your book of ideas
> With your alchemy
> O Come on,
> Send that stuff on down to me.

Earlier in the song, he demythologizes various literary figures, characterizing Karl Marx, who *"Squeezed his carbuncles while writing* Das Kapital," and Dylan Thomas, who *"Died drunk in St. Vincent's Hospital"* with much less reverence than usually attends them. He recasts them as human figures, afflicted by disease and drunkenness — common, human afflictions. The intended effect universalizes the creativity Cave sees as emanating from a divine presence. All of them, he reminds us, were merely suffering mortals, and the wellspring of creative potential those fortunate icons accessed

can and should be accessed in every person. The previous verse is directed toward evangelism:

> So if you got a trumpet, get on your feet, brother, and blow it
> If you've got a field, that don't yield, well get up and hoe it
> I look at you and you look at me and deep in our hearts know it.
> That you weren't much of a muse, but then I weren't much of a poet.

Although Cave has drastically reimagined the meaning of God, he maintains humanity's need for a relationship with the divine. He sees the creative potential within humanity as *"divinely granted"* but *"unlockable."* Metaphorical language of sending-down is suggestive of an orthodox cosmology. However, rather than suggesting his belief in a God somewhere out there in space, the reality is simpler: Cave is inhabiting the form of rock musicians to express his ideas in the same way he inhabits the form of a love song in *The Boatman's Call*. Cave is acting within a rock tradition that borrows from the blues, with its references to floods and other divine acts; the older cosmological language is probably better explained by the fact that he probably listened to a lot of records and thought the Old Testament sounded cool. Similarly, I don't think he believes that *"ivory and apes"* really attend God on a throne in heaven. Instead, his is a fundamentally mystical expression of God, because it speaks of communion with a divine presence through creative human acts. And because of the essential meaning communicated through those creative acts, all humanity needs Christ, the imagination. This is Cave's fundamental ethical principle: people should work to unlock their divinely-granted imagination.

WORKMANLIKE LOVE

Nick Cave is often described as a workmanlike musician. He is an extremely prolific artist, having written two novels, music for three first-run movies, and countless albums for three different notable bands. Now well-established, he works in an office composing songs and working on his various projects. He is a slave to muse Sophia, so to speak. The creative process has dominated his life, and love, to Cave, is similarly dominating. The titular track from *No More Shall We Part*, the album that followed *The Boatman's Call*, characterizes love as a contractual business arrangement. He sings, *"And no more shall we part/ your chain of command has been silenced now/ and all those birds would've sung to your beautiful heart/ anyhow."* The end of the song shifts and addresses God, pleading *"Lord, stay by me/ Don't go down/ I will never be free/ if I'm not free now."*

That understanding of love allows the albums before *The Boatman's Call* to be reexamined. They are albums of rebellion, with names like *Your Funeral, My Trial, Kicking Against the Pricks*, and *Tender Prey*. The railing of those albums is the story of Cave rejecting the despotic, uncreative God of the Old Testament and of the orthodoxy of his childhood. It is his personal apocalypse, and it is his 'born-again' story, to borrow a term. In the maniacally narcissistic "Lay Me Low," from 1994's *Let Love In*, Cave eulogizes himself. He lists figures from his childhood, including his teachers who say he was *"one of God's sorrier creatures,"* and the police chief, who says he was *"a malanderer, a badlander and a thief."* The funeral itself is a grand affair, wherein *"the sea will rage and the sky will storm"* and *"all man and beast will mourn."* He offers the same to anyone who cares to listen:

> If you wanna be my friend
> And you wanna repent
> And you want it all to end
> And you wanna know when
> Well, do it now, don't care how
> Take your final bow
> Make a stand, take my hand
> And blow it all to hell.

Salvation, then, is offered to anyone who cares

enough to destroy the oppressions of uncreative and dull thinking. "Take up the cross" indeed, Beiberites.

The condition of the world in Cave's theology is hyperbolically stark; to get that picture one needn't look any further than the matter-of-fact brutality of both the characters and the landscape in *The Proposition*. An overly simple reading might call Cave a hedonist, even a pessimist. With his slicked-back hair and sleazy mustache, it's certainly a tempting interpretation. This is Cave's image, his creation. The Epistle to the Hebrews refers to this Christ-as-image idea. The first chapter reads,

> Who being the brightness of his glory, and the express image of his person, and upholding all things by the word of his power, when he had by himself purged our sins, sat down on the right hand of the Majesty on high.

By choosing to portray all the guts and depravity of the human experience, and even relishing them, Cave effects a Christ-like *kenosis*. Depicting the world in a tragic way allows an experience with the tragic emotions of pity and terror, which in turn lead to an awareness of, as Joyce puts it, "the grave and constant sufferings" of humanity. By meeting the world on its own terms, in its 'un-awakened' state, he calls it to commune with the creative imagination. In order to do so, he must defile his own image, which is the central, Christ-like sacrifice of his art.

Andrew Phillip Smith

Cathar Country

The Languedoc is a beautiful region of southern France, bordering the Pyrenees, with Gascony to the West, Provence to the East. In contemporary France it is part of the combined Languedoc-Roussillon région, though part of the ancient territory has been shuffled off into the synthetic Midi-Pyrénées administrative territory. The River Aude twists its way through this hilly country, lending its name to the département, an older and more local and administrative division, roughly equivalent to a county. The name comes from *langue d'oc*, "the language of yes," the language of the South, named for its word for "yes," *oc* rather than the modern French *oui*, and different enough to modern French or even medieval French to qualify as a separate romance language. The pronunciation of French here isn't the same as the French we learn at school. *Vin* is pronounced more or less as an English speaker would pronounce the first syllable of "vintage" rather than with the elided vowel. The local wine is a light, fizzy white known as blanquette. Summers here are typically hot, winters wet and the area boasts an extraordinary 300 days of sunshine per year on average. The people are affable, appreciative of our attempts at French but happy to speak English. There is a small but noticeable British population of retirees and second home owners—Northern English couples clamming up whenever they need to speak the local language, tanned cockney estate agents rolling out fluent glottal-stop-inflected French. And, of course, the Languedoc was home to the Cathars.

As many readers will know, the Cathars or Albigensians (named after the city of Albi a little to the north, which we weren't able to visit) were dualist Christians regarded as heretics by the Catholic Church, who declared a crusade against them and enabled Northern French secular forces (France was merely the Northern kingdom at the time) to brutally besiege and massacre all those in the region who would not side with them. The overwhelming temporal victory was followed by the establishment of the Inquisition by the Spanish Dominic de Guzmán or Saint Dominic who pressed home their spiritual advantage against the remaining heretics. The Cathars are forever immortalised as victims, finding historical fame in the romantic tradition of the hopeless cause, a decentralised, rigorous, honest faith up against the political might of the pre-reformation Catholic Church.

It was at my wife's suggestion that we went there. She knew that I would like the Cathar connection and she had strong memories of a few weeks spent helping at an orphanage a little east of there when she was a teenager. We were tourists in an area where, though the people are cheerful, the economy seems a bit depressed. In advance of the trip I had picked up a guidebook titled *Cathar Country*. Originally published in 1992, the flyleaf proclaimed, in an unwieldy translation from the French, that the region needed to transform and restructure its economy by emphasising its cultural heritage, which of course is a euphemism for tourism.

The hook with which to snare the tourist trade, to lure them away from the coast or bounty of Provence, was to be the Cathars. Twenty years on from the publication of

that guide book the Cathar heritage is well-established as a holiday theme for the area. The variety of castle ruins—romantic, austere or devastated in turn, scattered around on hilltops or comprising the ancient cores of cities—have been rebranded as Cathar castles. Though most of them have some links to the Albigensians, having endured sieges and hosted atrocities, or sheltered Cathar Perfect, or having had Cathars among their noble families, none were built or maintained by or the Cathars. The Cathars left no architecture or art, nor even a substantial body of literature. Beyond the rumour of the lost treasure of Montségur, their only real legacy is the memory of them as the Good Christians. Yet these are the sites that anyone researching the Cathars would visit, and they are undeniably evocative of those who lived and died there.

"A cheap holiday in other people's misery" sang Johnny Rotten in "Holidays in the Sun." While this is hardly literally true of the Languedoc, which is generally a sunny, relaxed and cheerful region, I occasionally had the nagging feeling that in taking a holiday in Cathar country I was doing just that. History doesn't record very much of the simple, pure lives of these people, nor do the ruins primarily preserve the traces of lives lived well, spiritual plenitude vanished yet hinted at as in the ruins of an abbey or in the grandeur of a Gothic cathedral, or even in the strange power of a megalithic site. Like the history books, the stones remember blood and siege warfare, starvation, human holocaust, mutilation and massacre.

We flew in from Dublin with that rude, miserly, penny-pinching gobshite airline Ryanair, who also happened to offer cheap fares. Just about all the flights at the tiny, informal, slightly chaotic airport of Carcassonne were run by Ryanair and they obviously kept the airport, to mix metaphors, afloat.

Once we had landed we took the bus, aided by a very friendly driver and found our lodgings, passing through the modern town, past some dismal apartment blocks around to the citadel, the original fortified medieval city of Carcassonne.

Immediately siding with the enemy of the Cathars (I joke of course) we had booked in to an old Catholic abbey, just across the road from la Cité, the citadel of Carcassonne. The rooms were basic, with communal showers and toilets more suited to the groups of young people who occupied most of the other rooms than a middle-aged couple. We hadn't brought towels, so we had to pinch clean hand towels (temporarily I should add) from the communal area. It was no longer a working abbey but it had two chapels that still celebrated mass, plus a small museum of unexceptional religious art.

The citadel itself is huge, magnificent and well-maintained. Much of it had been rebuilt after the Cathar wars and had been restored and altered extensively in the nineteenth century by Viollet le Duc, who had also masterminded the restoration of Notre Dame de Paris. The conical fairytale castle towers were now roofed with the steep grey slate of Northern France rather than the native, gently angled terracotta tiles of the South. Another victory of the North over the Languedoc. In the castle walls I could make out the strata of the varied stone types and building techniques of each successive age, topped by the evenly cut blocks of relatively modern construction.

We had heard that the citadel was very touristy, and the rumours were correct. As soon as we entered the massive front gate, negotiating the young women in medieval costume who handed out flyers for forthcoming events, we saw the steep central narrow medieval street, filled with gift shops and eateries. Well, if airports can double as malls, why not medieval castles? The entire citadel was like this, packed full of retail and food outlets, with the exception of the outer walls, along which we could walk in relative peace and take photos of the surrounding countryside through the narrow views allowed by the arrow slits. Coming from a country filled with ancient fortresses I was taken back to childhood visits to the Roman, Norman, native and Victorian castles of Wales.

The citadel was busy, but on that first day it wasn't too bad. (When at the end of our trip we returned to Carcassonne I went back to la Cité and found it jam-packed, the tourist traffic so heavy that we were standing stationary in the main street, packed in with the other tourists like sardines in a tin). In the gravelled space outside the citadel there was a jaunty, old-fashioned carousel. A young woman in a red headscarf and blue pantaloons, about twenty years old, blew huge soap bubbles from a gigantic version of the bubble blowers we used as children, catching the circular frame in the breeze, soapy spheres floating off into the air, chased by children and popping against old people on benches, a cap out in front of her to collect money. All around I could hear a mishmash of tourist tongues plenty of French, but also German, Italian, Dutch Japanese and English in many accents.

A modern statue of Dame Carcas, legendary eponymous founder of the city, stands outside. An eight century widow of the lord of the castle, while it was under siege by Saracens Dame Carcas fed a pig with the remaining grain and threw the fattened beast over the castle walls. The besieging forces saw it and assumed that if such a sizeable pig could be wasted then the city's food stocks were so plentiful that they could defend the citadel for a long time and thus lifted the siege. She then rang all the city bells in celebration, hence the name "Carcas sonne", "Dame Carcas rings." In her modern guise as a statue she is serene and buddhalike.

A tourist train, the contraption actually a kind of bus with the front car shaped like a steam locomotive attached to a succession of wheeled carriages, rolled by. The holiday making passengers were entirely silent, listening to a recorded tour guide on their headsets. A local man, obstructed by tourists, brought into the castle boxes of lettuce stacked on his head. A small car with a Great Western Hotel logo drove into the citadel. The gift shops have plastic swords and shields, dragons and princesses, models of crusader knights, and Cathar knights, which look just like the crusader models on neighbouring shelves but with yellow Cathar or Languedoc crosses instead of the red crusader cross. I confess to buying a Languedoc cross in reconstituted stone (one arm of which snapped during the return flight) and a small gargoyle. These shops also stock the older kind of tourist memorabilia I remember adorning family mantelpieces: china plates and cups decorated with painted or transferred landscapes and coats of arms.

The first eating places offer fast food, halal kebabs (in memory of the Saracens?) and unkosher cheeseburgers but further in the restaurants are more typically French. Streets have names of local notables, including Trencavel and Dame Carcas. The costumed jongleurs, dames and knights are saved for the evening jousting tournaments and banquets. It's easy to despise the commercialism—indeed, it's the default option—but it gives some life to the mediaeval streets, beings employment to the town and the money to maintain the citadel structure, which is in fine nick. It's not Disneyland, not quite yet.

I'm part of a strange community, full of baseball-capped burghers in shorts who trade in postcards, figurines and, for some reason, all-white muslin cotton shirts, breeches and blouses from a shop called Blancs du Nil that sells white Egyptian cotton exclusively. There is also an Egyptian exhibition called Pharaoh: Mummies, Art and Culture. What is it doing here? Are we meant to be reminded again of the Saracens?

The most crass of the available activities must be La Maison Hantée, Das Geisterhaus, or the Haunted House. Do visitors really want to be haunted by the ghosts of those who died in the 1209 siege of Carcassonne? Of parched, starved old women and men, or infants dead from dysentery? It is not haunted by the Cathar Perfect, for they, according to their beliefs, have moved on to the heavenly realm.

We were there in the heat of August, the same

time of year in which the siege of Carcassonne took place. It took only two weeks for the city, swollen with sheltering local peasants, lacking any water source, to surrender.

When I am hot and thirsty I remember the Carcassonians besieged by French forces, the second city attacked in the campaign, their water cut off, surviving on rainwater from cisterns. When I am hungry, or when eating, I sometimes ponder the *endura*, a fast to death undertaken by newly initiated perfects, which allowed them to die in good standing, facing death by starvation in preference to the attentions of the Inquisition. We eat well in our week in France—monkfish, cassoulet, goat's cheese, duck, gazpacho, crème brulée. The Cathars had a strict dietary code. They were vegan, but, in accordance with medieval conceptions, ate fish, which were believed not to breed sexually, and hence to be in a separate category to beasts and birds. The restaurants of the Aude region are littered with special

"Cathar" menus, most of which contain large amounts of beef. In Carcassonne citadel there's a restaurant named Le Chaudron Cathare— the Cathar Cauldron—which summons up the image of a cauldron full of burning oil rather than stew.

The tour of the castle ramparts must be paid for. The price is a little steep and the queues long, so I skip it. My favourite oddity in the citadel is a museum of paper constructions, lovingly attended by their creator. There are miniature cities and vehicles, sculpted of paper

and card, but the triumph of the exhibition has to be a one-inch high paper model of the Statue of Liberty.

The modern city, which is still very ancient, is less sanitised than La Cité. In the street where we dine outside, a large woman who appears to be a Gypsy squats on the kerbside outside her front door, techno music blasting from her living room to the disgust of passing tourists.

We moved on to Esparaza, a small town on the Aude, where we stayed at a very nice bed and breakfast run by an English couple. They recommended Chris to, another Englishman, who gave tours. We had no car and I was reluctant to hire a car for a few day as I'm not keen on driving. An ex-policeman who had lived for some years in Algeria, conducting some sort of mysterious intelligence work, Chris drove us around all day for just €60. Probably in his late sixties he had extraordinary stamina, specialising in serious hill walking, and was an educated and entertaining companion rather than the lumpen flatfoot I had feared. From Esparaza we could see the hill of Rennes-le-Château, and that was our first destination. Rennes-le-Château is of course the site made famous by *The Holy Blood and the Holy Grail* by Baigent, Leigh and Lincoln and hence the *Da Vinci Code*. The mystery can be broken down into four sections: the bloodline of Jesus

inherited by the Merovingian kings of France; the secret society of the Priory of Sion, which preserved supposedly this knowledge through the ages; the activities of Bérenger Saunière, the priest of the village; and finally the sacred geography of the area in which, according to Henry Lincoln, five mountains make a pentacle, the lines of influence reinforced by man-made structures at certain points. The church in Esparaza falls on one of the lines that Lincoln has discovered.

The holy bloodline is entirely speculative (not that everything else in the *Holy Blood Holy Grail* theory is comprehensively documented), an element added by the three English-speaking authors who transformed a mystery of largely French interest into one with worldwide implications. The Priory of Sion has been shown to be a modern secret society which has perpetrated a hoax and, as far as I'm concerned the bloodline of Jesus was a nonstarter to begin with. But there is still plenty of uncertainty concerning the life of Saunière, the source of his wealth and his intentions in decorating the parish church and building his follies. The status of the large-scale pentacle is still controversial, but ancient societies all over the world have used and enhanced unusual landscape features for sacred purposes.

I must say that I loved Rennes-le-Château. After a fairly steep ascent we found ourselves at the physical centre of the mystery. The church is indeed unusual. Once through the porch the visitor is confronted with a scowling red devil supporting a conch shell stoop. Above the shell are salamanders, then four angels, presumably the archangels. These represent earth, water, fire and air respectively. Above them is a rosycross. The church decoration is gaudy fin-de-siècle, a style that I happen to love. The stations of the cross are based on templates common for the time but have peculiar additional details. There is definitely some strange imagery and a mysterious intention here.

The views are spectacular, with a circular valley surrounding the mountain. The village certainly feels as if it's at the centre of something. Saunière's house is now a museum, with memorabilia of his life and exhibits that describe the mystery. The Tower Magdala, built by Saunière, is slightly Disneyesque but peculiarly impressive. There is a pleasant garden. The little side chapel created by Saunière as a kind conservatory is open and one can look through into his salon, wonderfully 1890s, where he entertained Debussy and other notable guests. There is sign, "Les FOUILLES sont INTERDIT"—"excavations forbidden"—as the village has been plagued by treasure hunters since the late 1960s. Gift shops sell esoteric books, tarot cards and Buddha statues and they are mainly run by incomers, including a Dutch couple and a German couple. I was told that Henry Lincoln often holds forth in a village café, but today he was unfortunately absent.

I would have liked to have spent longer in Rennes-le-Château or to have revisited it but we had neither the time nor the transport to do this. The location and atmosphere were wonderful and the church and Saunière's house deserved further scrutiny. The mystery of Rennes may turn out to be unimportant in any absolute spiritual context—or even entirely invented— but I find the place fascinating and vivifying.

Uncanny mysteries or whacky New Ageism— take your pick—are also present at the nearby 1200m high mountain of Bugarach. Bugarach is hollow and inhabited by aliens who will manifest themselves in December 2012 when the world ends, revealing themselves by opening the top of the mountain as if it were the lid of a tagine, or so we are told. The local mayor is worried about the community being inundated when the significant date arrives and is requesting army backup. It's a dramatic mountain and I could well believe that, if UFOs visited us, they might pick a mountain in the south of France as their abode.

It was a hot day and our next location, the Gorge of Galamus involved a long walk around a narrow and twisting mountain road. After a picnic lunch we traipsed over to the mountainside Galamus Hermitage. This is a primitive chapel and hermit's cave built into the rock face. It was cool and calm in the ancient, sand-coloured chapel. There were two oddities in keeping with the esoteric ambience of the district. One was a Chi-rho, the two Greek letters that begin the name of Christ combined to form a hooked cross. The other was a carved stone version of the Sator square, an acrostic, palindromic magical square that can be read in four directions. *SATOR AREPO TENET OPERA ROTAS* can be read as a grammatical Latin sentence that can be interpreted as "Arepo the sower holds the wheels at work," which is not very meaningful in itself. However, the letters can be rearranged as a cross comprised of "Pater Noster" vertically and horizontally, with the single "N" being shared at the centre of the cross. There are two As and Os left over, which could represent Christ as alpha and omega. Curiously the oldest version of the magic square was found at Pompeii, curiously, and may therefore be pre-Christian. The stone in the Galamus chapel is smooth and accurately carved. I took it to be relatively modern but it may be older than I thought, though I have not been abler to find any dating for this particular version of the Sator square.

· My wife went to Salzberg later in the year and picked up a Sator Arepo talisman at a tourist shop, which she later gave to me for my birthday. It was packaged as "Keltische"—quite erroneously—due to the Celtic archaeological finds of nearby Hallstadt. The chapel and hermitage had a charming, magical feel to it and the Sator square was unexpected: our guide hadn't known of its significance.

Our last site for that day was the castle of Puilaurens. There was another steep climb in the heat and by this time I was hot and tired and slightly resentful. I would probably have called it a day but my wife's appetite for new experiences is stronger than mine and Chris, in his mid-sixties, was very fit and untroubled by what for him was a leisurely stroll. Coming back down from the castle we saw an old blind man who, helped along by a young woman, was using two walking sticks to ascend the path. Good for you, I thought.

This castle had a more tenuous connection to the Cathars, but the fortress was indeed used as a shelter. "In 1241, the Cathar deacon for Fenouillédes, Pierre Paraire stayed there, and towards 1245-1246, several Cathars were lodged here," so the tourist pamphlet told me. Cathars sought refuge after Montségur had capitulated but Puilaurens had to surrender around 1255. It's a typical ruined castle with some helpful wall signs describing the history. There were just a handful of visitors there, so the atmosphere was easy. It must have been difficult living in the mountaintop castles with no easy water supply, a steep ascent and food grown on the plain below.

One of the books that accompanied us was *The Discovery of France*, a rambling, fascinating investigation of the nature of France, stressing the fragmented nature of the country before the revolution and Napoleon's administrative reforms. The author Graham Robb describes a people known as *cagots* who are known to exist from 1000AD, mainly in the southwest of France, though also in Brittany and other areas. Known by a variety of similar names in different parts of the country, including *capots* in the Languedoc, and *cacous* in Brittany, they were a pariah caste, considered

to be a different race from the rest of the French. They had to enter churches by a separate porch, sit apart on separate benches, and even receive the host on the end of a stick. They were limited to carpentry and rope-making as trades for the men, midwifery for the women. All sorts of queer physical qualities were attributed to them. They were said to lack earlobes, have webbed hands and feet, peculiar eyes, and to bleed from the navel on Good Friday.

Though largely forgotten in modern France, they are of interest for this article because of the speculation about their origins.

"A group of cagots who sent a petition to Pope Léon X in the sixteenth century claimed to be the descendants of Cathar heretics who were exterminated in the Albigensian crusades in the thirteenth century. But the cagots predate the Cathars and there is no sign that their religion is unorthodox."

(*The Discovery of France* p. 45)

Still, the possibility is fascinating. Cagots do not seem to have been a distinct ethnic group, though they were forced to marry only within their own communities, nor did they have their own language, speaking the dialects of the region they lived in. This raises the possibility that there were multiple origins for the cagots and that people of varying origins were categorized as cagots. Among the suggestions are that the cagots were the descendants of lepers who returned from the crusades, or were Roman soldiers sent to spas in Gaul, that they were the descendants of Saracens, or that, since they were carpenters and many cagot communities lay on pilgrim routes, they were the remains of an itinerant carpenters' guild.

Why would a group of people who were

loathed and oppressed, yet attended church, claim that they were descended from massacred heretics unless there was some truth to the story? In addition to their thoroughly inferior status they would also be claiming a link to heresy, which would hardly have encouraged the Pope to help them. There may be some germ of truth in that particular group of cagots being descended from the Cathars. The mystery is not likely to be cleared up soon.

We moved again to settle for a few days at Quillan, a small town through which, like Esparaza, the river Aude ran. Formerly a centre of the hat-making industry, the hat museum was for us non-milliners less fascinating than the dinosaur museum with which it shared a huge shed. Quillan had acquired, through the work of Englishwoman Patrice Chaplin, links with the Saunière mystery. I read her most recent book *The Portal* on the trip. It describes an initiatory journey from Girona to Rennes-le-Château and Mount Canigou through a series of esoterically significant energy points. Though I found much of the symbolism and many of the factual claims to be rather hokey, for example that the Tour Magdala at Rennes-le-Château represented Isis to the Nephthys of a somewhat similar tower in Girona (although the town of Girona itself, we are told, is actually under the influence of Isis, not Nephthys), I quite enjoyed the book, and the amount of complaining that Patrice—a lady in her sixties—indulges in due to the physical exertion of the journey convinced me that she had certainly made the initiation.

I liked the quietness and slow pace of Quillan. Though there were many empty houses for sale at low prices and not much sign of local industry it felt like a healthy place. Each night we went the Place de la République, the town square, and had a pastis or a glass of blanquette or some other wine at one of the cafés. My favourite was run by a chaotic, shaven-headed, slightly camp character who stacked up the requests from his customers and carried them out in flurries of whirling activity until it all got too much and he would sit down and have a cigarette and a drink

with some friends and ignore everyone else. One time I sat there for nearly half an hour, catching his eye from time to time—"J'arriva," he assured me—till I successfully ordered a drink and then waited and waited and waited for it to arrive, before I gave up and when to a less charming but more efficient place across the road.

France is renowned as a country of smokers, but even here it is no longer allowed indoors in public places. In small bars everyone—clients and employees—will suddenly exit en masse and all start smoking together. No one supplies ashtrays so everyone just throws their butts into the gutter, if they are feeling responsible, or just onto the floor if not. But the most bizarre example of the French attitude to smoking was in a small restaurant in Quillan that specialised in fish. A table of two French couples were served their main fish course fresh our of the kitchen—and the fish there was excellent—and then the whole table promptly left the restaurant, ignoring the owner's pleading, and had a leisurely smoke, only returning to tuck in to the cooling food ten minutes later.

Other odd experiences that stick in the memory include a traditional knife grinder in the marketplace of a town whose name escapes me. In Limoux we found an odd wall decorated with a mixture of nationalist slogans, the tricolour and esoteric symbols, including stars of David drawn to resemble the tree of life, the motto "Nature=Morte", a reference to the sword of Damocles and what appear to be found objects on display. We visited the Musée des Automates, the Museum of Automatons, initially a little disappointed to find that they were all modern creations and not the elaborate and baroque clockwork devices portrayed in the rolling video on show. But we soon came under their spell. It was a little like being in a Neil Gaiman story as these human sized figures rocked back and forth metronomically, with a soundtrack of a hundred music boxes playing at different speeds. Medieval cat men, beaked aldermen, princesses in carnival masks, goat girls and ice maidens in bright synthetic fabrics

jerked their arms, nodded inexpressively, and repeated involuntary twitches out of synch with each other. The movements were limited, the designs too glossy and new and repetitive for my tastes, yet the overall effect was of entering a crazed fairyland of emotionless beings that whirred and jingled and twitched and sent a shiver up my spine.

Montségur was the most eagerly awaited site in the holiday and the most famous and infamous location in Cathar history. I was glad that the weather was cool and overcast given my difficulty with the heat and the steep climbs of the previous trip. As we approached Montségur via the windy roads the rocky outcrop came into sight again and again as we twisted around the hairpin bends. The castle held out against a crusader siege in 1244. When it looked as if the siege might at last have to be lifted a group of the Northern French Catholic army soldiers climbed their way up at night and established a foothold from which the castle could be attacked with siege engines. On the second of March the Montségurians surrendered and sought terms, and were told that they would be treated equally but that the Cathars would have to recant their faiths and submit themselves to the Inquisition. The Perfect refused. 200 of the Perfect delivered themselves up, and 16 believers, Cathars who had not taken on the strict conditions of the inner circle, took the initiation rite of the consolamentum to joined the other Perfect in death by fire. It was a temporal catastrophe but a spiritual triumph.

At Montségur village the mountain loomed above us. We visited the small museum, typical of French regional museums. Exhibit cases held a variety of small objects: clasps, keys, buckles, all from the time of the Cathars. The most memorable item, reproduced on various postcards, posters and promotional material, was a nicely fashioned pair of scissors. Cathars often worked as weavers and tailors, a renowned heretic's trade, and these were possibly Cathar scissors, perhaps used to cut out material for the black gowns worn by the Perfect. It is difficult to convey the intimacy of these scissors in that glass case.

Placards, mostly in French but with the occasional sentence or paragraph in English, described the course of the Albigensian war and the development of the siege. Large reproductions included a manuscript page of the Cathar ritual and a leaf of a Cathar Bible, probably identical to the Catholic Bible (though the Cathars didn't have a high opinion of the Old Testament), but translated into Occitan, the language of the South. Occitan refuses to die out and may be spoken as a first language by a million people, though these things are hard to estimate and the language remains in danger, with many parents not passing it on to their children.

The walk up to the castle was tough but not the hour-long slog I had somehow expected. The path was a mixture of mud and gravel, broad stone steps, wooden stays with eroded earth and irregular, embedded stones. I was wearing ordinary shoes with worn treads and my feet slipped occasionally, but I am cautious in these situations and no harm was done. My heart was beating fast, the sweat pouring down me, and we had to stop occasionally. I was glad the day was cool and overcast even if the wind had a bite to it, giving me slight earache. I felt that the physical discomfort somehow atoned for my status as a tourist, the mountain locations extracting an obligatory penance from even the most plastic traveller.

The castle, which was not identical to the structure the Cathars sheltered in, but had been rebuilt soon after, was simple in comparison to some of the other fortresses. I tried to imagine the Cathars living there. It was surely a harsh existence, assailed by blazing sun, biting wind or winter snow. The old lady in the ticket office, situated halfway up the mountain, was cheerful, enjoying practising her English and making jokes. She was there all seasons she said, and mimed having to poke a hole in the snow to see out of the booth in wintertime.

We climbed around to the side where the

French forces established the foothold that broke the siege. It must have taken unimaginable determination and certitude for the Cathars to surrender themselves to the Inquisition. They preferred to be burnt to death than to recant their faith.

As we took the path down I felt that I followed in their footsteps, intentionally visualized them filing down the difficult path. I found it took a fair amount of imagination in these places to bring the Cathars back to life. I tried to visualize the black-cowled Perfects of all ages and both sexes negotiating the difficult trail in pairs to their doom. At the bottom of the hill was an elegantly constructed bonfire, perhaps representing that on which they were consumed. A monument commemorates them. Though a fairly well-known image, it was erected only in 1970.

I'd hate to give the impression that I was constantly tortured by Gnostic angst over the contrast between the thirteenth century atrocities and our twenty-first century Ryanair tourism. The trip was wonderful We had good food, good local wine, pastis and blanquette, the local fizzy white wine. The Cathar sites were moving, though the presence of so many tourists made me uncomfortably aware of my own status. Books on the Cathars usually focus on the history of the Albigensian crusade and can easily disappear into a skeleton list of place names, the story moving from atrocity to atrocity, from town to town, but a visit to the land itself, despite the erosion of the centuries, the ravages of the heritage industry and the Cathar steak dinners, makes it all seem more real.

Stevan Davies

The Pre-Christian Odes of Solomon

In this essay I will argue that Christianity as we know it, a religion focused on Jesus of Nazareth, arose from an antecedent religion known to us through the Odes of Solomon. In the first part I will show that the general scholarly understanding of the Odes as products of early first century Christianity is mistaken and that they are not demonstrably Christian at all. In the second part I will show that the Odes represent the religion of the Churches of God that Paul first persecuted and then joined, and suggest that Jesus himself may have been associated with the Jewish cult that produced the Odes of Solomon, which I will call "Odes Judaism." I will show that principal ideas in the Odes are also to be found in the Gospel of John and in other ancient Christian writings, and argue that the temporal-causal arrow points from the Odes to the Christian texts, rather than vice versa.

PART ONE
THE RELIGION OF THE ODES OF SOLOMON

The Odes of Solomon are a collection of hymns that are generally believed to be Christian even though they represent a very peculiar variety of Christianity, one hard to classify using the standard scholarly types. James Charlesworth writes, for example, that "The Odes of Solomon were composed at a time when Gnosticism had not yet developed and when gnosis was a worldwide Spiritual way of thinking. They also come to us from a time when Judaism and Christianity had not yet gone their separate ways." [1] He believes that they derive from a religious group profoundly influenced by the spirituality of the Essenes and yet that the Odes are so similar in ideology to the Gospel and Letters of John that it is even possible "the Odist and John shared the same milieu, and it is not improbable that they lived in the same community." [2]

The Odes of Solomon are not Gnostic insofar as they do not argue for a cosmic dualism separating a perfect One from a fallen world, and they are in agreement with the standard Jewish view that God created this world out of his benevolence; there is no myth of the pre-cosmic fall of God or of God's Solphia, who then needs to be rescued by gnosis from this fallen or illusory world. However, the myth of rescue is clearly present throughout the Odes of Solomon. Human beings are enslaved or enchained in a prison existence wherein they are persecuted and in need of rescue. Rescue comes, at least from one of the Odes' metaphorical perspectives, from *gnosis*. This is most clear in Ode 17, which shows remarkable kinship to Gnostic ideas, although it does not presuppose a Gnostic myth of origins. Michael Lattke's translation of 17:7-9a reads,

> And he who knew me made me great, the Most High in his complete pleroma. And he glorified me by his benevolence and lifted up my gnosis to the height of Truth. And thence he gave me the way of his steps. And I opened the gates that were shut, and broke the bars of iron. [3]

There is a particularly significant connection between one of the greatest Gnostic works, the

Gospel of Truth, perhaps written by Valentinus himself, and Ode 7:20-21. In the Ode we hear (Lattke's translation),

> hatred will be lifted from the earth and be submerged together with jealousy. For non-gnosis has been destroyed, because the gnosis of the Lord has come.

The fundamental and reiterated theme of the Gospel of Truth is that when gnosis comes, illusion disappears: e.g. "but what comes into existence in him is knowledge, which appeared in order that oblivion might vanish and the Father might be known. Since oblivion came into existence because the Father was not known, then if the Father comes to be known, oblivion will not exist from that moment on."[4] This is a remarkable similarity of ideas.

One might suggest that while the problem the Odes of Solomon addresses is not formulated in terms of the Gnostic myth, the solution offered by the Odes is essentially Gnostic.

The Odes are known today from a variety of manuscripts and citations (all of which are discussed in detail by Lattke in his recent magisterial tome on the Odes) but experts differ on whether they were written originally in Syriac (so Charlesworth) or in Greek (so Lattke). [5] David Aune, having surveyed scholarly opinion, concludes that the Odes most probably were in originally written in Greek, but that there is no consensus.[6] There appears to be a general agreement in scholarship at present that they come from a very early period of Christian history. Lattke concludes that the date of the Odes of Solomon is "the first quarter of the second century C.E." and they represent "the overlap of early Judaism, early Gnosticism, and early Christianity."[7] Charlesworth basically concurs, writing that "the date of the composition is most likely some time before 125 CE." [8]

Many authorities locate the origin of the Odes somewhere in western Syria which, Charlesworth specifies, includes the region of Galilee. Lattke does not think it is possible to be very specific about the Odes' place of origin, but he does believe that while the affiliations of the Odes with the Letters of Ignatius of Antioch do not prove that they are of Antiochean origin, nevertheless those affiliations "do strongly suggest Syria as the area."[9] Robert Grant concluded that the Odes are most likely "composed in Syriac at Edessa." [10]

It is difficult to argue a negative, but I will try to show that the Odes of Solomon are not Christian. In the first place, nothing about Jesus of Nazareth is ever mentioned in them. Not one sentence of the Odes indicates that they derive from the religion that regards Jesus as its founder. They may be Christian in the sense that they are profoundly concerned with the concept of a human being who becomes Christ, but if this person is not uniquely Jesus, then we need to be careful how the word Christian is being used.[11]

Only if we assume from the outset, by hypothesis, that the Odes are Christian do we have any reason to think that the Odes derive from members of the religion focused on the life, death, resurrection of Jesus. No, in fact the Odes of Solomon are not Christian at all unless we redefine their Christianity to be a cult unrelated to the religion focused on Jesus of Nazareth. I suggest that this might indeed be the best way of understanding them, and that they derive from a form of Christianity for which Jesus of Nazareth was entirely irrelevant.

The supposed Christianity of the Odes is very hard to define, although in their vocabulary and phraseology they are certainly are similar to what one reads in early Christian writing, especially that from the Johannine community. However, while phrases in the Odes may sound familiar, the ideas they communicate are not. As Robert Grant wrote in 1944, "In regard to Christian doctrines inherited from Judaism [the Odes of Solomon] do not mention forgiveness, atonement, or in fact, sin. The only circumcision is that of the heart (Ode 11:1-2), while the offering of the Lord is righteousness and purity of heart and lips (20:5)."[12] Grant continues, "As for doctrines more specifically

Christian, they do not speak of resurrection and ascension (though these may be implied in Christ's victory), nor of baptism and the Eucharist."[13] Major themes that are vital to the Christian religion are missing in the Odes of Solomon. Grant quotes a conversation with his friend Arthur Darby Nock: "Professor Nock has observed to me in this connection, we can probably conclude that the Christ of the Odes of Solomon was not really born, did not really live, was not really crucified, did not really die."[14]

One can go further. The Odes do not mention Jesus in any sense; his name is never used, nor do the Odes contain a single one of his sayings, nor do they mention even one event in which the gospels say he participated. The "cross" supposedly appears twice in the Odes of Solomon (Odes 27 and 42), but only when translators such as Charlesworth take the Syriac (*qaysa*) or Greek (*xylon*) word for wood or tree and translate it as "cross." Less tendentious translators do not do this. The first English translator, Rendel Harris, used the word "wood." Lattke's recent translation gives, for Ode 27 "

I stretched out my hands and hallowed my Lord, because the spreading out of my hands is his sign, and my stretching [up] is the wood, which is upright;

(The passage in Ode 42 is nearly identical). Charlesworth and others have assumed that "wood" must be "the cross" and that the physical position of the one speaking is cruciform. Accordingly, while Charlesworth's version of Ode 27 is

I extended my hands and hallowed my Lord, For the expansion of my hands is His sign. And my extension is the upright cross,

Lattke argues that the speaker stands with arms upraised, stretched up and outwards, not in a cruciform shape.[15] This matters a great deal because if Lattke is correct (and his recent tome

of commentary makes him the world's leading expert on the Odes) then there is no reference to cross or crucifixion in the Odes anywhere. One should note that arboreal imagery is rather common in the Odes. For example, in Ode 11 the speaker becomes a tree in the garden of God:

Blessed, O Lord, are they who are planted in Your land, and who have a place in Your Paradise; and who grow in the growth of Your trees, and have passed from darkness into light."[16]

In Ode 38 the speaker says he

"was established and lived and was redeemed, and my foundations were laid on account of the Lord's hand; because He has planted me, for He set the root, and watered it and endowed it and blessed it, and its fruits will be forever."

The speaker standing in a manner that suggests a tree does not in any way require one to presume that the speaker represents the cross of Jesus. One cannot validly conclude from these two instances (Odes 27 // 42) of the term wood (*xylon* / *qaysa*) that the Odes refer to the crucifixion of Jesus of Nazareth.

Some might argue that there are specific references to Christian themes in Ode 19, which discusses a virgin birth, and in Ode 24 where a dove flutters above the Messiah. But in both cases the imagery in the Odes is utterly unlike any that has ever been associated with the Christian conception of Mary or of the Spirit-dove in the story of Jesus' baptism. In Ode 19 we hear that the Father's breasts are full and that He is milked by the Spirit so that his milk runs into the cup which is the Son. The milk from the Father's breasts is the metaphorical semen that "the womb of the Virgin caught, and she conceived and gave birth." This is hardly an expansion of the Matthean or Lukan account! It is something wholly different. While in later centuries some Christians occasionally spoke of the milk of Christ, that is the not the metaphor used here, where the Son is the cup containing the milk of the Father.

The only other reference to a Virgin comes in Ode 33, which is a reference to God's Wisdom; the passage reads "*The Perfect Virgin stood up proclaiming and crying out and saying 'Sons of men, turn back, and their daughters, come, and leave the ways of this Corruption and draw near to me....*'" (5-7). This is not a reference to Mary but to the female Wisdom who speaks in passages such as this one from Proverbs 8:1-5:

> Does not wisdom call out? Does not understanding raise her voice? At the highest point along the way, where the paths meet, she takes her stand; beside the gate leading into the city, at the entrance, she cries aloud: 'To you, O people, I call out; I raise my voice to all mankind. You who are simple, gain prudence; you who are foolish, set your hearts on it.'

Ode 19 also contains a trinity of terms "Father," and "Son," and "Spirit," that became, of course, crucial to later Christian theology, but the terms are hardly unique to Christianity. The use of the concept "Father" for God, and the discussion of God's Spirit are common in Judaism, only the "Son" is unusual in that theological context. This trinity of terms is unusual in earliest Christianity, occurring only once as such in the New Testament (Matthew 28:19), but it is not a set of concepts that is unique to Matthew. The Spirit of Christ and the Spirit of the Father are conceived synonymously by Paul, who also refers to the Spirit of the Son (Romans 8:9-16, Galatians 4:6)). I am arguing, however, that the Odes community preceded and strongly influenced branches of earliest Christianity and so the fact that both communities occasionally utilize what came to be known as Trinitarian vocabulary indicates ideological connection, but it does not give us evidence of chronological priority. When the Trinitarian terms are listed in Ode 23, however they appear to be a later

interpolation; line 21 refers to a letter entirely written by the finger of God, but line 22 lists its authors as the Father and the Son and the Holy Spirit.

As for the dove, we hear in Ode 24:1-2 (Lattke): "*The dove flew onto the head of our Lord Messiah, because he was her Head. And she cooed on/over him, and her voice was heard...*" This might, at a stretch, appear to have something to do with the account in Mark 1:10 but as the passage continues on we quickly enter wholly alien territory, (3-4) "*and the inhabitants were afraid, and the sojourners were disturbed,. The birds gave up their wing [beat], and all creeping things died in their hole,*" that soon becomes cosmic mythos, (5-6), "*and the primal deeps were opened and covered. And they sought the Lord like those who are about to give birth, and/ but he was not given to them for food, because he was not their own,*" One does not have to raise the question of what kind of Christian theology identifies the Messiah as the head of the Spirit (assuming that the Odes' dove is symbolic of the Spirit, which is very far from obvious) to realize that the conjunction of the words "dove" and "Messiah" here have nothing whatsoever to do with Mark's scene of the baptism of Jesus by John.

The Odes of Solomon are an extraordinary mixture of the incomprehensible (e.g. the bizarre accounts of the impregnation of a symbolic virgin with the Father's milk; the fluttering flight of a deadly dove who opens the door to primal deeps) with the platitudinous. The Odes are replete with boilerplate praise formulae that would not be at all out of place in a Christian church today or, for that matter, a synagogue, or a mosque, or a convocation of worshippers of Govinda. To give just one of many possible examples, Ode 40:1-2 reads (Lattke's translation):

> As honey drips from the honeycomb of bees, and milk flows from the woman who loves her children, so also my hope is on thee, my God. As a spring gushes out

its water, so my heart gushes out praises for the Lord, and my lips bring forth a hymn to him.

Nothing about this sort of poetic piety is specific to Christianity.

THE TRANSFORMATION FROM HUMAN TO DIVINITY

What makes the Odes particularly interesting is their propensity to shift back and forth from poetic speech that seems to emerge from a human worshipper to speech that seems to emerge from a divine being, a Messiah, a Son of God. These speakers are so interwoven within various Odes that translators have added in "ex ore Christi" before some sentences and "ex ore Odist" before others to help readers keep supposedly different characters separate. The original texts, however, see no need to try and separate speakers in this way. In Ode 10, for example, we hear that

The Lord has directed my mouth by His Word, and has opened my heart by His Light. And He has caused to dwell in me His immortal life, and permitted me to proclaim the fruit of His peace. To convert the lives of those who desire to come to Him, and to lead those who are captive into freedom.

So far we hear the voice of a human being but the remainder of the Ode appears to be spoken by a divine person:

I took courage and became strong and captured the world, and the captivity became mine for the glory of the Most High, and of God my Father. And the Gentiles who had been dispersed were gathered together, but I was not defiled by my love for them, because they had praised me in high places. And the traces

of light were set upon their heart, and they walked according to my life and were saved, and they became my people forever and ever.

As is often the case in the Odes, we do not have here two separate people speaking, one human and one divine, but one person speaking who has been transformed from human to divine, a person in whom dwells God's immortal life who becomes a savior with a people whom he has saved. Presumably those who are saved are now in the same condition he is, once captives but now in freedom.

For a similar example we read in Ode 29 at first the words of a human person who has been transformed:

According to His mercies He exalted me, and according to His great honor He lifted me up. And he caused me to ascend from the depths of Sheol, and from the mouth of death He drew me. And I humbled my enemies, and He justified me by His grace. For I believed in the Lord's Messiah, and considered that He is the Lord.

This transformed person immediately begins to speak as the Messiah who drew him and transformed him,

He revealed to me His sign, and He led me by His light. And He gave me the scepter of His power, that I might subdue the devices of the people, and humble the power of the mighty. To make war by His Word, and to take victory by His power. And the Lord overthrew my enemy by His Word, and he became like the dust which a breeze carries off.

If we do not insert separate speaker categories into the translation, and the originals contain nothing of that sort, then the one who ascends and is justified is also the one who has the scepter of power and who humbles the power of the mighty.

It is important to realize that the Odes are not just the product of speculation, wishful thinking, believer's faith or some other use of poetic imagination. Rather, the Odes, when they reflect a transformation of a human person to a divine person, ultimately derive from a particular type of human experience, one that is documented everywhere and through all times. That experience is a form of psychological dissociation that we can call "Spirit possession," a type of experience that is probably a genetically determined possibility available to anyone with the right cultural conditioning and group expectation. This conclusion follows simply from the observation that spirit possession seems to occur throughout the world in virtually all religious settings.[⊠]

The Spirit possession experience is logically prior to any explanation of the experience. The experience can be described in secular terms as follows: one's primary personality is set aside or minimized and a secondary personality occurs. The secondary personality may speak fluently or incoherently and it may control the body well or poorly. Modern psychology will define this experience as a form of dissociation and discuss its origins and nature in reference to states of mind or measure the experience with an electroencephalograph.[⊠] In religious settings, however, the experience of such personality dissociation will usually be explained as the arrival into a person of an external secondary personality which will be understood to be that of God, a Spirit, an Ancestor and so forth depending on the local theology. Personality dissociation that has negative consequences will be understood to be the result of a demon, positive consequences will be associated with the arrival of a beneficial Spirit. Within a Judaic cultural setting (and within settings historically derived from the Judaic) the Holy Spirit is the term most often used. In secular terms "Holy Spirit" is an explanatory paradigm for positively valued experiences of personality dissociation in Judaic cultural settings.

The experience of Spirit possession is not that of a person experiencing, but rather of a person ceasing to experience while being replaced by another who does experience. The first person may or may not remember anything of what the second person experienced. In Spirit possession it is paradigmatic that one individual is two persons. In the experience of Spirit possession a single body alternates persons who inhabit it, there being one person there some of the time and another person there some of the time. In terms of the Odes of Solomon, a single body is transformed by the addition of a second person so that the first person becomes the second person, although presumably the active domination of the second person is occasional and the first person is normally dominant.

If the Odes derive from a kind of possession experience, then the odists will understand themselves sometimes to be speaking as the possessing divine entity and sometimes as themselves. Insofar as they have become a Spirit, they can speak sometimes as themselves transformed and sometimes as the Spirit within them. Speaking as Spirit, for example, the Odist speaks of descent, of arrival in this world from a world beyond this world. Speaking as a human merged with Spirit, the Odist speaks of ascent, of arrival in the paradise beyond this world, of becoming a divine person. Ode 36: (Lattke's translation)

The Spirit of the Lord rested upon me, and she lifted me up to the height and set me on my feet in the height of the Lord before his pleroma/ fullness and his glory. While I gave praise by the composition of the odes, she brought me forth before the face of the Lord. And although I was a (son of) man, I was called the Shining One, the Son of God, while I was glorious among the glorious and was great among the great.

For according to the greatness of the Most High, so she made me, and according to his renewal he renewed me. And he anointed me from his perfection, and I was/became one of those beside him.

And my mouth was opened like a cloud of dew, and my heart gushed forth a flood of righteousness. And my access was in peace and I was established in the Spirit of the plan of salvation. Hallelujah.

We find the following stages of transformation in Ode 36:

1. The Spirit of the Lord arrives; the speaker has an experience that receives this culturally conditioned explanation.

2. The experience is understood to include ascent to the presence of God, a common theme in Jewish mysticism.

3. The speaker, who is a human, a son of man, becomes a new type of being, here called "the Shining One," and "the Son of God." Charlesworth, assuming that the speaker is Jesus, assumes also that the Christian title "Son of Man" used sometimes in the Gospels for Jesus as a cosmic being should be used in translating this part of the Ode, and so he writes: "because I was the Son of Man, I was named the Light, the Son of God." But Lattke is not so tendentious; the phrase "son of man," is a Semitic language commonplace for any human being. As Lattke translates it, a human person becomes the anointed Son of God; Charlesworth understands the Ode to be about Jesus, the unique Son of Man.[16]

4. The speaker is transformed toward divinity by being remade "according to greatness" and "renewed."

5. The speaker is "anointed," and so is by definition a christ or a messiah, i.e. one who has been anointed.

6. The speaker is located in the heavenly space, "one of those beside him."

Ode 36 describes the speaker's experience as a Spirit-caused ascent resulting in transformation from a human status to a divine or heavenly status as anointed Son of God. There is no reason to doubt that if the speaker can experience this one time he can experience it repeatedly. Since many of the Odes speak of what is evidently the same experience understood more or less in the same way, we can assume that this type of experience is available to members of the Odes community generally; it is evidently their prototypical experience and as far as we know the main point of their community life.

The speaker in the Ode becomes the Son of God and, through the Spirit of God, is anointed to become a being in the heavenly world. He takes on the past and the future of the Son of God, as various Odes describe it. To become Son of God or Messiah is to absorb both the Messiah's history and his mission. His history is to have escaped from the shackles and imprisonment of the world below, of Sheol, and his mission is to act as an ideal example for other humans. In more mythological terms, he brings them salvation from above so that they might recapitulate his career by escaping the shackles and imprisonment of the world below, ascending through the Spirit to become Son of God, and then bringing others salvation and so on.

We find an excellent example of such a transformation in Ode 17 where the speaker, having been unchained, becomes the liberator of others whose chains he destroys. Ode 17 begins with a transformation story: "*Then I was crowned by my God, and my crown was living. And I was justified by my Lord, for my salvation is incorruptible. I have been freed from vanities, and am not condemned.*" In this instance the transformation is not described as an ascent but as liberation. "*My chains were cut off by His hands, I received the face and likeness of a new person, and I walked in Him and was saved. And the thought of truth led me, and I went after it and wandered not. And all who saw me were amazed, and I seemed to them like a stranger.*" The speaker is a new person, newly unchained, now a stranger in the world from which he came. The Odes' process of transformation identifies the speaker not only with labeled categories of being (Son of God, Shining One, Anointed) and with categories of religious excellence (saved, renewed) but also with a mythological pattern, here one of bondage and freedom:

And from there He gave me the way of His steps, and I opened the doors which were closed. And I shattered the bars of iron, for my own shackles had grown hot and melted before me.And nothing appeared closed to me, because I was the opening of everything.

The speaker, transformed, can now facilitate the transformation of others. As the Ode begins the speaker's chains are cut off, now the speaker shatters bars and opens doors for others.

And I went towards all my bound ones in order to loose them; that I might not leave anyone bound or binding. And I gave my knowledge generously, and my resurrection through my love. And I sowed my fruits in hearts, and transformed them through myself. Then they received my blessing and lived, and they were gathered to me and were saved because they became my members, and I was their Head. Glory to You, our Head, O Lord Messiah.

The Lord Messiah is both the savior and a status that one might strive to attain, the goal and culmination of the Odes religious quest, so that the speaker in the Ode is himself the saved savior.

The Odes of Solomon present a "saved savior" model such that potentially any and all human beings can receive the Spirit, ascend to the place of God, and be transformed into a Son of God to serve as a model so as to facilitate the saving transformation of others. Accordingly, the Odes shift deliberately back and forth between a human speaker and a divine speaker or, as some translators have it, between the Odist and Christ. One must bear in mind, however, that an Ode will be spoken by a single individual and reflect the experience of the individual who composed it.

The idea that the Odist and Christ are two separate persons is mistaken. The Odes speak of the transformation of the speaker (the "Odist") into the one spoken about ("Christ"). The mythological career of the Christ was that he was in bondage below but escaped his bonds and soared into heaven, which is also the metaphorical career of the Speaker who was liberated from chains and taken into heaven from here below. There is, in the Odes, a mythological Christ prototype that is assumed by the speaker, the successful human being ("son of man") who becomes the Son of God. If we think about this in terms of the Spirit-possession paradigm common throughout the world, then it is no great surprise that one person can speak as both a human and a divine being.

As discussed above, there is no mention of Jesus in the Odes anywhere, no mention of the crucifixion anywhere, not one saying of Jesus or miracle story about him found in any gospel is referenced in any of the Odes. When the Odes speak of mythological activities of the savior, they are activities that have never been connected with Jesus. For example, the Odes' motif of escaping imprisonment and breaking shackles of iron is not mentioned in any account of Jesus' life. In a manner not characteristic of Christianity the speaker in Ode 22 is given the power to destroy the seven headed serpent, as well as the power to free others from bondage, as we can see in Lattke's translation:

He who brought me down from the high places which are above, and has brought me up from the places in the depth below,

which nicely shows the commensurability of the savior who descends and the saved who ascends, and

He who has scattered my enemies and my adversaries. He who has given me authority over bonds, to release them. He who has smitten the serpent with seven heads by my hands. He has set me up over its root so that I might wipe out its seed.

Stories like this are simply not connected to the tradition of Jesus of Nazareth in any way. They are stories where the human speaker and a divine personage shift identities back and forth. The divine person has scattered the enemies and adversaries of the human speaker who then receives authority to release people from bonds (a standard role of the savior in the Odes). The speaker's hands destroy the seven headed serpent, whatever that might be, and the speaker becomes the cosmic warrior who will wipe out the seed of the serpent.

The Odes characteristically blur the distinction between the speaker and the spoken-of, between the son of man and the anointed Son of God. While the Odes share some language and conceptions with the Christianity associated with Jesus of Nazareth, they have nothing to do with him.

In his fascinating book on the New Testament Christological Hymns, which are Philemon 2:6-11, Colossians 1:15-20, Ephesians 2:14-16, 1 Timothy 3:16, 1 Peter 3:18-22, Hebrews 1:3, and the Prologue to the Gospel of John, Jack T. Sanders finds that the hymns "all seem to present generally the same myth of the redeemer, involving his participating in creation, his descent and ascent to and from the world, and his work of redemption."[17] "It may reasonably be assumed that this mythical drama has some background in the history of religions, that the way was already prepared in the general (or in some particular) religious milieu of early Christianity for the formulation of this particular myth—if the myth had not in reality already been formulated."[18] Sanders argues that the similarities in the Christological hymns and the Prologue to John "necessitate some kind of unified explanation of the historical religious background of all the hymns together, not of any one in isolation."[19] His observation that there is a common redeemer myth embedded in a variety of New Testament hymns leads him to believe that this myth existed before the rise of the Christian religion so that there was, in a sense, a pre-Jesus Christianity in existence, one that was then adapted to the movement that became the Jesus-oriented Christian religion.

Sanders believes that the background to the New Testament Christological hymns "is in all probability to be sought in pre-Christian Judaism," a form of pre-Christian Judaism that spoke of a "divine figure that was in the image (likeness, form) of God, i.e. that it possessed equality with God, that it participated in creation and embodied the All, that it descended from the sphere of the divine to the sphere of the mortal, that it in some way entered into human existence, i.e. became identified with human existence for the sake of the revelatory task."[20]

After having analyzed the canonical New Testament Christological hymns, Sanders takes up the analysis of the Odes of Solomon. He studies the Odes' connection to the themes of the canonical Christological hymns and comes to the strong conclusion that their "parallels with the New Testament Christological hymns are so close as to imply either influence from one to the other, or influence from a common background. Thus one must ask, 'Did these elements come into the Odes of Solomon from Christianity, or from somewhere else?'"[21] After considerable discussion, he concludes that the Odes of Solomon contain only a few, and perhaps no, signs of Christian influence. The few that they do seem to contain probably, in his view, and in the opinion of other scholars whom to whom he refers, derive from later scribal interpolations. In Sanders' opinion, the Odes of Solomon originate from a Jewish group that was in existence shortly before the rise of Christianity.[22]

Sanders notes that "the possibility that the myth in the New Testament Christological hymns was already intact prior to its use by Christianity is still further increased when it is seen that the redeemer myth of the Odes of Solomon is connected with a stage of hypostatization of divine qualities less developed than the stage present in the New Testament Christological hymns."[23] He argues that the mixture of ideas found in the Odes of Solomon probably arose independently of the New Testament and therefore, "*then presumably also prior to it;* therefore, the possibility is increased that the element of cosmic reconciliation, which completes the act of redemption, had already become a part of the developing myth lying behind the New Testament Christological hymns *prior to its appropriation by Christianity.* The redeemer of the Odes of Solomon certainly effects redemption by incorporating the redeemed, as is clear from Ode 17:14f."[24] While a "myth" is known to us only as it is found in ancient texts, it once was the centerpiece of a social movement, of a cult whose practices, whatever they might have been, were far more extensive than simply propagating a myth. Accordingly, when Sanders proposes that there was a myth that preceded the rise of Jesus-oriented Christianity and one that came to be incorporated into that Christianity, he is proposing that a cult, an assembly of like-minded people, existed. This fact is trivially obvious, but it can be overlooked by textual scholarship.

Not only does Sanders conclude that the Odes of Solomon are evidence of a pre-Jesus Jewish Christianity that incorporated the main themes of crucially important New Testament Christological hymns, he does something few other scholars ever do: he looks north. It should be, but often is not, obvious that there were cultural influences on Galilee, and Samaria, and even Judea that come from the north, from Syria, Tyre, Sidon, Damascus, Antioch, influences on Judaism that were not Judean in origin. We should especially bear in mind the fact that Paul of Tarsus, when he was first initiated (by God, he would say) into the Christian faith, had an experience that took place near a Christian community in Damascus, and that he spent some of his early years with a Christian community in Antioch, and that he saw no purpose in visiting Jerusalem until three years of his time as a Christian had passed.

There were, of course, religions in the ancient world near Palestine that were not Judaism and Jewish people and Jewish cults were influenced to lesser or greater degrees by those religions. In reading the Odes of Solomon, Jack T. Sanders is struck by the frequency of their use of the word "Lord." That word leads to some ambiguity for

two reasons. First, it is not always clear when the term "Lord" refers to God and when the word "Lord" refers to the secondary figure of the Son or Messiah. Second, influenced by their Christian backgrounds, modern scholars will tend to assume that "Lord" refers to the Lord Jesus Christ even though there is no place in the Odes where this is evident.

Sanders suggests that the word "Lord" in Hebrew, which is "Adon," the plural of which, "Adonai" is commonly used in Judaism as the name or title of the Jewish God, may have entered the community of the Odes of Solomon from another religious tradition than Judaism, the tradition that worshipped Adon, the Lord, as God, the religion of the worship of Adonis. Sanders writes that, "Adonis, it should be remembered, is the western designation of Tammuz (or, viewed otherwise, Tammuz is regularly designated simply 'the Lord'), and his influence was felt on Jewish religion before the time of Ezekiel, as is attested by Ezek. Viii.14: 'Then he brought me to the entrance of the north gate of the house of the Lord; and behold, there sat women weeping for Tammuz.'"[25] Sanders does not push this point of view very far, he writes that "the eclecticism present in the Odes of Solomon prevents a final explanation of the character of the redeemer they present simply in terms of a fusing between concepts from Judaism and from the cult of Adonis; still, the Odes of Solomon seem to attest that Judaism could, under some outside influence, give birth to at least one myth of redemption similar to that displayed in the New Testament Christological humans, and yet apparently independent of the New Testament tradition."[26] Looking to the north, as Sanders did, will remind us of the fact that the people of Judea, and even more so the people of Samaria and of Galilee were influenced by a host of different religious ideas and systems.

Leaving aside possible connections to the religion of Adonis to the north, the Odes do have a strong relationship with the mystical tradition of late second-Temple Judaism to the south near Jerusalem. April de Conick writes that

"It is apparent that during the Second Temple Period, an esoteric tendency was developing and manifesting itself within different varieties of Judaism including the Philonic corpus, the sectarian communities of the Therapeutae and Qumran, apocalyptic circles, and rabbinic teachings. This early Jewish mysticism filtered into Christianity, Gnosticism, and the Hekhalot literature, teaching that, after proper preparations, one could seek to ascend into heaven in order to gain heavenly knowledge and a transforming vision of the deity."[27] This is the background of some of the Odes of Solomon.[28]

From the Dead Sea Scrolls; hymn 4Q491-C we hear of the ascent of a person to the presence of God and that person's identification with the holy beings who reside there: "I am reckoned with the gods and my abode is in the holy congregation. [My] desi[re] is not according to the flesh, and everything precious to me is in the glory [of] the holy [habit]ation. [Wh]om have I considered contemptible? Who is comparable to me in my glory? Who of those who sail the seas shall return telling [of] my [equa]l? Who shall [experience] troubles like me? And who is like me [in bearing] evil? I have not been taught, but no teaching compares.... [with my teaching]. Who then shall attack me when [I] ope[n my mouth]? Who can endure the utterance of my lips? Who shall arraign me and compare with my judgment [... Fo]r I am reck[oned] with the gods, [and] my glory with that of the sons of the King."[29] The Odes of Solomon too identify the one who ascends with the divine beings who are in God's presence, as we will discuss below.

David Aune writes, in connection to Ode 38:1 specifically, where we hear "I went up to the light of truth as if into a chariot and the truth took me and led me," as well as to Odes 36:1-2, 11:16-17, 20:7, 38:1, 36:1-2, that "the mention of a chariot within a context where a trip to the celestial Paradise is in view calls to mind Gershom Scholem's claim that Paul's use of the term "Paradise" in II Cor. 12:3 together with an experience of mystical transport puts the apostle of the Gentiles in the tradition of Jewish Merkabha ("chariot") mysticism.[30] The

Antiquity of this variety of Jewish mysticism is attested by the discovery of the so-called Angelic Liturgy (4QS1) at Qumran, revealing that the Essenes of Qumran were occupied with the Throne or Chariot mysticism so characteristic of medieval Jewish mysticism." [31]

Aune concludes with these remarks: "To summarize, the Odes of Solomon appear to be a collection of prophetic or charismatic hymns of praise and thanksgiving which were of central importance in the cultic worship of Christian communities in Syria. The Spirit of God is the agent who enables the cult leader and the congregation to participate in eschatological salvation through the proleptic experience of participating in the future heavenly worship of God within the setting of an earthly community assembled for worship. The participation of the congregation in this experience is demonstrated by the frequent shift from 'I' to 'we' in the Odes, the characteristic use of plural imperatives, and the final 'Hallelujah.'"[32] This summary characterizes the communitarian setting of the Odes quite well, although I do not believe that "Christian" here should be understood to refer to the religion founded upon Jesus of Nazareth. Be that as it may, the religion of the Odes is surely as he describes it, a cult comprised of people who are focused on a mystical prophetic experience closely related to the ascension mysticism of second temple Judaism. As such the religion of the Odes presumably was attractive to intellectuals who appreciated the beauty of the Odists' compositions and who could undergo the spiritual disciplines necessary to the experiences of ascension mysticism.

April DeConick has pointed out significant connections between pre-Christian Jewish ascension mysticism and some of the sayings found in the Gospel of Thomas, particularly the dialogue of saying 50 and the mystical revelation of sayings 83 and 84.[33] She also observes that the Odes of Solomon share motifs with certain Thomasine passages, noting that saying number 108 of the Gospel of Thomas: "Jesus said: He who drinks from my mouth will become like I am, and I will become he. And the hidden things will be revealed to him," derives from the same wisdom-based conceptual background as Ode 11:6-9

> And speaking waters touched my lips from the fountain of the Lord generously. And so I drank and became intoxicated, from the living water that does not die. And my intoxication did not cause ignorance, but I abandoned vanity, and turned toward the Most High, my God, and was enriched by His favors. I rejected the folly cast upon the earth, and stripped it off and cast it from me. And the Lord renewed me with His garment, and possessed me by His light.

Indeed, the motif of "stripping off" also can be found in Thomas' gospel, for saying 37 says: "His disciples asked him: When will you appear to us? When will we see you? Jesus replied: When you strip naked without shame and trample your clothing underfoot just as little children do then you will look at the son of the living one without being afraid." Motifs such as these probably stem from the Jewish wisdom tradition.

The Odes of Solomon are part of the development of Jewish mysticism in the later second Temple period. Ideas they contain are found also in hymns from the Dead Sea scrolls' Essene community and in sayings attributed at an early time to Jesus of Nazareth. The Odes are ideologically connected with forms of Judaism that preceded Christianity and with forms of Christianity, but nothing they contain requires them to be dated to a time after the lifetime of Jesus of Nazareth.

THE INFLUENCE OF ODES JUDAISM IN THE RISE OF CHRISTIANITY

PAUL'S RELIGION OF TRANSFORMATION

Before the hardening of Christianity into The Church in the later second century, much of the Christian religion was the same as the Odes religion, although the Odes are not Christian. The fundamental identity of savior and saved that is found in the Odes is also a fundamental idea in the early Christianity oriented to Jesus. I will discuss that theme as it appears in two major sources, the letters of Paul and the Gospel of John, stressing the fact that in both texts the Savior, Son of God, Messiah, whom those texts identify with Jesus, is identified with the individuals who are saved through the experience of the Spirit who enters into and possesses the individuals. I see no reason to doubt that the experiences discussed in John's Gospel under the category "Paraclete," and by Paul of Tarsus under the category "Spirit," are fundamentally the same. Certainly they have been assumed to be the same throughout the history of Christian theological discussion.

Paul's letters are the earliest known Christian documents. Paul identifies himself as the saved savior when he writes in Galatians 2:20: "I have been crucified with Christ and I no longer live, but Christ lives in me." This identification of the saved with the savior is fundamental to Pauline Christianity and not just an idiosyncratic experience of the apostle himself. As he sees it, "God sent his Son, born of a woman, born under the law, to redeem those under the law, that we might receive adoption as Sons. Because you are his Sons, God sent the Spirit of his Son into our hearts, the Spirit who calls out, 'Abba, Father.' So you are no longer a slave, but God's Son; and since you are his Son, God has made you also an heir," Galatians 4:4-7 and cf. Romans 8:14-16). Translators often try to distinguish the Son (capitalized) from the people who have become son (not capitalized) via the Spirit, or even to use "Son" for the one and "child" for the other. But in the Greek they are not distinguished. As Paul can say "I no longer live, but Christ lives in me," so can any Christian transformed by the experience called the Spirit of the Son say, "I am the Son of God," just as he may say "I am Christ" if Christ lives in him.

One must remember that the Spirit is an explanatory hypothesis for certain kinds of experience rather than an entity out there in the external world, and that the Spirit experience is the substitution of one personality for another so that one becomes that which one believes oneself to be possessed by. While these fundamental factors in possession are considered obvious facts when applied to our understanding of demonic possession, or when one discusses possession phenomena in other cultures, it is surprisingly difficult to find this applied to possession in early Christianity. "If you receive the Spirit of Christ you become Christ" sounds preposterous, even though it is a simple restatement of the possession paradigm, and there is every reason to think that when Paul says that Christ lives in him (Gal. 2:20) this is because he has received the Spirit of Christ (Rom. 8:9). It is hard for many to think that receiving the Spirit of the Son means to Paul that you become the Son despite the fact that Paul says so. The difficulty arises from the fact that Christianity stopped being a possession-oriented religion in the mid-second century CE and henceforth for two thousand years it has been a Christian commonplace that whatever you might say about Christ the Son of God, you are not him and you cannot become him.

Paul insists that "You are not in the realm of the flesh but are in the realm of the Spirit, if indeed the Spirit of God lives in you. And if anyone does not have the Spirit of Christ, they do not belong to Christ. But if *Christ is in you*, then even though your body is subject to death because of sin, the Spirit gives life because of righteousness. And if the Spirit of him who raised Jesus from the dead is living in you, he who raised Christ from the dead will also give life to your mortal bodies because of his Spirit who lives in you." (Romans 8:9-11). Christ who is in you is synonymous with 1) the Spirit of God, 2) the Spirit of Christ and 3) the Spirit of him who raised Jesus from the dead, all in one paragraph! Recall that in Ode 36 the speaker ascends through the Spirit and becomes the Son of God. According to Paul, one receives the Spirit of the Son and becomes the Son of God or one who receives the Spirit of Christ has Christ is in

him so that, like Paul, he can say it is not I who live but Christ who lives in me. There is quite a fluid vocabulary in these texts, one that reaches its furthest extent perhaps when the Spirit finds itself renamed Paraclete in the Gospel of John.

David Aune believes that the Odes of Solomon are the sort of hymns Paul describes with the term *odai pneumatikai* or "spiritual songs" in Col. 3:16 and that "a member of the Pauline circle connects this term even more closely with inspired utterance: 'Be filled with the Spirit, addressing one another in psalms and hymns and spiritual odes.'" (Eph. 5:18b-19).[34] He believes that such odes were sung during ecstatic congregational worship "enabling the Christian community assembled for worship to encounter a proleptic experience of worshipping God in the presence of heavenly angelic beings in Paradise.[35] We also find, in Ephesians 2:4-6, a passage that could have come directly from one of the Odes of Solomon describing, in the past tense, heavenly ascent to Paradise: "But because of his great love for us, God, who is rich in mercy, made us alive with Christ even when we were dead in transgressions—it is by grace you have been saved. And God raised us up with Christ and seated us with him in the heavenly realms in Christ Jesus." The religious experiences advocated in Pauline Christianity seem to have been strikingly similar to those advocated in the Odes of Solomon.

TRANSFORMATION IN THE GOSPEL OF JOHN

I won't make many arguments of my own regarding John's Gospel but I will take advantage of the conclusions drawn by the great Johannine scholar Raymond Brown, who recognizes that the Spirit-Paraclete that comes to dwell within Christians transforms them into what Jesus also was. Brown writes of John 17:20-26 that, "from the viewpoint of a later and more precise theology, one might like to have a sharper differentiation than John provides between God's incarnation in Jesus and God's indwelling in the Christian—in other words between natural Sonship and general Christian sonship."[36] Further, Brown concludes that the Spirit "carries on the earthly work of Jesus. The Paraclete/Spirit is not corporeally visible and his presence will only be by indwelling in the disciples," and so "the presence of Jesus after his return to the Father is accomplished in and through the Paraclete. Not two presences but the same presence is involved."[37] "It is our contention," Brown writes, "that John presents the Paraclete as the Holy Spirit in a special role, namely, as the personal presence of Jesus in the Christian while Jesus is with the Father."[38] Indeed, "the Paraclete is to Jesus what Jesus is to the Father."[39]

Brown concludes that, "The one whom John calls 'another Paraclete' is another Jesus," and so "Jesus' promises to dwell within his disciples are fulfilled in the Paraclete."[40] Like Paul, John assumes an identity of the Spirit-possessed person that would validate an identity of that person with the Messiah, or the Son of God, or even with Jesus himself. John's Gospel claims that one can learn the teachings of Jesus through the Paraclete, which means in real cultic life that when a person living after the time of Jesus' death who is possessed by the Paraclete speaks, the words will be attributed to Jesus; as Brown translates John 14:26: "the Paraclete, the Holy Spirit, that the Father will send in my name, will remind you of all that I told you [myself]." The sayings of Jesus found in John's Gospel, which are radically different from sayings found in other sources (Mark, Thomas, Q) derive from Jesus, to be sure, but this Jesus is the Paraclete speaking in Greek through the mouths of persons in a state of possession by his Spirit.[41] While the vocabulary is diverse, the underlying assumption is simple: through a particular type of experience understood to be that of an externally existing Spirit entering into him and transforming him, a person becomes another divine person so that, as Brown put it, there is "the personal presence of Jesus in the Christian."[42]

Ode 12:12: "For the dwelling place of the Word is man," is remarkably similar to John 1:14, "the Word became flesh and dwelt *in* us."

While the Greek sentence in John's Gospel (ὁ λόγος σὰρξ ἐγένετο καὶ ἐσκήνωσεν ἐν ἡμῖν,) is usually translated "the word became flesh and dwelt *among* us," the Greek word ἐν can be translated with either the English preposition "in" or "among." The preposition "in" construes the passage to refer to the Word potentially dwelling within any human being; the preposition "among" understands the Word to be one unique human being, Jesus. This is something of an archetypal case, for understanding the sentence one way reveals an underlying religion of transformation behind the Johannine prologue where the Word dwells within us, while construing it the other way reveals a religion focused on worshipping a unique divine person, Jesus, who once lived among us. I argue that Christianity did move from the former type of religion, transformative, to the latter type, Jesus-centric, in the course of its first century of existence. The prologue to the Gospel of John may have first expressed a transformative understanding of the Word "in" us only to be incorporated into a biographical narrative where, in that context, it henceforth is to be understood as a unique reference to Jesus dwelling "among" us.

Charlesworth finds the ideas of Johannine Christianity to be so similar to ideas found in the Odes of Solomon that he concludes that the two must arise from a common milieu. "It is improbable that the Odes systematically borrowed from John," he writes, "the most probable solution, at this stage in our research, is that both the author of John and the odist contemporaneously inhabited not only the same milieu but perhaps the same community."[43] If there were, as I argue here, pre-Christian communities of Odes Judaism, the Gospel of John perhaps represents the next stage in the development of those communities themselves as they merge with the cult that arose from the followers of Jesus of Nazareth.

To summarize my observations so far:

1. The Odes of Solomon are not Christian in

the sense that they do not show any awareness of the religion that is oriented to Jesus of Nazareth.

2. The Odes of Solomon feature an experience of transformation such that through the experience of Spirit and ascent, individuals identify themselves as Christ or Son of God and their own speech, history and mission can be understood to be those of the Christ or Son of God.

3. Principal texts of the Christian religion oriented to Jesus of Nazareth also speak of an experience of transformation such that through the experience of Spirit, individuals can identify themselves as Christ or the Son of God.

It is clear to me, as it has been clear to everyone who has studied the Odes of Solomon, that the ideas and phraseology of the Odes is quite similar to that found in early Christianity. This does not mean that the movement arising from Jesus of Nazareth led to the writing of the Odes of Solomon, although this is presently the standard scholarly opinion. Rather, I believe that the temporal arrow, or arrow of causality, should be pointed in the opposite direction. I think it is more likely that the Odes of Solomon existed before Jesus of Nazareth was ever born, than that the Odes of Solomon emerged from the Jesus of Nazareth cult.

INTERTEXTUALITY OF THE ODES OF SOLOMON

Evidently, the people who wrote about the Odes in the earliest times for which we have records believed that the Odes were Jewish hymns composed at roughly the same time as the Psalms of Solomon, c. 50 BCE[44]. If we must separate ancient religious writing of the Palestinian region into two great volumes, the Hebrew Bible and the New Testament, then the Odes of Solomon belong in the Hebrew Bible category, to be labeled perhaps Hebrew Bible apocrypha. That is how they were regarded in the ancient world, so far as we know. Both the manuscript evidence and the evidence from lists of ancient religious texts (stichometria—discussed by Lattke) show that the Odes of

Solomon were always copied in sequence with the Psalms of Solomon.[45] Further, in ancient stichometria they were included in the category of Hebrew Bible apocrypha along with the Psalms of Solomon, the Wisdom of Solomon and the books of Maccabees.[46] Lattke writes "whether there was ever a collection limited to the Odes of Solomon (i.e., without the Psalms of Solomon) is unknown."[47] He observes that Lactantius, writing in c. 305 CE, "doubts neither the (prophetically inspired) authorship of the Odes of Solomon nor their place in the canon of his OT."[48] In ancient times both the Psalms of Solomon and the Odes of Solomon were regarded as Jewish writings, distinct from writings of the Christian religion. As with all of the texts of the Hebrew Bible, Christian authors felt free to make use of them as sacred scripture, but the Christian use of a text does not, of course, make that text a Christian text.

Lattke writes that "the dependence of the Odes of Solomon on—or their relation to—the Johannine corpus (especially John and 1 John) has always been highlighted. But it only became clear with the completion of this commentary that in addition to the pseudo-and deutero-Pauline letters (especially Colossians, Ephesians, and 1 Timothy) Hebrews, and the letters ascribed to Peter (1 Peter), all seven of the authentic Pauline epistles, the Synoptic Gospels (especially Matthew), and possibly Revelation had all exerted a quite surprising influence in the shaping of the Odes of Solomon."[49] All that, but there is not one quotation from any of those sources in any of the Odes! Even great scholars forget that shared religious concepts and phraseology move from person to person in ways outside the lines of documentary utilization.

Claims that the Odes of Solomon are *dependent* on the Johannine corpus requires clear literary proof via cause-and-effect intertextuality. Claims that there is *a relation between* the Johannine corpus and the Odes corpus means that people sharing ideas interacted with each other, and that is quite a different thing, one having no necessary temporal or causal arrow connected with it. Literary intertextuality means that the one written manuscript pre-existed another that depends on it, while ideological relationships are much more fluid in terms of timelines. So, while one does find similarities between phrases or ideas or vocabulary in the Odes of Solomon and in a wide variety of early Christian writings, there is not thereby any certain arrow of time and causality. Professor Charlesworth and others have found a host of intertextual commonalities between the Essenes' Dead-Sea scrolls and the Odes of Solomon; the Dead-Sea scrolls were completed and hidden away before most of the New Testament authors had written their texts.

Professor Lattke is mistaken when he reasons, from the similiarities he finds between one set of documents and another, that the one set *therefore* pre-existed and exerted a causal influence on the other. I see no reason to conclude from ideological and phraseological similarities that a whole host of New Testament texts "exerted a quite surprising influence in the shaping of the Odes of Solomon."[50] On the contrary, I think it is much more likely that the Odes of Solomon exerted quite a surprising influence in the shaping of the New Testament. I mean only that ideas and phrases found in the Odes of Solomon were written before the time when similar ideas and phrases were written into the New Testament, and that the community behind the Odes of Solomon was in existence before there were any Christian communities oriented to Jesus of Nazareth. I have no reason to believe that any New Testament author had ever read any of the Odes, or that any author of the Odes had ever read any of the New Testament.

The Odes of Solomon, I believe, came first; the writing in the New Testament was later, perhaps a generation or two later. I believe that the ancients who placed the Odes of Solomon alongside the Psalms of Solomon and who included both texts in their lists of Hebrew Bible apocryphal books had it right. I believe that the reason Jesus of Nazareth is not known by name, or by quotation, or by deed, or by stories of crucifixion and resurrection anywhere in the Odes of Solomon is because they were written before the time of Jesus' ministry. I think that the Odes come from the period 50 BCE—25 CE, roughly the time that many of the Dead Sea scrolls were produced and not far from the period that is commonly assigned to the Psalms of Solomon.

PAUL OF TARSUS AND THE ODES OF SOLOMON

Earlier in this essay I discussed how Paul (and John, and others, such as the author of Ephesians 2:6) believed, along with the authors of the Odes of Solomon, that a human being could be transformed through the Spirit of the Son into a Son of God, a Christ, and that Paul believed this had occurred to him, for Christ now lives in him—he has had the experience called "the Spirit of Christ." At the beginning of his letter to the Galatians Paul tells us how he understands that experience first to have occurred in his own life: Galatians 1:13-2:1a

For you have heard of my previous way of life in Judaism, how intensely I persecuted the church of God and tried to destroy it. I was advancing in Judaism beyond many of my own age among my people and was extremely zealous for the traditions of my fathers. But when God, who set me apart from my mother's womb and called me by his grace, was pleased to reveal his Son in me so that I might preach him among the Gentiles, my immediate response was not to consult any human being. I did not go up to Jerusalem to see those who were apostles before I was, but I went into Arabia. Later I returned to Damascus. Then after three years, I went up to Jerusalem to get acquainted with Cephas and stayed with him fifteen days. I saw none of the other apostles—only James, the Lord's brother. I assure you before God that what I am writing you is no lie. Then I went to Syria and Cilicia. I was personally unknown to the churches of Judea that are in Christ. They only heard the report: "The man who formerly persecuted us is now preaching the faith he once tried to destroy." And they praised God because of me. Then after fourteen years, I went up again to Jerusalem. (NIV)

This account is supplemented by stories in Luke's Acts of the Apostles and in other letters of Paul's (Acts 9:1-2; 22:4-5; and 26:9-1; 1 Cor 15:9; and Phil 3:6)., but the autobiographical account in Galatians tells us enough.

Paul's conversion takes place about 33 CE. Udo Schnelle in his recent comprehensive study of Paul dates the conversion to 33 CE, and Jerome Murphy-O'Connor does so too, but the conversion has been dated as late (!) as 35 CE.[54] Jesus' crucifixion is dated by some to 30 CE but many scholars conclude that 33 CE is the correct date. (Raymond Brown says that he cannot decide between 30 and 33.). The period between Jesus' crucifixion and Paul's conversion may have been as much as five years or even less than one year if the crucifixion and conversion both occurred in 33 CE. Evidently the churches that Paul persecuted covered a remarkably large geographical area. Presumably Paul spent some period of time persecuting them, for he says he intensely persecuted the churches and tried to destroy them. There is no reason at all to believe that such persecution started and ended with Paul himself. Presumably he had associates. It probably preceded his participation, and later on it may have segued as a historical process into the persecution of churches organized by the followers of Jesus of Nazareth.

According to Paul's eyewitness testimony there were churches to be persecuted that extended from Jerusalem through Judea and Galilee at least to Damascus and quite possibly into Arabia, whence Paul traveled immediately after his conversion experience. Given the time frame, as little as one year (33 CE) to no more than five (30 CE to 35 CE) it is impossible that the religion of Jesus of Nazareth the crucified and resurrected Savior managed to begin, then expand, then spread out as a network of church communities from Jerusalem and Judea past Samaria through Galilee and all the way Damascus while engaging activities so nefarious as to spur persecution, and then to suffer the consequent intense and destructive persecution about which Paul reports. I think that it is likely that our assumption that Paul persecutes a network of Christian churches founded through the mission of Jesus of Nazareth and his immediate family (James, Mary) and disciples (Peter, John, etc.) is wrong. Rather, there seems to have been a network of communities oriented to the Judaism of the Odes of Solomon that existed well before c. 33 CE stretching at least from Jerusalem to Damascus.

Paul adds some extraordinary information about the situation prior to his conversion when he reports in First Corinthians that he first told the Corinthian Christians something he had himself been told, which is that the risen Jesus appeared, in order, to Cephas, the Twelve, and "to over five hundred brothers at once, of whom the greater part are still alive, although some have died," (1 Cor. 15:6) and after that to James, then to all the apostles and finally to Paul himself. Paul reports that all of this took place in the brief period prior to Paul's conversion in 35 CE or before, during the time of Paul's active persecution of the churches. We should not underestimate the fact that Paul finds it reasonable that there would have been more than five hundred Christians gathered in one place all experiencing something they came to regard as an appearance of Jesus. Further, by telling us that many of them are still alive, Paul claims there are eyewitness participants in this event who can confirm it. One might suppose that the numbers given are exaggerated but the significant fact for our purpose is that Paul believes it could have taken place, which in turn confirms the impression one receives from his reports of persecuting churches from Jerusalem to Damascus that there were an awful lot of Christians at an awfully early time. Presumably the hundreds of people he mentions in 1 Cor. 15:6 had gathered for some purpose other than watching the skies in hopes of seeing Jesus. What actually happened then is a puzzle, to be sure, but the fact is that Paul believes himself supported by hundreds of potential eyewitnesses in reporting that over five hundred people at one time were gathered together pursuant to some sort of Christian activity ca. 30—34 CE. This means that there was a much more extensive Christian religious movement at that period than is generally assumed.

Paul quotes the churches in Judea as having heard from other churches in the network that "the man who formerly persecuted us is now preaching the faith he once tried to destroy," and Paul regards this as a statement of fact. If so, and this is Paul reporting on Paul's own life and experience and so is a uniquely strong piece of evidence, Paul joined a network of churches that taught Pauline Christianity.

He did not join not some sort of hypothetical Q-sayings oriented communities concerned about the apocalyptic kingdom to come, as Bart Ehrman, Dominic Crossan and others argue arose in Galilee and Judea (if anything did) in response to the teachings of Jesus.[51] The discontinuity between the historical Jesus as he has been constructed by scholars throughout the past century and the form of religion preached by the apostle Paul is so overpowering that some conclude that there was no historical Jesus at all.[52] Some others believe that Paul invented the Christianity he preached *ab novo* or, as he would say, from divine revelation, but Paul reports to us that he has joined with a group of communities that were preaching the religion that he himself began to preach, and since the religion Paul preaches is one focused largely on the experience of the transformational Spirit of God/Christ/Son it is not difficult to argue that the churches he first persecuted and then joined were focused largely on the experience of the transformational Spirit of God/Christ/Son as was the Jewish religion of the Odes of Solomon.

In the Odes of Solomon we may hear the feelings of those who were persecuted. For example, in Ode 28 the speaker says,

I am ready before destruction comes, and have been set on His immortal side. And immortal life embraced me, and kissed me. And from that life is the Spirit which is within me. And it cannot die because it is life. Those who saw me were amazed, because I was persecuted. And they thought that I had been swallowed up, because I seemed to them as one of the lost. But my injustice became my salvation. And I became their abomination, because there was no jealousy in me. Because I continually did good to every man I was hated. And they surrounded me like mad dogs, those who in stupidity attack their masters because their thought is depraved, and their mind is perverted.

This description of the self as a righteous person rescued from entrapment and persecution is part of the Odes' soteriological vision of human beings who are in bondage and rescued by a savior whom they themselves become, but it also may also reflect their social reality as a Jewish community persecuted by Jewish authority. In Ode 5 we hear the speaker declare:

My persecutors will come but let them not see me. Let a cloud of darkness fall upon their eyes; and let an air of thick darkness obscure them. And let them have no light to see, so that they cannot seize me. Let their designs become hardened, so that whatever they have conspired shall return upon their own heads.

This passage is a curse formulation quite similar to curses found in ancient magic. It certainly sounds as if it derives from people who are persecuted in reality not just in their mythic self-perceptions. These words may come from the people who lived in communities persecuted by the likes of Paul, and who later came to say "The man who formerly persecuted us is now preaching the faith he once tried to destroy," (Gal. 1: 23).

Paul is a Christian because, he says, the Son of God was revealed in him (ἀποκαλύψαι τὸν υἱὸν αὐτοῦ ἐν ἐμοί,) so that henceforth Christ would live in him ((ζῶ δὲ οὐκέτι ἐγώ, ζῆ δὲ ἐν ἐμοὶ Χριστός). Furthermore, Paul believes that the Son of God enters into members of his community so that they too become Sons of God and so forth. In other words, the primary experience of conversion that convinces Paul that the communities he was persecuting had it all right all along is an experience that is central to the Odes of Solomon. I believe that the churches of Christ that existed in c. 33 -35 CE of whom Paul speaks, and which Paul joined, the Church of God, or the Churches of Judea that are in Christ, were oriented to the type of Jewish religion manifested by the Odes of Solomon. Presumably some of those churches used the Odes of Solomon in their worship services. Those churches featured the experience of people being possessed by the Spirit of God understood to be the Spirit of the Son or the Spirit of Christ and so, when God revealed his Son *in* Paul, much to Paul's astonishment Paul experienced what the people whom he had been persecuting also had experienced. Paul claims with no evident doubt in his mind that his gospel, his Christianity, is the same as the Christianity of the network of churches he persecuted and it is not entirely unreasonable to think that Paul might have been right.

When God revealed his son *in* Paul the first thing Paul did was to go to Arabia. Only after three years did he go to Jerusalem, and then only for a fortnight to speak with no more than two people who had known Jesus. This does not indicate to me that Paul had any significant interest in Jesus' life or teaching, quite the opposite. He seems initially to have joined a religious movement where the historical Jesus of Nazareth was of no particular interest. Bear in

mind that all Paul knows of Christianity at this point is antagonistic information that supports the view that it should be persecuted. That is not nothing; people who persecute movements have some idea of what it is they are persecuting. But if the network of churches that Paul persecuted was based on the life and teachings of Jesus of Nazareth and if God revealed His Son in Paul so that Paul now affirmed that the movement he persecuted was the true Churches of God, he would have gone first to Jerusalem, or Capernaum, and not to Arabia. However, if the Odes represent a form of Christianity without a focus on Jesus, then Paul could begin to preach what he formerly condemned without thinking that he needed to find out more about Jesus. In that case, though, what would motivate Paul to speak so fervently about Jesus Christ and him Crucified? Paul clearly separates two things we put together. About the life, personality, miraculous deeds and wise inspired sayings of Jesus he evidently cares nothing at all. He seeks no information about such things and nothing about them is ever mentioned in his letters, but about Jesus Christ the crucified and risen Christ he cares a great deal.

JESUS OF NAZARETH AND THE ODES OF SOLOMON

It is clear in the first chapter of Mark's Gospel that Jesus of Nazareth comes repenting his sins to John's baptismal rite, has the experience of the Spirit coming *into* him, (καὶ τὸ πνεῦμα ὡς περιστερὰν καταβαῖνον εἰς αὐτόν). He is henceforth regarded by some as the Christ the Son of God (Mark 1:1). Mark's story of Jesus is transformational, Jesus was an ordinary human being (cf. Mark 6:1-6) who is changed by Spirit possession experience into the Spirit possessing him, which is the Spirit of the Son, or the Spirit of Christ.

If the Odes community existed before the time of Jesus, existing from Judea through Galilee to Damascus then it may have influenced Jesus' understanding of himself. If he was familiar with a community represented by the Odes he would have anticipated that his experience of possession would be transformation into a Christ, a Son of God, as Mark's Gospel indicates that he did. Evidently he quickly turned this condition into a remarkably successful career as a healer and exorcist, or so all of the synoptic gospels report. When Jesus arrived in Jerusalem for a Passover he was arrested and executed and, his body having been removed from a temporary entombment, stories of his resurrection began to be told.

If Jesus believed that the Spirit of God had come into him then it would be expected that the Spirit spoke through him about itself, that being a fundamental factor in religious practices based on Spirit-possession throughout the world. The Odes are in theory spoken by the Spirit through the mouth of the transformed human odist (e.g. Ode 16:5: "I will open my mouth, and His Spirit will speak through me the glory of the Lord and His beauty,") and so the Spirit speaking through the ones it possesses is a feature of the Odes. I suggest that it is not unreasonable to think that some of the sayings in the Gospel of John, or perhaps the style of some of those sayings, derive from the speech of Jesus of Nazareth when the Spirit was speaking of itself through him. There is even one such saying in Q (Luke 10:22)

Jesus' associates evidently understood him to be Christ or Son of God, but they did not regard this condition to be one they might themselves aspire to. To them Jesus was a unique case, the only Christ the only Son of God. But Jesus may not have understood himself that way and so may have suggested that the Spirit might potentially come to all of his associates, a circumstance they came to call "being baptized in the Spirit." We hear that they did become possessed on Pentecost by the Spirit that they believed Jesus had sent to them (cf. Acts of the Apostles 2:1-13, 33, and *passim*). One finds in Paul's letters and in the Johannine corpus the idea that one can become Christ through the Spirit, but in both cases one specifically becomes Jesus Christ, whom John identifies as Paraclete and whose crucifixion and resurrection were central to Paul's religion. In the cases of Paul and John we

have an amalgamation of the ideas found in the Odes, that one can become Christ the Son of God through the Spirit, and an idea not found in the Odes that Jesus of Nazareth was Christ the Son of God in a unique fashion.

If Paul's reports about his own experiences are reliable, there was a network of possession oriented churches stretching from Jerusalem to Damascus, one whose realm of influence therefore inevitably passed through Galilee. This network of churches practiced a form of religion that, through Paul's idiosyncratic interpretation, came to be what we call Christianity. Jesus of Nazareth himself may have been affiliated with this movement and, by the time he was executed, have become a prominent member of it because, as Mark insists, Jesus had had a very successful medical career in Galilee and southern Syria, a career founded on his ability as "the Holy One of God" to drive out demons.[53]

Paul testifies, and the Odes themselves seem to confirm, that Jewish legal authorities, in part consisting of Pharisees like Paul, sought to destroy the religion of the Odes by attacking the members of the Odes communities. If such persecution had been going on for some time we probably should regard the Odes Judaism as a form of Syrian Judaism that was forced to be secretive, hidden away, and defensive. Repeatedly the Odes speak of persecution, e.g. in Ode 28 "Those who saw me were amazed, because I was persecuted. And they thought that I had been swallowed up, because I seemed to them as one of the lost. But my injustice became my salvation," and it stands to reason that the people who found their ecstatic religious transformations an escape from real persecution would keep a low profile in ordinary society. The Odes communities probably kept to themselves and tried to avoid publicly giving their Pharisaic enemies reason to attack.

Jesus, however, acted publicly and attracted a significant number of followers some of whom imitated his practice (cf. e.g. Mark 6:7-13) so that his influence spread rapidly and successfully. During his lifetime the Jesus movement may have became a public form of the Odes

Judaism, although his followers believed that the movement focused uniquely on the person of Jesus himself. The Odes religion regarded the career of the savior as recapitulating the feelings of people transformed by possession, released from imprisonment and bondage into liberation and escape, to ascent and transformation, so that they can now liberate others, break the bonds of others, kill dragons, and so forth. The Jesus movement, however, identified the savior with a particular person, especially with his crucifixion and resurrection (a special case of bondage and liberation).

The Odes would have you become a Christ and they speak generally about ascent and descent, bondage and liberation, etc., but the Jesus movement would have you become Jesus Christ and understand yourself to have died and risen with him, or so Paul understood it. Paul evidently joined the Odes Judaism that he had been persecuting, but he had been influenced in Jerusalem by the followers of Jesus who led him to believe that the movement was specifically oriented toward Jesus Christ. The Odes Judaism as Paul understood it was not one offering Christ status to anyone who achieved certain experiences but one that spoke particularly about Jesus Christ crucified.

If the Odes of Solomon are the remnant of a Jewish cult of a Pauline type that existed before Jesus, we might understand what happened way back when. Jesus became part of the Odes movement but rather than simply practicing g within the community he launched a highly public and highly successful career as a Spirit possessed exorcist. People outside the Odes may have thought him to uniquely be the Son of God and Christ but the Odes community had any number of members who were Son of God and Christ. After his death his associates believed him to be unique and the Jesus of Nazareth religion began, featuring Jesus of Nazareth as the prototypical spirit-possessed Christ who sends the spirit to possess all of his followers (so the Acts of the Apostles).

Paul persecuted the Odes community itself, one which was rather well established around 33 CE but as its persecutor while he knew something of it he hardly knew it well. Paul conflated the Odes Christianity with the Christianity that identified the Christ with the crucified and risen Jesus to achieve the form of religion evident in his letters. Whether this conflation was his own contribution, or whether it had started within the Odes communities themselves thanks to the missionary efforts of Jesus' associates, I cannot tell.

Subsequently, the Johannine community produced a set of sayings attributed to Jesus some of which had to do with the Paraclete. The Johannine Paraclete sayings retained the Odes' old perspective that everyone who receives the Spirit becomes the Son but added the specification that Jesus Christ is the Son who dwells within his followers via the Paraclete. The sort of in-dwelling language for transformation is found in the Odes of Solomon. For example, in Ode 32 we read:

The Lord has directed my mouth by His Word, and has opened my heart by His Light. He has caused to dwell in me His immortal life, and permitted me to proclaim the fruit of His peace, to convert the lives of those who desire to come to Him, and to lead those who are captive into freedom. I took courage and became strong and captured the world, and the captivity became mine for the glory of the Most High, and of God my Father.

and in Ode 32: "To the blessed ones the joy is from their heart, and light from Him who dwells in them; And the Word of truth who is self-originate, Because He has been strengthened by the Holy Power of the Most High; and He is unshaken forever and ever." The Johannine idea of Spirit possession speaks of the power of the Spirit and of Jesus coming to dwell within Jesus' followers. As we read in John 17:20-23

I pray also for those who will believe in me through their message, that all of them may be one, Father, just as you are in me and I am in you. May they also be in us so that the world may believe that you have sent me. I have given them the glory that you gave me, that they may be one as we are one— I in them and you in me— so that they may be brought to complete unity."

Raymond Brown wrote of passages such as this one: "The one whom John calls 'another Paraclete' is another Jesus ... Jesus' promises to dwell within his disciples are fulfilled in the Paraclete."[54] To experience, as Ode 32 puts it, "light from Him who dwells in them" or to receive the glory that God gave to Jesus, as John 17:22 phrases it, cannot be two different things from two unrelated forms of first century Judaism. They are, I think, substantially and essentially the same thing. But while the Gospel of John focuses on Jesus of Nazareth, the Odes never do. Therefore, I think, the Odes came first and then Jesus, and then Paul's gospel, John's Gospel, and the religion of Christianity.

The communities behind the Odes were not ordinary folks but people with the special mental dispensations and the time for disciplined reflections that entitle them to be called "mystics." Theirs is not a religion that is likely to spread rapidly into a large semi-literate or illiterate population of relatively poor people, as early Christianity did. But when people associated with Jesus of Nazareth experienced mass possession experiences on the day called Pentecost and they quickly began to enable others to experience Spirit possession experiences, that movement achieved major success and came to incorporate the prexisting mystical cult that produced the Odes of Solomon in part through the conversion of Paul of Tarsus. In essence, a Jewish mystical cult with a limited number of disciplined members became a Gentile-oriented pentecostal cult that spread throughout the ancient world.

CONCLUSION

I propose that the following occurred:

A: Before 25 CE there was a network of communities stretching from Jerusalem to Damascus whose religious ideas are to some degree preserved for us through some of the hymns they chanted, the Odes of Solomon. Those communities believed that humans could be transformed into Christ or the Son of God through an experience understood in terms of the Spirit that we can understand in terms of the generic category of spirit possession.

B: Jesus of Nazareth was affiliated with or influenced by one of those communities. He came to understand himself as one transformed into Son of God and Christ through an experience understood in terms of the Spirit. He was rather widely regarded as one transformed into Son of God or the Holy One of God and thereby was able to have a brief but successful career as an exorcist-healer and to gather a cadre of associates who regarded him as being, uniquely, Christ and Son of God.

C: The communities of Odes Judaism were persecuted through Judean police power and Paul carried out such persecution. However, Paul, to his surprise, experienced what those communities advocated, believed that the Son of God had been revealed in him, and he began to spread their form of religion into Gentile areas. Paul understood the Odes religion in reference to the much more public career of Jesus of Nazareth, whose associates identified him as crucified and risen Christ. Paul conflated the Odes religion with the idea that Jesus is Christ to produce a form of Christianity that offered people the possibility of identification through the Spirit with Jesus Christ crucified.

D: Jesus' associates, who understood him to have been the unique Son of God and to have been the only Christ, had "Pentecostal" experiences of Spirit possession that were thought to derive from Jesus Christ now in heaven with God. The success of Christianity in spreading throughout the Roman Empire was based largely on the success of Christian missionaries in inducing Spirit possession in people in diverse areas, presumably through methods similar to those that are utilized by Pentecostal missionaries today.

E: Johannine Christians believed that possession by the spirit Paraclete would transform them so that they might believe that Jesus dwells in them and that they can speak words of the spirit, understood to be Jesus' words recalled to them. Their experiences mean to them that they are now the presence of the Son of God, Jesus, on the earth; it is possible that some of the communities of Odes Judaism became Johannine Christian churches. The Johannine community may be the principal form in which Odes Judaism came to exist after the rise of Christianity oriented to Jesus of Nazareth.

F. By the mid-second century Jesus the Christ came to be regarded as a separate divine being to be worshipped as God. The Spirit was separated as an independent divine Person. The Christian religion ceased to be fundamentally concerned with Spirit-possession, which was left to fringe groups and heretical cults.

I suggest that we should reverse Professor Lattke's observation that the Johannine Gospel and Letters, the epistles of Paul both authentic and pseudepigraphal, the Synoptic Gospels, the letter ascribed to Peter and even Revelation "exerted a quite surprising influence in the shaping of the Odes of Solomon."[55] It is more likely that the influence went the other way, not that a very wide range of texts came to influence a single set of Odes in a process completed before 125 CE but that the Odes represent the Jewish religious movement out of which Christianity arose so that the Judaism of the Odes (not the specific literary Odes themselves) lies at the root of Pauline Christianity and Johannine Christianity and even the Christianity of Jesus of Nazareth. Accordingly, the influence of that kind of religion is to be found practically everywhere, from the Letter to the Galatians to the speech of Jesus in John 17 to the Gospel of Thomas.

The arrow of temporal-causal influence should be reversed. The Odes of Solomon are not influenced by virtually all varieties of early Christianity but the religion and phraseology of the Odes of Solomon preceded and influenced virtually all those varieties. The Syrian Odes' form of Judaism may have been more influential on Jesus of Nazareth than Judean Temple Judaism was. The religion of the Odes, coupled with the idea of a Jesus Christ crucified, was substantially the Gospel of Paul and, in quite a different way, is at the root of the Gospel of John. To see that these are not idle speculations you need only realize that it is a relatively recent idea that the Odes are Christian and c. 125 CE in date. People of ancient times thought the Odes of Solomon were as Jewish as the Psalms of Solomon and of roughly the same date. I think they were right.

NOTES

1 Charlesworth, James. *Critical Reflections on the Odes of Solomon, Volume One*, Sheffield UK: Sheffield Academic Press, 1998 p. 18

2 Ibid. p. 229

3 Lattke, Michael. *The Odes of Solomon* (Hermeneia Series) Philadelphia PA: Fortress Press 2009. Lattke retains the Greek "pleroma" and "gnosis" in his translation.

4 Attridge, Harold and George MacRae translators, in James M. Robinson, ed., *The Nag Hammadi Library*, revised edition. HarperCollins, San Francisco, 1990.

5 Ibid. p. 11, and Charlesworth p. 15

6 Aune, David. *The Cultic Setting of Realized Eschatology in Early Christianity*, Leiden: Brill, 1972: "a majority of scholars concerned agree that Greek was the original language in which the Odes were composed." p. 167 and n. 5 where Aune lists 16 major scholars who believe that Greek was the original language and 10 who believe that the original language was Syriac.

7 Lattke, p. 1

8 Charlesworth, *Critical Reflections* p. 15

9 Lattke, p. 11

10 Grant, Robert., "The Odes of Solomon and the Church of Antioch," *Journal of Biblical Literature*, Vol. 63, No. 4, Dec., 1944 p. 377

11 We need to bear in mind that the word "Christ" is the Greek version of the Hebrew term "Messiah" and that both simply mean "an anointed person." However, in Judean religio-political language the words Messiah and Christ came to mean anointed in the sense of being a person ceremonially anointed to be the king of Judea. The last such king in the lineage of David, a man named Zedekiah, died in 586 BCE, but some Judeans speculated that God would eventually intervene and install a Davidic descendant as the Judean king, give him supernatural power to liberate the land, and help him to bring an end to wickedness; that man came to be called the Messiah or the Christ. While this is the original meaning of the term, it is not the way the term is used in the Odes of Solomon or in most of the later Christian texts.

12 Ibid. p. 364

13 Ibid.

14 Ibid. p. 365

15 Lattke, p. 380.

16 Unless specified otherwise in the text, I will use the translation of James Charlesworth, found in his work *The Odes of Solomon: Edited, with Translation and Notes* Oxford UK: Clarendon Press, 1973.

17 Cf. for example, Bourguignon, Erika. *A Cross-Cultural Study of Dissociational States*. Columbus: Research Foundation, Ohio State University. 1968 Bourguignon, Erika. *Possession*. Chandler & Sharp Series in Cross-cultural Themes. San Francisco: Chandler & Sharp Publishers. 1976 Cohen, Emma. "What is Spirit Possession? Defining, Comparing, and Explaining Two Possession Forms" *Ethnos*, Nol. 73 No. 1, March 2008 (pp. 1-25)

18 Cf. e.g. Oohashi, T., Kawai, N., Honda, M., Nakamura, S., Morimoto, M., Nishina, E., Maekawa, T. 2002. Electroencephalographic measurement of possession trance in the field. *Clinical Neurophysiology*, No. 113, pp. 435-445.

19 Translators of ancient Christian texts incorporate a considerable amount of commentary into their translations through their use of capitalization although no ancient language distinguished words in that way.

20 Sanders, Jack T. *The New Testament Christological Hymns: Their Historical Background*, Cambridge UK: Cambridge University Press, 1971 p. 24.

21 Ibid. p. 25

22 Ibid. p. 57

23 Ibid. pp. 96-97

24 Ibid. p. 104

25 Ibid. p. 113

26 Ibid. p. 114

27 Ibid. p. 113 (italics added)

28 Ibid. pp. 109-110

29 Ibid. p. 113

30 De Conick April, *Seek to See Him: Ascent and Vision Mysticism in the Gospel of Thomas*, Leiden: E. J. Brill, 1996. p. 38.

31 For example, Ode 38: "I went up into the light of Truth as into a chariot, and the Truth led me and caused me to come. And caused me to pass over chasms and gulfs, and saved me from cliffs and valleys. And became for me a haven of salvation, and set me on the place of immortal life."

32 For the full translation refer to http://www.qumran.org/js/qumran/hss/4q491

33 Scholem, Gershom, *Major Trends in Jewish Gnosticism*, New York: Schocken, 1941 pp. 16f.
34 Aune, n.1 p. 186, and cf. Dupont-Sommer, Andre. *The Essene Writings from Qumran*, London: Peter Smith, 1973 pp. 332-35
35 Aune, pp. 182-183.
36 50a Jesus said: If they ask you "Where are you from?" reply to them "We have come from the place where light is produced from itself. It came and revealed itself in their image." 50b. If they ask you "Are you it?" reply to them, "We are his sons. We are chosen ones of the living father." 50c. If they ask you "What is the sign within you of your father?" reply to them, "It is movement. It is rest." 83. Jesus said: The images are revealed to people. The light within them is hidden in the image of the father's light. He will be revealed. His image is hidden in his light. 84. Jesus said: You are pleased when you see your own likeness. When you see your images that came into being before you did, immortal and invisible images, how much can you bear?

37 Aune, p. 177
38 Ibid. p. 179
39 Brown, Raymond. The Gospel According to John (xiii-xxi): Anchor Bible Series, Garden City NY: Doubleday and Company, 1970 p.779
40 Ibid. pp. 644, 645.
41 Ibid. p. 1139.
42 Ibid. p. 1140.
43 Ibid. p. 1141.
44 Davies, Stevan. Jesus The Healer: Possession, Trance and the Origins of Christianity, New York NY: Continuum Press, 1995 pp. 151-169.
45 Brown p. 1139
46 Charlesworth, *Critical Reflections*, p. 216
47 The Psalms of Solomon are eighteen hymns similar in style to the canonical psalms. Today they exist only in Greek but they were originally Hebrew. One of the psalms describes the death of the Roman general Pompey (48 BCE) and they can be dated c. 70 BCE—40 BCE overall. They defend the legalism of the Pharisees against the supposed immorality of the Saducees and they distain the Hasmonean dynasty and priesthood. Occasionally the Psalms of Solomon discuss "the Lord Messiah" and envision him as a political figure, a human person given special powers by God, who will battle successfully to liberate Israel from foreign occupation and install a reign of righteousness forever. Until that time the Psalms of Solomon believe that God properly allows his people to suffer as punishment for their sins. While these Psalms are bound together with the Odes in ancient text collections, and both may derive from roughly the same time period, they are from two different Jewish communities and reflect quite different ways of thinking even when they refer to the same subject such as the Messiah.

48 Lattke pp. 1-2
49 Ibid.
50 Ibid. p. 5 n. 32
51 Ibid. p. 2
52 Ibid. pp. 13-14
53 Ibid.
54 Schnelle, Udo. *Apostle Paul: His Life and Theology*, Grand Rapids, MI: Baker Academic, 2005, p. 87. Murphy - O'Connor, Jerome. *Paul: A Critical Life*, New York, NY: Oxford University Press, 1998, p. 7
55 Crossan, John Dominic. *The Historical Jesus*, New York NY: HarperOne 1993. Ehrman Bart. *Jesus: Apocalyptic Prophet of the New Millennium* New York NY: Oxford University Press, 1999

56 Cf. Doherty, Earl. *The Jesus Puzzle: Did Christianity begin with a mythical Christ?* Ottawa CA: Canadian Humanist Publications 1999
57 Cf. Davies, Stevan, *Possession, Trance and the Origin of Christianity*, Bardic Press, 2012 Note that since the Gospel of John is a work of fiction, and because the Gospels of Matthew and Luke rely entirely on Mark's Gospel for their biographical frameworks, the story of Jesus in Mark's Gospel is the only one we have that can possibly be at all accurate. Jesus' reputation as a spirit-possessed healer was very great and very widespread, according to Mark.
58 Brown, p. 1141
59 Lattke, pp. 13-14

Stevan Davies/Rendel Harris

The Odes of Solomon

Originally published in *The Odes And Psalms Of Solomon Vol. II: The Translation with Introduction And Notes*
By Rendel Harris and Alphonse Mingana, London : Longmans, Green & Company. 1920
Reprinted in *The Lost Books of the Bible and the Forgotten Books of Eden, Collins-World Publishers*
Available on the internet at various sites including,
http://www.goodnewsinc.net/othbooks/Odesolmn.html
http://carm.org/ Odes-of-solomon

[I have changed this translation by revising archaic English usage and most of the theological capitalizations — Stevan Davies]

ODE I

1 The Lord is upon my head like a crown and I shall not be without him.
2 The crown of truth was woven for me, and it caused your branches to bud in me;
3 For it is not like a withered crown that does not bud
4 But you live upon my head and you have blossomed upon my head.
5 Your fruits are full-grown and perfect. They are full of your salvation.
(Hallelujah.)

ODE II

This
Ode is missing.

ODE III

1 . . . .
2 And (his) members are with him, and on them do I depend, and he loves me.
3 For I should not have known how to love the Lord, if he had not loved me.
4 For who is able to distinguish love, except one that is loved. Where his rest is, there also am I. For with the Lord Most High and Merciful, there is no grudging.
7 I have been united (to Him), for the lover has found the beloved in order that I may love him that is the son, I shall become a son.
9 And he that has pleasure in the living one, will become living.
10 This is the Spirit of the Lord, which does not lie,
Which teaches the sons of men to know his ways.
11 Be wise and understanding and vigilant. Hallelujah.

ODE IV

1 No man, O my God, changes your holy place, nor is (one able) to change it, and put it in another place.
2 Because he has no power over it, for your sanctuary you designed before you made places.
3 That which is the elder shall not be changed by those that are younger than itself; you have given your heart, O Lord, to your believers.
4 you will never fail, nor will you be without fruits;
5 For one hour of your faith is more precious than all days and years.
6 For who is there that shall put on your grace,

and be injured?

7 For your seal is known, and your creatures are known to it.

8 And the hosts possess it, and the elect archangels are clad with it.

9 you have given us your fellowship; It was not that you were in need of us, but that we are in need of you.

10 Distil your dews upon us, and open your rich fountains that pour forth to us milk and honey.

11 For there is no repentance with you; nor that you should repent of anything that you have promised.

12 And the end was known to you;

13 For what you gave, you gave freely so that you may not draw back and take them again.

14 For all was known to you as God and set in order from the beginning before you;

15 And you, O Lord, have made all things. Hallelujah.

ODE V

1 I will give thanks unto you, O Lord because I love you;

2 O Most High, do not you forsake me, for you are my hope.

3 Freely I have received your grace I shall live thereby.

4 My persecutors will come but let them not see me.

5 Let a cloud of darkness fall on their eyes, and let an air of thick gloom darken them.

6 And let them have no light to see, that they may take hold upon me.

7 Let their counsel become thick darkness, and what they have cunningly devised, let it return upon

their own heads.

8. For they have devised a counsel, and it has come to nought.

9 They have prepared themselves maliciously, and were found to be ineffective.

10 For my hope is upon the Lord and I will not fear.

12 He is as a garland on my head, And I shall not be moved ;

14 And if (all) things visible should perish, I

shall not die

15 Because the Lord is with me, and I am with him. Hallelujah.

ODE VI

1 As (the hand) moves over the harp, and the strings speak;

2 So speaks in my members the Spirit of the Lord, and I speak by his love.

3 For he destroys what is foreign, and everything is of the Lord.

4 For thus he was from the beginning, and (shall be) to the end.

5 That nothing should be his adversary, and nothing should stand up against him.

8 For there went forth a stream, and became a river great and broad. It swept away everything, and broke up and carried away the Temple.

9 And the restraints (made) by men were not able to restrain it, nor the arts of those whose (business it is to) restrain water.

10 For it spread over the face of the whole earth and it filled everything.

11 All the thirsty upon earth were given to drink (of it) and thirst was done away and quenched

12 For from the Most High the draught was given.

13 Blessed then are the ministers of that draught, who have been entrusted with his water,

14 They have assuaged the dry lips, and the will that had fainted they have raised up

15 And souls that were near departing they have held back from death,

] 6 And limbs that had fallen they have straightened and set up.

17 They gave strength to their coming and light to their eyes.

18 For everyone knew them in the Lord and they lived by the water an eternal life. Hallelujah.

ODE VII

1 As is the motion of anger over evil, so is the motion of joy over the beloved, and brings in of its fruits without restraint.

2 My joy is the Lord, and my motion is towards Him; this path of mine is excellent.

3 For I have a helper, to the Lord. He has shown himself to me without grudging in his simplicity; because his kindness has diminished his awesomeness.

4 He became like me that I might receive him. In similitude was he reckoned like me, that I might put him on.

5 And I did not tremble when I saw him because he was gracious to me.

6 Like my nature he became, that I might learn him, and like my form, that I might not turn back from him.

7 The father of knowledge is the word of knowledge;

8 He who created wisdom is wiser than his works.

9 He who created me when yet I was, knew what I should do when I came into being;

10 Wherefore He pitied me in His abundant grace and granted me to ask from him and to receive from his sacrifice

11 For he is incorrupt, the perfection of the worlds and the Father of them.

12 He has given him to appear to them that are His so that they may recognize him that made them and that they might not suppose that they came of themselves.

13 For it is to knowledge he has appointed his way; he has widened it and extended it and brought it to all perfection.

14 He set over it the traces of his light and it proceeded therein even from the beginning to the end.

15 For by Him He was served. And He was pleased with the Son.

16 And because of his salvation he will take possession of everything. And the Most High shall be known in his saints

17 To announce to those that have songs of the coming of the Lord that they may go forth to meet him and may sing to him, with joy and with the harp of many tones.

18 The seers shall go before him and they shall be seen before him

19 And they shall praise the Lord in his love because he is near and sees.

20 And hatred shall be taken from the earth and along with jealousy it shall be drowned

21 For ignorance has been destroyed because the knowledge of the Lord has arrived.

22 Let the singers sing the grace of the Lord Most High and let them bring their songs

23 And let their hearts be like the day, and like the excellent beauty of the Lord, their harmonies and let there be nothing without life, nor without knowledge, nor dumb.

24 For (the Lord) has given a mouth to his creation to open the voice of the mouth towards him and to praise him

25 Confess his power and show forth his grace. Hallelujah.

ODE VIII

1 Open yourselves, open your hearts to the exultation of the Lord

2 Let your love abound from the heart, and even to the lips

3 To bring forth fruits to the Lord, a holy life and to talk watchfully in his light.

4 Rise up and stand erect, you who were sometimes brought low

5 You who were in silence, speak out, (Now) that your mouth has been opened.

6 You who were despised be lifted up now that your righteousness has been lifted up,

7 For the right hand of the Lord is with you and he will be your helper.

8 And peace has been prepared for you, before ever your war happened.

9 Hear the word of truth and receive the knowledge of the Most High

10 Your flesh does not know what I am saying to you, nor your raiment what I am showing to you;

11 Keep my secret, you who are kept by it. Keep my faith, you who are kept by it.

12 And understand my knowledge, you who

know me in truth;

13 Love me with affection, you who love;

14 For I do not turn away my face from them that are mine, for I know them.

15 Before they came into being, I took knowledge of them, and on their faces I set my seal.

16 I fashioned their members; my own breasts I prepared for them that they might drink my holy milk and live thereby.

17 I took pleasure in them, and I am not ashamed of them.

18 For my workmanship are they, and the strength of my thoughts.

19 Who then shall stand up against my handy work? Or who is there that is not subject to them?

20 I willed, and fashioned mind and heart, and they are mine, and by my own right hand I set my elect ones.

21 And my righteousness goes before them and they shall not be detached from my name for it is with them.

22 Pray and abide continually in the love of the Lord; you beloved ones, in the beloved and you who are kept, in him that lived (again), and you that are saved, in him that was saved.

23 And you shall be found incorrupt in all ages to the name of your father.

Hallelujah.

ODE IX

1. Open your ears and I will speak to you.

2. Give me your souls, that I may also give you my soul.

3. The Word of the Lord and his good pleasures, the holy thought that he has thought concerning his Messiah.

4. For in the will of the Lord is your life, and his intention is (your) everlasting life, and your end is incorruptible.

5 Be enriched in God the father, and receive the intention of the Most High. Be strong and be redeemed by his grace.

6 For I announce peace, to you his saints, that none of those who hear may fall in war.

7 And that those who have known him may not perish, and that those who receive (Him)

may not be ashamed.

8 An everlasting crown is Truth. Blessed are they who set it on their heads.

9 A stone of great price (it is), and the wars were on account of the crown.

10 And righteousness has taken it, and has given it to you.

11 Put on the crown in the true covenant of the Lord and all those who have conquered shall be inscribed l in his book.

12 For their inscription is the victory, which is yours, and she (victory) sees you before her, and wills that you shall be saved.

Hallelujah.

ODE X

1. The Lord has directed my mouth by his word, and he has opened my heart by his light.

2. And he has caused deathless life to dwell in me, and gave me to speak the fruit of his peace;

3. To convert the souls of those who are willing to come to him and to lead captive a good captivity for freedom.

4. I was strengthened and made mighty and took the world captive, and (the captivity) became to me for the praise of the Most High and of God my father.

5 And the gentiles were gathered together who had been scattered abroad, and I was unpolluted by my love (for them) because they confessed me in high places.

6 And the traces of the light were set upon their hearts, and they walked in my life and were saved, and they became my people forever and ever.

Hallelujah.

ODE XI

1. My heart was cloven and its flower appeared, and grace sprang up in it and it brought forth fruit to the Lord.

2. For the Most High circumcised (my heart) by his Holy Spirit, and exposed towards him my affection. 1 And filled me with his love.

3 And his circumcising of (my heart) became my salvation, and I ran in the way, in his peace, in the way of truth.

4 From the beginning and even to the end I

received his knowledge.

5 And I was established upon the rock of truth, where he had set me up.

6 And speaking waters drew near my lips from the fountain of the Lord plenteously.

7 And I drank and was inebriated with the living water that does not die, and my inebriation was not one without knowledge,

8 But I forsook vanity

9 And I turned to the Most High my God, and I was enriched by his bounty

10 And I forsook the folly cast away over the earth, and I stripped it off and cast it from me.

II And the Lord renewed me in his raiment, and possessed me by his light;

12 And from above he gave me rest without corruption and I became like the land which blossoms and rejoices in its fruits

13 And the Lord (was) like the sun (shining) upon the face of the land.

14 My eyes were enlightened, and my face received the dew

15 And my nostrils had the pleasure of the pleasant odor of the Lord.

16 And he carried me into his Paradise, where the abundance of the pleasure of the Lord is

17 And I worshipped the Lord on account of his glory

18 And I said, Blessed, O Lord, are they that are planted in your land, And who have a place in your p;aradise,

19 And that grow in the growth of your trees, and have changed from darkness to light.

20 Behold! All your servants are fair, they who do good works and turn away from wickedness to your pleasantness.

21 And they have turned away from themselves the bitterness of the trees, when they were planted in your land.

22 And everything became like a remembrance of yourself, and a memorial forever of your faithful servants.

23 For there is abundant room in your paradise and nothing is useless therein but everything is filled with fruit.

24 Glory be to you, O Lord, the delight of paradise forever.

Hallelujah.

[Note, in line two and three I replaced "clave" and "cleaving" with "circumcised" in accordance with Charlesworth and Lattke's translations. Charlesworth has "pruned" for "cloven" in line one. -- S.D,]

ODE XII

1. He has filled me with words of truth, that I may speak the same.

2 And like the flow of waters, flows truth from my mouth, and my lips showed forth its fruits

3.And caused its knowledge to abound in me, because the mouth of the Lord is the true word, and the door of his light;

4 And the Most High has given him to his worlds. (Worlds) which are the interpreters of his own beauty and the repeaters of his praise and the confessors of his thought and the heralds of his mind and the instructors of his works.

5 For the swiftness of the word is inexpressible and like his expression is his swiftness and his sharpness, and his course has no limit.

6 Never (does the word) fall, but ever it stands.

8. His descent and his way are incomprehensible.

7 For as his work is, so is his limit

9. For he is the light and the dawn of thought

8 And by him the worlds spoke one to the other, and those that were silent acquired speech.

9 From him came love and concord and they spoke one to the other what they had (to tell)

10 And they were stimulated by the word, and they knew him that made them because they came into concord.

11 For the mouth of the Most High spoke to them and the interpretation of himself had its course by him.

12 For the dwelling-place of the word is man, and his truth is love.

13 Blessed are they who by it have comprehended everything, and who have known the Lord by his truth. Hallelujah.

ODE XIII

1 Behold! The Lord is our mirror, open your eyes and see them in him

2. And learn the manner of your face, and tell forth praises to his Spirit,

3 And wipe off the filth from your face, and love his holiness and clothe yourselves with it

4 And you will be without stain at all times with him.

Hallelujah.

ODE XIV

1 As the eyes of a son to his father, so are my eyes at all time towards you, O Lord

2 For with you are my consolations and my delights.

3 Turn not away your mercy from me, O Lord, and take not your kindness from me.

4 Stretch out to me, my Lord, at all times, your right hand, and be my guide even to the end, according to your good pleasure.

5 Let me be well-pleasing before you, because of your glory and because of your name let me be saved from the Evil One.

6 And let your gentleness, O Lord, abide with me, and the fruits of your love.

7 Teach me the Odes of your truth that I may bring forth fruit in you

8 And open to me the harp of your Holy Spirit, that with all (its) notes I may praise you, O Lord.

9 And according to the multitude of your mercies so shall you give to me, and hasten to grant our petitions

10 And you are able for all our needs.

Hallelujah.

ODE XV

1 As the sun is the joy to them that seek for its daybreak, so is my joy the Lord

2 Because he is my sun, and his rays have lifted me up, and his light has dispelled all darkness from my face.

3 In him I have acquired eyes, and have seen his holy day;

4 Ears I have acquired, and I have heard his truth.

5 The thought of knowledge I have acquired, and I have been delighted by him.

6 The way of error I have left and I went towards him, and I have received salvation from him abundantly.

7 And according to his bounty he has given to me, and according to his excellent beauty he has made me.

8 I have put on incorruption through his name, and I have put off corruption by his grace.

9 Death has been destroyed before my face and Sheol has been abolished by my word.

10 And there has gone up deathless life in the Lord's land, and it has been made known to his faithful ones, and has been given without stint to all those that trust in him.

Hallelujah.

ODE XVI

1 As the work of the husbandman is the ploughshare, and the work of the steersman is the guidance of the ship so also my work is the psalm of the Lord in his praises.

2 My craft and my occupation are in his praises because his love has nourished my heart, and even to my lips his fruits he poured out.

3 For my love is the Lord and therefore I will sing unto him.

4 For I am made strong in his praise, and I have faith in him.

5 I will open my mouth, and his spirit will utter in me the glory of the Lord and his beauty;

6 The work of his hands and the fabric of his fingers

7 For the multitude of his mercies, and the strength of his word

8 For the word of the Lord searches out the unseen thing, and scrutinizes his thought.

9 For the eye sees his works, and the ear hears his thought.

10 It is he who spread out the earth, and settled the waters in the sea;

11 He expanded the heavens, and fixed the stars

12 And he fixed the creation and set it up, and he rested from his works

13 And created things run in their courses, and work their works and they know not how to

stand (still) and to be idle.

14 And the hosts are subject to his word.

15 The treasury of the light is the sun, and the treasury of the darkness is the night.

16 And he made the sun for the day that it might be bright, but night brings darkness over the face of the earth

17 And (by) their reception one from the other they speak the beauty of God.

18 And there is nothing that is without the Lord, for he was before anything came into being.

19 And the worlds were made by his word and by the thought of his heart.

20 Glory and Honor to his name. Hallelujah.

ODE XVII

1 I was crowned by my God, and my crown is living

2 And I was justified by my Lord, and my salvation is incorruptible.

3 I was loosed from vanities. And I am not condemned. The choking bonds were cut off by his hand.

4 I received the face and the fashion of a new person, and I walked in him and was redeemed.

5 And the thought of truth led me, and I walked after it and did not wander.

6 And all that have seen me were amazed, and I was supposed by them to be a strange person.

7 And he who knew and brought me up, is the Most High in all his perfection. He glorified me by his kindness, and raised my thought to the height of Truth.

8 And from there he gave me the way of his steps, and I opened the doors that were closed

9 And I broke in pieces the bars of iron but my own iron (bonds) melted and dissolved before me.

10 And nothing appeared closed to me because I was the opening of everything.

11 And I went towards all the l bondsmen to loosen them, that I might not leave any man bound and binding

12 And I imparted my knowledge without grudging, and their request to me with my love.

13 And I sowed my fruits in hearts, and

transformed them through myself

14 And they received my blessing and lived, and they were gathered to me and were saved.

15 Because they became to me as my own members,and I was their head

16 Glory to you our Head, the Lord Messiah. Hallelujah.

ODE XVIII

1 My heart was lifted up and enriched in the love of the Most High, that I might praise him by my name.

2 My members were strengthened that they might not fall from his power.

3 Sickness removed from my body, and it stood for the Lord by his will, for his kingdom is firm.

4 O Lord, for the sake of them that are deficient, Do not deprive me of your word,

5 Nor, for the sake of their works, do you restrain from me your perfection.

6 Let not the luminary be conquered by the darkness, nor let truth flee away from falsehood.

7 Let your right hand bring our salvation to victory, and receive from all quarters, and preserve whomever is affected by ills.

8 Falsehood and death are not in your mouth, my God, but your will is perfection.

9 And vanity you do not know, neither does it know you.

10 And error you do not know, neither does it know you.

11 And ignorance appeared like dust, and like the scum of the sea;

1 And vain people supposed that it was (something) great, and they came to resemble it and became vain

13 And the wise understood and meditated (thereon) and were unpolluted in their meditations for such were in the mind of the Lord.

14 And they mocked at those who were walking in error

15 And on their part they spoke truth, from the inspiration which the Most High breathed into them.

16 Praise and great comeliness to his name. Hallelujah.

ODE XIX

1. A cup of milk was offered to me and I drank it in the sweetness of the delight of the Lord.
2. The son is the cup, and he who was milked is the father, and he who milked him is the Holy Spirit.
3. Because his breasts were full, and it was not desirable that his milk should be spilt to no purpose.
4 And the Holy Spirit opened his bosom and mingled the milk of the two breasts of the father,
5 And gave the mixture to the world without their knowing, and those who take (it) are in the fullness of the right hand.
6 The womb of the virgin took (it) And she received conception and brought forth
7 And the virgin became a mother with great mercy.
8 She travailed and brought forth a Son without incurring pain, for it did not happen without purpose.
9 She had not required a midwife, for he delivered her.
10 And she brought forth, as a man, by (God's) will, and she brought (him) forth with demonstration and acquired (him) with great dignity;
11 And loved (him) in redemption, and guarded (him) kindly, and showed (him) in majesty.
Hallelujah.

ODE XX

1 I am a priest of the Lord, and to him I do priestly service
2 And to him I offer the offering of his thought.
3 For his thought is not like (the thought of) the world, nor (like the thought of) the flesh nor like them that serve carnally.
4 The offering of the Lord is righteousness and purity of heart and lips,
5 Offer your 1 reins (before Him) blamelessly, and let not your heart - do violence to heart nor your soul do violence to soul.
6 you shall not acquire a stranger . . . neither shall you seek to deal guilefully with your neighbor,

7. Nor shall you deprive him of the covering of his nakedness.
7 But put on the grace of the Lord without stint, and come into his paradise and make you a garland from his tree
8 And put it on your head and be glad, and recline on his rest
9 And his glory shall go before you, and you shall receive of his kindness and his grace and you shall be fat in truth in the praise of his holiness.
10 Praise and honor to his name.
Hallelujah.

ODE XXI

1 My arms 1 I lifted up on high, even to the grace of the Lord
2 Because he had cast off my bonds from me and my Helper had lifted me up to his grace and his salvation.
3 And I put off darkness, and clothed myself with light
4 And my soul acquired members free from sorrow or affliction or pain.
5 Increasingly helpful to me was the thought of the Lord, and his incorruptible fellowship.
6 I was lifted up in the light, and I passed before Him and I became near to him, praising and confessing him.
8 He made my heart overflow, and it was found in my mouth, and it shone upon my lips.
9 And upon my face the exultation of the Lord increased, and his praise likewise.
Hallelujah.

ODE XXII

1 he who brings me down from on high, and brings me up from the regions below
2 And who gathers the things that are betwixt, and throws them to me,
3 He who scattered my enemies and my adversaries,
4 He who gave me authority over bonds, that I might loosen them;
5 He who overthrew by my hands the dragon with seven heads, and set me at his roots that I might destroy his seed —
6 You were there and helped me, and in every

place your name was round about me.

7 Your right hand destroyed his wicked venom and your hand leveled the way for those who believe in you

8 And it chose them from the graves, and separated them from the dead and covered them with bodies

10 And they were motionless, and it gave (them) energy - for life.

11 Your way was without corruption and your face; you brought your world to corruption, that everything might be dissolved and renewed,

12 And that the foundation for everything might be your rock, and on it you built your kingdom and you became the dwelling-place of the saints.

Hallelujah.

ODE XXIII

1 Joy is of the saints! Who shall put it on but they alone?

2 Grace is of the elect! Who shall receive it but they who trust in it from the beginning?

3 Love is of the elect! Who shall put it on, but those who have possessed it from the beginning?

4 Walk in the knowledge of the Most High and you shall know the grace of the Lord without grudging to his exultation and to the perfection of his knowledge.

5 His thought was like a letter, and his will descended from on high,

6 And it was sent like an arrow that is violently shot from the bow.

7 Many hands rushed to the letter, to seize it and to take it and to read it.

8 It escaped from their fingers, and they were frightened at it and at the seal that was on it.

9 For they were not permitted to loosen the seal, for the power that was over the seal was greater than they.

10 But those who saw it went after the letter, that they might know where it would alight, and who should read it, and who should hear it.

11 But a wheel received it, and (the letter) came over it

12 And there was with it a sign of the kingdom and of the government.

13 The wheel mowed and cut down everything that was moving;

14 And it destroyed many things that were adverse, and it spanned the rivers

15 And crossed over and rooted up many forests, and made a broad path.

16 The head went down to the feet for down to the feet ran the wheel, and that which had come upon it.

17 The letter was one of recommendation for there were included in it all districts

18 And there was seen at its head, a head which was revealed the son of truth from the Most High father;

19 And he inherited and took possession of everything, and the thought of the many was brought to naught,

20 And all the apostates became bold and fled away, and the persecutors became extinct and were blotted out.

21 And the letter became a great tablet, which was wholly written by the finger of God.

22 The name of the Father was upon it, and of the Son and of the Holy Spirit, To rule forever and ever.

Hallelujah.

ODE XXIV

1 The dove flew over the head of our Lord the Messiah, because he was her head

1 And she sang over him, and her voice was heard,

3 And the inhabitants were afraid, and the sojourners trembled.

4 The birds took to flight, and all creeping things died in their holes.

5 The abysses were opened and closed. They were seeking for the Lord, like (women) in travail.

6 He was not given to them for food because he did not belong to them,

7 and the abysses were submerged in the submersion of the Lord, and they perished in the thought which they had existed in from the beginning.

8 For they travailed from the beginning, and

the end of their travail was life.

9 And every one of them that was defective perished for it was not permitted to them to make a defense for themselves that they might remain;

10 And the Lord destroyed the imaginations of all them that had not the truth with them regarding the Messiah.

11 For they were defective in wisdom, they who were lifted up in their hearts,

12 And they were rejected, because the truth was not with them.

13 For the Lord disclosed his way, and spread abroad his grace

14 And those who understood it know his holiness.

Hallelujah.

ODE XXV

1 I was rescued from my bonds, and unto you, my God, I fled.

2 For you were the right hand of my salvation, and my helper.

3 You have restrained them that rise up against me, and they were seen no more

4 Because your face was with me, which saved me by your grace.

5 But I was despised and rejected in the eyes of many, and I was in their eyes like lead

6 And I acquired strength from yourself, and help.

7 You set me a lamp at my right hand and at my left, that in me there may be nothing that is not bright.

8 I was covered with the covering of your spirit, and I removed from me the raiment of skins,

9 For your right hand lifted me up, and removed sickness from me.

10 I became mighty in your truth and holy by your righteousness.

11 All my adversaries were afraid of me. I became the Lord's by the name of the Lord

12 And I was justified by his gentleness, and his rest is forever and ever.

Hallelujah.

ODE XXVI

1 I poured out praise to the Lord for I am his,

2 And I will speak his holy song, For my heart is with him.

3 His harp is in my hands, and the Odes of his rest shall not be silent.

4 I will cry unto him from my whole heart; I will praise and exalt him with all my members.

5 For from the East and even to the West is his praise;

6 And from the South and even to the North is his confession;

7 And from the top of the hills to their utmost bound Is his perfection.

8 Who can write the Odes of the Lord, or who can read them?

9 Who can train his soul for life, that his soul may be saved?

10 Who can rest on the Most High, that from his mouth he may speak?

11 Who is able to interpret the wonders of the Lord? He who interprets would be dissolved, and that which was interpreted will remain.

12 For it suffices to know and to rest, for in the rest the singers stand

13 Like a river which has an abundant fountain, and flows to the help of them that seek it.

Hallelujah.

ODE XXVII

1 I expanded my hands, and I sanctified (them) to my Lord. For the expansion of my hands is his sign.

2 And my expansion is the upright wood.

ODE XXVIII

1 As the wings of doves over their nestlings and the mouths of their nestlings towards their mouths, so also are the wings of the Spirit over my heart.

2 My heart is delighted and leaps up, like the babe who leaps up in the womb of his mother;

3 I believed; therefore I was at rest for faithful is he in whom I have believed. He has richly blessed me, and my head is with him.

4 And the sword shall not divide me from him nor the scimitar.

5 For I was ready before destruction came, and I have been set on his immortal pinions.
6 Deathless life embraced me and kissed me.
7 And from that (life) is the spirit within me, and it cannot die, for it lives.
8 They who saw me marveled at me because I was persecuted,
9 And they supposed that I was swallowed up for I seemed to them as one of the lost.
10 But my oppression became my salvation.
11 And I was their scorn because there was no wrath in me.
12 Because I did good to every man I was hated.
13 They circled round me like mad dogs who ignorantly attack their masters,
14 For their thought is corrupt and their understanding perverted.
15 But I was carrying water in my right hand, and their bitterness I endured 1 by my sweetness.
16 And I did not perish, for I was not their brother, nor was my birth like theirs.
17 They sought for my death and could not (accomplish it) for I was older than the memorial of them, and vainly did they cast lots against me.
18 Those who came after me sought without cause to destroy the memorial of him who was before them.
19 For the thought of the Most High cannot be anticipated, and his heart is superior to all wisdom.
Hallelujah.

ODE XXIX

1. The Lord is my hope; In him I shall not be confounded.
2 For according to his praise he made me, and according to his goodness 1 even so he gave unto me.
3 And according to his mercies he exalted mc, and according to his excellent beauty he set me on high.
4 And he brought me up out of the depths of Sheol, and from the mouth of death he drew me.
5 And I laid my enemies low, and he justified me by his grace.
6 For I believed in the Lord's Messiah, and he appeared to me that he is the Lord.
7 And he showed me his sign, and led me by his light;
8 And he gave me the rod of his power; hat I might subdue the imaginations of the people, and to bring down the power of the men of might.
9 To make war by his Word, and to take victory by his power.
10 And the Lord overthrew my enemy by his Word, and he became like the stubble which the wind carries away.
11 And I gave praise to the Most High because he exalted his servant and the Son of his handmaid.
Hallelujah.

ODE XXX

1 Fill you water for yourselves from the living fountain of the Lord for it has been opened to you,
2 And come all you thirsty and take a draught, and rest by the fountain of the Lord.
3 For fair it is and pure, and it gives rest to the soul.
4 Much sweeter is its water than honey, and the honeycomb of bees is not to be compared with it.
5. It flows from the lips of the Lord, and from the heart of the Lord is its name.
6. It came unlimited and invisible, and until it was set in the midst they did not know it.
7 Blessed are they who have drunk from it, and rested thereby.
Hallelujah.

ODE XXXI

1 The abysses were dissolved before the Lord, and darkness was destroyed by his appearance.
2 Error went astray and disappeared from him, and (as for) Falsehood, I gave it no path, and it was submerged by the truth of the Lord.
3 He opened his mouth and spoke grace and joy, and he spoke a new (song of) praise to his name.
4 And he lifted up his voice to the Most High,

and offered to him the sons that were in his hands.

5 And his face was justified; for thus his Holy Father had given to him.

6 Come forth, you that have been afflicted, and receive joy.

7 And possess your souls by grace, and take to you immortal life.

8 They condemned me when I rose up, me who had not been condemned.

9 They divided my spoil, though nothing was due to them.

10 But I endured and held my peace and was silent, that I might not be moved by them.

11. But I stood unshaken like a firm rock that is beaten by the waves and endures.

12 And I bore their bitterness for humility's sake, that I might redeem my people and inherit it.

13 And that I might not make void the promises to the patriarchs to whom I was promised for the salvation of their seed. Hallelujah.

ODE XXXII

1 To the blessed the joy is from their hearts, and light from him that dwells in them,

2 And the word from the truth who is self-originate.

3 For he has been strengthened by the holy power of the Most High, and he is unperturbed forever and ever. Hallelujah.

ODE XXXIII

1 Grace ran again and left the corruptor and came down upon him to bring him to naught.

2 He made utter destruction from before him and devastated all his array,

3 And he stood on a lofty summit and cried aloud from one end of the earth to the other.

4 He drew to him all those who obeyed him, and he did not appear as an evil person

5 But a perfect virgin stood who was proclaiming and crying and saying,

6 "O you sons of men, return you, and you their daughters, come you;

7 And leave the ways of that corruptor, and draw near unto me

8 And I will enter into you and bring you forth from destruction, and I will make you wise in the ways of truth.

9 Be not destroyed nor perish.

10. Hear me and be saved for the grace of God I am telling among you.

11 By my means you shall be redeemed and become blessed; I am your judge;

12 Those who have put me on shall not be injured but they shall possess incorruption in the new world.

13 My chosen ones have walked in me, and I will make known my ways to them that seek me, and I will make them trust in my name. Hallelujah.

ODE XXXIV

1 There is no hard way where there is a simple heart nor is there any barrier where the thoughts are upright,

2 Nor is there any storm in the depth of the illuminated thought.

3 The one who is surrounded on every side by open country is freed from doubts.

4 The likeness of that which is below is that which is above,

5 For everything is above, and below there is nothing, but it is believed to be by the ignorant.

6 Grace has been revealed for your salvation; Believe and live and be saved. Hallelujah.

ODE XXXV

1 The dew of the Lord distilled rest upon me, and it caused a cloud of peace to rise over my head

2 That it might guard me continually. It became salvation to me.

3 Everybody was shaken and affrighted, and there came forth from them a smoke and a judgment,

4 But I was keeping quiet in the ranks of the Lord. More than shadow was he to me, and more than support.

5 I was carried like a child by its mother, and he gave me milk, the dew of the Lord.

6 I grew great by his bounty, and I rested in his perfection,
7 And I spread out my hands in the lifting up of my soul, and I directed myself towards the Most High,
And I was redeemed with him.
Hallelujah.

ODE XXXVI
1 The Spirit of the Lord rested on me, and (the Spirit) raised me on high;
2 And made me to stand on my feet in the high place of the Lord, before his perfection and his glory while I was praising (him) by the composition of his
Odes.
3 (The Spirit) brought me forth before the face of the Lord, and although a son of man, I was named the luminary, the son of god, and the greatest among the great ones.
5 For according to the greatness of the Most High, so she made me, and like his own newness he renewed me
6 And he anointed me from his own perfection, and I became one of those that are near to him.
7 And my mouth was opened like a cloud of dew, and my heart gushed out, as it were, a gush of righteousness;
8 And my access (to Him) was in peace, and I was established in the Spirit of Providence.
Hallelujah.

[Note: in line 1 I adopted Lattke's emendation of "I rested in the Spirit of the Lord" -- SD]

ODE XXXVII
I stretched out my hands to the Lord and to the Most High I lifted my voice and I spoke with the lips of my heart.
2. He heard me when my voice reached him.
3 His word came to me, and gave me the fruits of my labors,
4 And gave me rest by the grace of the Lord.
Hallelujah.

ODE XXXVIII
1 I went up into the light of truth as into a chariot, and the truth led me and brought me

2 And carried me across hollows and gulfs.
From the cliffs and reefs it preserved me,
3. And became to me a haven of salvation, and set me on the arms of immortal life.
4 And it went with me and made me rest and suffered me not to err because it was and is the truth.
5 I ran no risk because I walked with him, and I made no error in anything, because I obeyed him,
6 For error fled away from him, and would not meet him.
7 But truth was proceeding in the right way, and whatever I did not know he made clear to me,
8 All the drugs of error and the plagues of death which are considered to be sweet (beverage).
9 And I saw the destroyer of the corrupter when the bride who was being corrupted was adorned, along with the bridegroom who corrupts and is corrupted.
10 And I asked the truth, "Who are these?" and he said to me, "This is the deceiver and error.
11 And they imitate the beloved and his bride, and they lead astray and corrupt the world.
12 And they invite many to the banquet,
And give them to drink of the wine of their intoxication.
13 They make them vomit up their wisdom and intelligence, and they deprive them of understanding.
i4 Then they leave them, and so these go about like madmen and corrupt."
15 And I was made wise so as not to fall into the hands of the deceiver and I congratulated myself that the truth had gone with me.
16 I was established and lived and was redeemed, and my foundations were laid by the Lord; For he planted me.
17 For he set the root, and watered it and fixed it and blessed it, and its fruits will be forever.
18 It struck deep and sprang up and spread wide, and it was full and was enlarged.
19 And the Lord alone was glorified, in his planting and his husbandry,
20 In his care and in the blessing of his lips, in the beautiful planting of his right hand,

21 And in the splendor of his planting, and in the thought of his mind.
Hallelujah.

ODE XXXIX

1 Mighty rivers are the power of the Lord that carry headlong those that despise him
3 And entangle their paths, and sweep away their fords
3 And carry off their bodies and destroy their souls.
4 For they are more swift than lightning, and more rapid.
5 But those who cross them in
faith shall not be moved,
6 And those who walk on them without blemish shall not be afraid.
7 For the sign in them is the Lord and the sign becomes the way of those who cross in the name of the Lord.
8 Put on, therefore, the name of the Most High and know him, and you shall cross without danger, while the rivers shall be subject to you.
9 The Lord has bridged them by his word, and he walked and crossed them on foot,
10 And his footsteps stand (firm) on the waters, and were not erased. They are as a beam that is firmly fixed.
11 And the waves were lifted up on this side and on that, and the footsteps of our Lord Messiah stand (firm)
12 And are not obliterated, and are not defaced.
13 A way has been appointed for those who cross after him, and for those who agree to the course of his faith and who adore his name.
Hallelujah.

ODE XL

1 As the honey distils from the comb of the bees, and the milk flows from the woman that loves her children, so also is my hope on you, my God.
2 As the fountain gushes out its water, so my heart gushes out the praise of the Lord, and my lips utter praises to him.
3 And my tongue is sweet in his intimate converse and my limbs are made fat by the sweetness of his Odes.

4 My face is glad with his exultation, and my spirit exults in his love, and my soul shines in him.
5 The fearful one shall confide in him, and redemption shall in him stand assured.
6 His gain is immortal life and those who participate in it are incorruptible.
Hallelujah.

ODE XLI

1 Let all the Lord's bairns praise him, and let us appropriate the truth of his faith, and his children shall be acknowledged by him.
3 We live in the Lord by his grace, and life we receive in his messiah,
4 For a great day has shined upon us and marvelous is he who has given us of his glory.
5 Let us, therefore, all of us unite together in the name of the Lord, and let us honor him in his goodness,
6 And let our faces shine in his light, and let our hearts meditate in his love by night and by day.
7 Let us exult with the joy of the Lord.
8 All those that see me will be astonished, for from another race am I.
9 For the Father of Truth remembered me, he who possessed me from the beginning,
10 For his riches begat me, and the thought of his heart.
11 His word is with us in all our way, the savior who makes alive and does not reject our souls.
12 The man who was humbled and was exalted by his own righteousness.
13 The son of the Most High appeared in the perfection of his father
14 And light dawned from the word that was previously in him.
15 The messiah is truly one and he was known before the foundations of the world that he might save souls forever by the truth of his name.
16 Let a new song arise to the Lord from them that love him.
Hallelujah.

ODE XLII

1 I stretched out my hands and approached my Lord, for the stretching out of my hands is his sign

2 And my expansion is the outspread wood that was set up on the way of the righteous one.

3 And I became of no use to those who knew me, for I shall hide myself from those who did not take hold of me,

4 But I will be with those who love me.

5 All my persecutors have died and they sought after me who proclaimed about me because I am alive.

6 I rose up and am with them and I will speak by their mouths

7 For they have despised those who persecute them. I threw over them the yoke of my love. Like the arm of the bridegroom over the bride, so is my yoke over those that know me.

9 As the couch that is spread in the chambers of the bridegroom and the bride, so is my love over those that believe in me.

10 I was not rejected, though I was reckoned to be so, and I did not perish though they thought it of me.

11 Sheol saw me and was in distress; death cast me up and many along with me.

12 I have been gall and bitterness to it and I went down with it to the extreme of its depth,

13 And the feet and the head it let go for it was a not able to endure my face.

14 And I made a congregation of living men amongst his dead men and I spoke with them by living lips in order that my word may not be void.

15 And those who had died ran towards me and they cried and said, "son of God, have pity on us

16 And do with us according to thy kindness and bring us out from the bonds of darkness

17 And open to us the door by which we shall come out to you, for we perceive that our death does not touch you.

18 Let us also be saved with you, for you are our Savior."

19 And I heard their voice and I laid up their faith in my heart

20 And I set my name upon their heads

for they are free men and they are mine. Hallelujah.

Andrew Phillip Smith

Round Table: a Story

"Here's to Facebook."

The four men clinked glasses, three of them pints of beer, one white wine.

"That's the shittiest toast I've ever raised a glass to," said Phil.

"Ah, the wonders of social networking. Click your way through six degrees of separation and you end up where you started, with your old school chums," said Matt.

The pub was quiet, typical of the older kind of London pub, well maintained, brass and dark-stained wood, stained glass windows advertising the brewer Youngs. Yet it was distinctive in its lack of a jukebox and no flat screen televisions, a pub mostly for the middle-classed and middle-aged, for those who liked their real ale and conversation.

"Well, Matt and I have kept in touch over the years, so there's nothing miraculous about that. We manage to meet up for a drink a couple of times a year. We had dinner at my place a couple of years ago but Maggie and Judith didn't get on too well, so we've only done that the once. You really ought to get Judith to volunteer though, Matt."

"I'll let her come up with the idea, Phil."

Phil's upturned nose and bright eyes prevented his face from holding any expression other than cheeky innocence for more than a few seconds.

"I managed to stayed in touch up to the mid-90s," said Robin. "I even went to your wedding Phil. The first one, anyway. Are you married, Wyn? Not everyone admits to it on their Facebook pages"

"No, I'm not," said Wyn, "Came close a couple of times. If I found the right woman and wanted to start a family I might."

At the mention of Wyn's Facebook page Matt grimaced. "You can tell a lot about people from Facebook. Hallelujah, Wyn."

Wyn gave a shy little smile, his already ruddy, rough cheeks reddening a little more. Wyn's face was coarser than the others', his body bulkier and his hands rougher as if he had been used to physical work at some point. His accent still had some Welsh in the vowels. His family had moved to London when he was eleven. The other three had well-spoken English accents with varying degrees of fashionable London mockney. Even Rubin with his well-rounded vowels, included the occasional fashionable glottal stop.

The conversations continued, breaking up into parts and reforming, cycling through the possible permutations of two, three and even four people.

Robin had been talking to Matt about some teacher who had recently died, and Phil to Wyn about the recession. Both trains of discussion ended simultaneously and the group was left in silence, the talk from neighbouring tables spilling out into their consciousness. It was Phil, ever the easy talker, who spoke first.

"Well, this is about the four of us, about us all catching up. So let's involve the whole table. What can we do to keep us all together?"

"Oh Christ, you're not proposing one of your drinking games are you?" said Matt. His glass of wine stood still untouched on the table before him.

"I'm not into drinking games either," said Wyn.

"Fuzzy duck. Ducky fuzz. Does he?" Reminisced Robin.

"Let's get another round in anyway," proposed Wyn.

"I'll sit this one out," said Matt. He shifted back a little, his height suddenly noticeable, his long face hinting disapproval.

Robin returned with a pint of bitter in each hand for him and Phil and a lager for Wyn.

"OK," said Phil, "questions then? What's the worst thing you've ever done?"

"Well, the worst thing I remember you doing, Phil," said Robin, "was having a wank during the fourth year physics exam."

""Yeah, well, I finished early," said Phil.

"You can probably last a lot longer these days," said Robin.

"I can remember some of the things you used to get up to, Robin," said Phil.

"OK then, forget the teenage misdemeanours," said Phil, "Let's make it the worst thing you've done since leaving school."

"I bet you've been preparing your answer," said Matt, "and it's not the worst thing you've ever done at all." You'll just give us a sop, a little bit embarrassing but not that bad. "

"What's yours then?"

"I dropped a Mars bar wrapper on the street once instead of putting it in the bin. You've been a bit quiet Wyn, you next."

Wyn wasn't smiling, and shrugged, "I'll pass on that one."

"Hallelujah," said Matt again.

"You said that before," said Robin, "What's the joke?"

"Haven't you looked at Wyn's Facebook wall?"

"Do I look like the kind of man who has time to trawl through people';s Facebook walls?"

"Well you seem to have enough time to play Farmville."

"Farmville's different. That's my relaxation."

"Well, Wyn's a Christian. He's a believer. He's born again."

Wyn sat there impassively, his mouth a straight line on his ruddy face. He was well familiar with the general antagonism to Christianity among a large proportion of the English.

"What denomination?" asked Robin?

"Baptist," replied Wyn.

"Don't tell me you're one too," said Matt.

"Not exactly. I'm a Gnostic."

"Me too," said Phil. For a moment Robin stared incredulously at Phil, but then Phil went on,"I'm agnostic."

"Is that a joke?"

"No. I genuinely feel that we can't really know about these things."

"Oh, an agnostic. Well you might say that I'm the opposite of that. I'm a Gnostic. Gnosticism. *Guh-nosti-cism.* I believe that the way to knowledge of God, or the divine, or whatever you want to call it, is through direct experience. I follow the ideas and the myths of the ancient Gnostics."

"The heretics?" said Wyn, finally grinning.

"Shit, that sounds even worse than being a Baptist," said Matt.

"So what do you think of it all then, as if I couldn't guess?"

"Religion? It's a load of crap."

"See, I think that's too broad. As for the existence of God, I just don't see how we could know. I'm not a religious person, but you have to admit that religion's done some good for humanity in its time and despite all the crap, as you call it, it still does some good. "

"Yeah, like in Northern Ireland," said Matt.

"I was in the forces in Northern Ireland," said Wyn. "It was brutal. Yeah, the IRA were all Catholics and the loyalist paramilitaries were all Protestants. You can't argue with that. But religion wasn't the cause."

"It certainly helped it along though," interjected Robin.

"Yeah, but it wasn't the cause. I didn't have the time or the inclination to think much about it while I was there but I've read about it since, and discussed the history with some Irish people, and it was British policy that was at fault. Originally. Most of us were trying to keep the peace when I was there. I have my problems with Catholicism but it was actually outlawed in Ireland for a long time. No wonder there were strong feelings about it. And those protestant communities are there because Elizabeth I established plantations and moved in Scots settlers. It's complicated, it's complicated."

He was getting a little fiery now. "And the sectarians in Ulster were behaving a an unchristian way. You can't blame a religion based on love and redemption and charity for all the violence that went on there. Some of the things I saw, man!"

For a moment the other three felt out of their depth.

"The problem with mainstream religion," Robin began, "is that it forgets about inner transformation."

His chubby face was passive in repose but surprisingly determined when he was making a point.

"New age!" shouted Matt.

"It gets caught up in external observance and dogma and sectarianism. The inner transformation—what I call Gnosis—has to come first. I believe that most value is in the esoteric side of religion. The outer religion will always be there—unless Matt exterminates it of course—but within that there will always be a core of people, not necessarily high up in the hierarchy—who have true spiritual development."

"Well, that makes some sense I suppose," said Robin the reconciliator.

"It's fucking elitist I suppose you're part of the

spiritual inner circle, Robin." Matt approximated a laying on of hands, "You have consciousness, my son."

"Well, I have had genuine spiritual experiences."

"Isn't it wonderful what schizophrenia can do for you," said Matt.

"Fuck off!" said Robin.

"I've got to agree with Matt there," said Wyn, "That's elitist. Christianity is for anyone, not just those who think they deserve it. Christ gives his love to all who will receive it. And believe me, so-called external Christianity can transform people. When someone receives Christ he doesn't spend his time meditating and playing with tarot cards."

"What do they do then?"

"We help people."

"In what way?"

"Speaking for myself, I work with teenagers from troubled backgrounds. I help out with a soup run for the homeless once a week. I've put in time with a few charities, and done much more besides. And there are people who contribute much more than I do."

Robin looked disgruntled but added, "I don't use tarot cards, as it happens."

Phil said, "I haven't done much for charity, apart from buying a lot of clothes from Oxfam, but I always have a nagging feeling that I ought to."

Matt responded, "I have a standing order payment to a homeless charity each month, and I didn't have to get religion to do that. So do you do anything charitable, Rob?"

"As a matter of fact, I agree that charity should be primarily the domain of religion any more. It's part of society as a whole. Though of course religion is one of the major influences on establishing charity as a principle, and still one of the major sources of charity work. I don't particularly like the mega charities, with all that bureaucracy and commercialism. One thing I never do is sign up for those pay-every-month schemes that people approach you about in the High Street. I know they're just kids, students usually, but they're doing it because they get paid to canvas. It's not as clean. I usually give a bit of change to homeless people on the street, mainly the older ones or the women. And I do other things too. Including regular payments."

"Now you're all making me feel guilty. But it's good what you're doing, Wyn," said Phil, "But it's not just one-way giving is it?"

"What do you mean?" he bridled a little.

"Well, I've seen some of those Christian soup runs and they're always quoting the Bible to the homeless people, and trying to lure them along to church. One of the helpers gave me a card telling me that Christ loves me."

"Maybe he thought you looked homeless, Phil," said Robin, smiling.

"It's called shabby chic, Robin."

"So?" said Wyn. "Yeah, we do try to spread the word of God. You think the homeless are going to get themselves out of that mess by reading Richard Dawkins?"

"At least Dawkins makes sense. You don't need religious gobbledegook to do charity."

"I preferred Christopher Hitchens' book myself. God Is Not Great. Dawkins is too much of evangelist. Though he comes across as very C of E and out of touch."

"But what he says is right. There's no real argument against Darwinian evolution. I bet you're a creationist, Wyn."

"As it happens I believe in intelligent design. Everything evolved in the way scientists say, but the whole process was directed by God."

"That's just creationism by the back door. OK, so you don't have to believe that it was all done in seven days or that humans were riding around on dinosaurs, but you're trying to have the best of both worlds without thinking them through properly. What kind of intelligent designer creates the human appendix, or Alzheimer's or shortsightedness or animals that devour their young?"

Matt had long legs. He pushed his chair back, balancing it on the two legs.

"Right, " said Robin, "but this is where Gnosticism has better answers. The material world was created by a lesser God, an ignorant demiurge."

"How does that work?" asked Phil.

"Well, there's this big myth going on in the background—which I don't take literally" he glanced at Matt. "The highest, unknowable source of divinity emanated out all these divine beings called aeons. The last of them, Sophia, fell from grace, gave birth to a monstrosity called Yaldabaoth. He created the material world without knowing about the spiritual realm above him. So all the evil in the world is due to the imperfect creation of the demiurge, and not to the true God."

Matt was obviously thinking things through, playing with the beer mat, using it to make shapes with a thin puddle of beer on the table, then he said, "It sounds like passing the buck to me."

"How come?"

"Well, if the true God hadn't come up with all his divine beings in the first place the last one wouldn't have fallen and we wouldn't have what you call the material world."

"It keeps God free from blame, yes. It's a process of God coming to know himself, through which we ourselves come to know ourselves and the universe. Some Gnostics believed that this is all a process of God coming to know himself. By coming to know ourselves and to experience gnosis we partake of the divine world and help to restore it. It's a world view. I don't claim to have empirical evidence for a lot of it, but it provides a meaningful view of life. And it's not just an intellectual approach. It provides me with a helpful attitude to personal suffering and other human issues. After all, what's your answer to the purpose of the universe? It just is? If there's no purpose to the universe and everything is just due to blind chance, everything from the big bang and the laws of physics to evolution, then there is no ultimate meaning. I find that meaningless and nihilistic. "

"Well, shouldn't we be basing our "worldview" as you call it on hypothesis and experimentation, on truth, rather than whether it suits us or not?"

"I agree," said Wyn.

"You do?" said Matt, rolling his eyes.

"I do. I believe in Christ because Christ is truth."

"Only because you believe in it. That's pretty circular."

"So you actually believe that a man came back to life?"

"Yeah, of course I do. It's a foundation of my faith. But he wasn't just a man, he was the son of God"

"A zombie God. Night of the Living Jesus. Gasp at the open wounds. He's staggering towards you, arms out, the yes rolling back in

their bloodshot sockets. . . "

"Take it easy Matt," said Phil, "This is something he believes in."

"See, that's where the Gnostic view once again makes a lot more sense. Gnostics say that Jesus rose spiritually.

"Look, I wasn't the one who brought all of this up. I'm always happy to spread the gospel but I came here to meet old friends, not to argue about atheism."

""Hmmm," said Robin, "You think we're arguing about atheism, Matt seems to think we're arguing about religion."

"Robin reckons we're arguing about heresy, " said Wyn.

Robin said, "But I do agree about the nihilism. Gnosticism recognises the difficult nature of the world, but all the same it has a sense of purpose. Whereas Christianity doesn't really explain the existence of evil satisfactorily. I don't mind admitting that Christianity can genuinely transform people, but it seems rare to me."

"Theology isn't really my thing. I'm more of a practising Christian. Evil comes from the lack of God."

"But how can a scorpion or an earthquake or a brain-damaged baby be due to a lack of God if that same God—your god—created the world, intervenes in it occasionally and is a personal God?"

"I don't claim to have the answer, but I do not that my faith has changed me, and if more people were Christians there would be less suffering in the world. And more strength to cope with the suffering that exists.."

"I'm enjoying this," said Matt.

Robin turned on Matt, "I agree that atheism is nihilistic. If everything human can be explained by Darwinism then there really isn't any meaning to life, and nature and history give us every justification to treat each other cruelly."

"Very few atheists are social Darwinists. You're assuming that meaning has to come from some kind of higher source. There's no reason why human beings shouldn't treat each other decently. Meaning just comes from personal satisfaction and doing the kind of things that we were built to do. Part of that satisfaction is treating people decently. Things like altruism and morality could well have entered through natural selection because they're beneficial for survival. We were made to help each other."

"So we're built to do things are we? Sounds like your an intelligent design believer on the quiet," said Robin.

"It's just a figure of speech," said Matt.

"Your turn, Phil," said Robin.

"I just don't know," said Phil.

"What a cop out," said Wyn.

"At least I admit I don't know."

"So did I," said Wyn.

"Yeah, but then you went on about faith and made it obvious that you think you do know."

"OK Wyn," said Matt, "I'll bit. What is this great redemption you've been hinting at? What changed a Welsh lager lout into an upstanding member of the God squad?"

"Well now we're back to the worst things you've ever done. I raped a woman," he said simply.

There was silence again at the table. The barman pulled a rack of glasses from the dishwasher and started to unload them, the clattering ;loud against the sudden quietness of the four men.

"It was in 1989. I'd just finished a term of duty in Northern Ireland. I was wound up. My head wasn't right. I'd had a night of drinking and some speed and I met a woman at a club. We went back to her place."

He paused, not for dramatic effect, but as if groping for the memory.

"I misread the signs. She just wanted to talk. She went on and on and I made a move, but I didn't listen to her. She was saying no, but not very directly. I didn't listen."

He stopped again and looked down at his glass, took a sip, his knotty fist wrapped tensely around the glass, his pale freckled skin contrasting awkwardly with the golden, fizzy lager.

"I've paid my debt to society. I had time to think in prison. More than just that. There was a chaplain there who was a good man and understood about these things. I found God and offered myself up to him. It changed my life"

Well, it's difficult to argue with that," admitted Matt.

In reaction tot he uneasy silence the talk turned to jobs, to hobbies, to women, but then they remembered Wyn's crime. They had another couple of rounds. The landlord called last orders but they each of them felt they had had enough and ought to be going.

As they were leaving Matt said to Wyn, "Sorry, I didn't know about all that. I didn't mean to put you on the spot like that."

He held out his hand. Wyn took it, "It's OK. I'm ashamed of what I did but I'm not ashamed of admitting to it."

Robin turned to Wyn and said, "I've had difficult experiences in my life too, and done things that I wish I hadn't. I'll leave it at that."

They parted, Wyn and Matt finding that they both needed the same tube station, Robin taking a bus, Phil hailing a cab. Down a service alley two cats fought with each other, their hideous yowls organic against the hum of traffic. An old woman, probably Irish, crossed herself as she passed a large, modern and ugly church. Robin got onto the bus but it only went a few yards before the traffic lights turned red. A young man, bare-chested in tracksuit bottoms, shouted as he left an all night grocery shop. The stars were concealed by the street lights. The city ground onwards.

Dean F. Wilson

Gnosticism in Enochian Magic

Enochian magic is a system of esoteric practice that was reputedly delivered by numerous angelic entities to magician, mathematician and astrologer Dr. John Dee and skryer Edward Kelley in Renaissance times. The system, which was transmitted over the course of many years, includes a complex array of tools, magical tables, and an entire language, purported to be that of the angels.

The communications between Dee and the angels were also highly flavoured in theological material that was overtly Christian, but also subtly Gnostic, in form, a point that many magicians and scholars of Enochian magic have noticed over the years, including Geoffrey James, Donald Tyson and Aaron Leitch.[1]

A number of scholars argue over the definition of Gnosticism, with some, like Michael Allen Williams, suggesting that the word is somewhat of a misnomer.[2] For this article I will be employing Gnosticism as a blanket term for a series of sects and traditions from before and after the time of Christ, with many of the more popular forms of it, such as the Valentinian school, espousing esoteric Christian doctrine. However, other groups made use of Jewish, Neoplatonic, and even Pagan symbolism and teachings, some independently and others combined. While the various Gnostic groups had very different views and practices, they usually shared a common appreciation of *gnosis*, the experiential knowledge of the divine.

One of the most striking sessions recorded in Dee's diaries was on June 8, 1584, which revealed some shocking doctrines that were largely Gnostic in persuasion. The session on that day proved generally fruitless, as there was no apparition in the stone, but Kelley talked about his conversion to God and a series of doctrines that "wicked spirits" transmitted to him:

".....That Jesus was not God.

.....That no prayer ought to be made to Jesus.

.....That there is no sin.

.....That mans soul doth go from one body, to another child's quickening on animation.

.....That as many men and women as are now, have always been: That is, so many human bodies, and human souls, neither more nor less, as are now, have always been.

.....That the generation of mankind from Adam and Eve, is not an History, but a writing which hath an other sense.

.....No Holy Ghost they acknowledged.

.....They would not suffer him to pray to Jesus Christ; but would rebuke him, saying, that he robbed God of his honour, etc."[3]

These doctrines were extremely radical for the time and likely shook Dee's Protestant faith, but it seems that he was able to maintain his world view by dismissing it all as "blasphemous" and a "manifold horrible doctrine". While Dee was not exactly the most orthodox of Christians, he was very devout, and the suggestion that many of the teachings he believed in were not true likely came as a big surprise, one that he would not readily accept.

The working from this date is not very clear about whether or not these views were espoused by the Enochian angels or were given to Kelley at some time before he came into contact with Dee. At first it seems like it might have happened at some earlier time when Kelley was working with evil spirits, but it is important to remember that Kelley regularly dismissed the Enochian entities as being demons, and this may have been one of those times.

Another important point is that for several sessions after this one Kelley was unable to see anything in the shewstone, which left Dee wondering what they might have done wrong. Dee gives one of the potential reasons for the no show as a caveat from one angel, who tells them: "This Action shall never come to pass, until there be no remembrance of wickedness, or Hell left amongst you."[4] Dee appears to have viewed this as a command to rid themselves of sin, but it may also have been a command to rid themselves of the *thought* of sin—i.e. to no longer worry about such orthodox views, which is particularly apt if they put forward the doctrine that there is no sin. It may have been that Dee and Kelley's refusal to accept this supposedly sinful doctrine that resulted in the angels being unwilling to communicate with them for a time.

Regardless of where these teachings came from, there are many parallels between them and the teachings of Gnostic groups and texts. For example, the idea that Jesus was not God, that they should not pray to Jesus, and that there was no Holy Ghost could be seen in terms of the Gnostic view that Jesus is an Aeon, an emanation of God, but not God himself, and that, indeed, we all can be anointed like Jesus to free ourselves from the shackles of the world.

The dismissal of the Holy Ghost is harder to reconcile with Enochian teachings, which attribute a line of the Great Table to the *Spiritus Sanctus*, Latin for "Holy Spirit". It may have been that the entities were dismissing the Christian view of the Holy Spirit (noting the use of the term "Holy Ghost" instead) without actually dismissing the Holy Spirit altogether. In Gnosticism the Holy Spirit can be likened to Sophia, the feminine aspect of God that is often paired with Jesus and can thus be seen as equally part of, or an emanation of, God, but not God in totality.

The suggestion that there is no sin is an equally devastating revelation to a Christian world view. However, this was not alien to Gnostic theology, with some Gnostics readily rejecting the idea of original sin, because the God of the Old Testament was often seen as the Demiurge, a fake god, and the tasting of the fruit from the Tree of Knowledge of Good and Evil was often not seen as an evil act, but as the first awakening of gnosis in humanity, one that was punished by the jealous Demiurge. A popular Gnostic view is that we all have a spark of the divine within us and that we are trapped here, the result of the evil or ignorance of a false god rather than the greed and selfishness of humanity.

One of the biggest revelations was that "man's soul doth go from one body, to another child's quickening on animation", or, in other words, reincarnation. This was a very radical view for the time, but not so for Gnostics, who widely believed in reincarnation. For example, one Basilidean text reads:

Indeed, the apostle has said, 'I was once alive apart from the law', at some point or other. That is (Paul means), before I came into this body, I lived in the kind of body that is not subject to the law: the body of a domestic animal or a bird. [5]

The Secret Book of John tells us:

That soul will be made to follow the guidance of another in which the spirit of life resides, and by that other it attains salvation, and so is not cast into flesh again.[6]

Another Gnostic text, *The Book of Thomas the Contender*, states:

For, the visible parts of humankind will perish, since the instrument of their flesh is going to perish. And when it is dispersed it will come to reside among visible things, among things that are seen. And next, because of the love of the faith, which they formerly had, the fire that can be seen torments them. They will be regathered to the visible realm.[7]

The Gnostic viewpoint was generally similar to the Buddhist idea of *samsara*, which is the cycle of rebirth which leads to suffering in the mortal world. The Gnostic would attempt to free him or herself from this cycle and return to the *Pleroma*, the Fullness of God.

Tying in with this belief in reincarnation was the suggestion to Kelley that there are the exact number of people now as there has always been, which makes sense with a literal belief in reincarnation, but does not necessarily hold up to inspection with the facts about population growth around the world, with growth from several hundred million people in the Middle Ages to several billion today.

The idea that the tale of the generation from Adam and Eve is "a writing which hath an other sense", not a literal history, is strongly Gnostic, as many of the Gnostics viewed scripture as an allegory, not historical fact. One very clear example of this is *Ptolemy's Epistle to Flora*, which reads:

Finally, the third subdivision is the symbolic and allegorical part, which is after the image of the superior, spiritual realm: the saviour changed (the referent of) this part from the perceptible, visible level to the spiritual, invisible one.[8]

Another example is Herakleon's commentary on the Gospel of John[9], which is filled with references to one thing signifying something else and once again the mention of "another sense". Herakleon's exegesis was one of the first in existence, and also one that bore the symbolic

meaning of the gospel into consideration more than many others.

Even if we accept the revelations on June 8, 1584 as not being the work of the Enochian angels, there are many other parallels between Enochian magic and Gnosticism in the magical system itself.

One of the strongest links can be found in the view of the cosmology of the universe. In Gnosticism there is usually a singular divine source, followed by successive emanations of the divine called Aeons, which, depending on the source text, tended to be viewed as places, beings or states of consciousness. A very strong parallel can be found in the 30 Enochian Aethyrs, which could easily be linked with the 30 Aeons of the Valentinian tradition. Other Gnostic traditions had a different number of Aeons, but the principle was essentially the same. The Qabalistic tradition of the Sephiroth on the Tree of Life, which Dee was well versed in, is also particularly Gnostic in style, having been partially influenced by it, particularly via the Lurianic tradition, a popular Qabalistic school based on the teachings of Renaissance rabbi Isaac Luria, with many of his concepts still used by Qabalists and Hermeticists today.

The parallel is even stronger in the *Pistis Sophia*, an important Gnostic document that was for a long time, until the discovery of the Nag Hammadi collection in 1945, the best source of Gnostic teaching. It reads:

And moreover Jesus had not told his disciples the total expansion of all the regions of the great Invisible and of the three triple-powers and of the four-and-twenty invisibles, and all their regions and their aeons and their orders, how they are extended—those which are the emanations of the great Invisible—and their ungenerated and their self-generated and their generated and their light-givers and their unpaired and their rulers and their authorities and their lords and their archangels and their angels and their decans and their servitors and all the houses of their spheres and all the orders of every one of them."[10]

Here we see mention of the Aeons, which can be likened to the Aethyrs. Ruling over them there appear to be "three triple-powers", which is similar to the three governors which rule each Aethyr (barring the last one, TEX, which has four). The mention of "four-and-twenty invisibles" could have some relationship with the 24 Seniors of the Enochian system. The various ranks of angels mentioned could be seen in relation to the numerous ranks of angels on the Great Table.

Later in the text there are references to various gates that are passed through, which is very similar to the many gates mentioned in relation to Liber

Logaeth and the Enochian Calls. This passage also mentions the number 49, which is of pivotal importance to Enochian magic, both in terms of the 49x49 tables of Liber Logaeth, the 49 Bonorum, the 49 Calls, and many other references to this important number within the system:

And I left that region behind me and ascended to the first sphere, shining most exceedingly, forty-and-nine-times more brightly than I had shone in the firmament. It came to pass then, when I had reached the gate of the first sphere, that its gates were shaken and opened of themselves at once."[11]

Some magicians and scholars have suggested that the God mentioned in the Enochian Calls is actually the Demiurge. There is some support for this in the Calls themselves. For example, the First Call mentions *Iad Balt*, which translates as "the God of Justice". It is hard not to see the resemblance of this to *Ialdabaoth*, one name attributed by Gnostics to the Demiurge. The link between the Demiurge and the harsh god of the Old Testament is also apparent in the translation, as Yahweh was very much a "God of Justice", a very different divine being to the loving God exemplified in the New Testament, something that many ancient Gnostics picked up on.

While some may dismiss the similarity of these words as no more than mere coincidence, let me point out several other similarities between some Enochian and Greek and Latin words. The most obvious examples are the Enochian words *Christeos* ("let there be"), *Iehusoz* ("mercy"), *Luciftias* ("brightness") and *Babalon* ("harlot"), which are strikingly similar to the Greek *Christos* ("the annointed"), Latin

Iehus ("Jesus"), Latin *Lucifer* ("light-bearer") and the Whore of Babylon mentioned in the Book of the Revelation of St. John the Divine. It is clear that these Enochian words share a relationship with other common words in the Christian lexicon, and it is just as likely that *Iad Balt* does the same within a Gnostic Christian framework.

Enochian scholar Geoffrey James argues that Kelley might have been consciously or unconsciously lifting material from other sources, including Gnostic works:

If Kelly was plagiarizing some as-yet undiscovered manuscript, it may have been Gnostic in origin, as significant parallels exist between the Angelical keys and certain Gnostic texts.[12]

James points out a surprising similarity between a common phrase in the Enochian Calls, *Zacar Ca Od Zamran*[13] ("Move, therefore, and show yourselves"), and an invocation in the *Pistis Sophia*, which reads *Zama Zama Ozza Rachama Ozai*.[14] There is no known translation for these words, which are most likely a form of glossolalia. The *Pistis Sophia* describes them as "five words of those from the height"[15], echoing the frequent mention of "the Highest" in the Enochian Calls.

From the wording used in the Calls, the being who is speaking is clearly the Creator, and yet the end of the First Call reads: "I am the servant of the same your God, the true worshipper of the Highest." The Call appears to start in the point of view of the Creator and shift to the point of view of the magician towards the end, but it could also be possible that the Creator, or Demiurge from a Gnostic perspective, is still speaking here and is actually acknowledging that there is a higher power than him.

The number seven is particularly important in both Enochian magic and Gnosticism. Many Gnostic texts mention the number frequently. For example, the *Pistis Sophia* tells us that we are to forgive sins "not only unto seven times, but unto seventy times seven".[16] A Mandaean text called *The Soul's Deliverance* talks about seven enemies, which are also mentioned in several other Gnostic texts, including *Poimandres*, where the "seven rulers" (or archons) are seen as the seven planets. *The Gospel of Mary* tells of the ascent of the soul past "the seven powers of wrath"[17], representing forces of bondage. This is very similar to the attribution of the planets to many seven-fold entities within the Enochian system, though these are not necessarily seen in as negative a light as that of many Gnostic texts.

Perhaps one of the most striking parallels can be found in a passage in Dee's diaries about the Daughter of Fortitude, which is very similar to the Gnostic text *Thunder, Perfect Mind*. To best illustrate their similarities I will quote first the full text of Dee:

I am the Daughter of Fortitude, and ravished every hour, from my youth. For behold, I am Understanding, and science dwelleth in me; and the heavens oppress me, they covet and desire me with infinite appetite: few or none that are earthly have embraced me, for I am shadowed with the Circle of the Stone,[18] and covered with the morning Clouds. My feet are swifter than the winds, and my hands are sweeter than the morning dew. My garments are from the beginning, and my dwelling place is in myself. The Lion knoweth not where I walk, neither do the beast of the field understand me. I am deflowered, and yet a virgin: I sanctify, and am not sanctified. Happy is he that embraceth me: for in the night season I am sweet, and in the day full of pleasure. My company is a harmony of many Cymbals, and my lips sweeter than health itself. I am a harlot for such as ravish me, and a virgin with such as know me not: For lo, I am loved of many, and I am a lover to many; and as many as come unto me as they should do, have entertainment. Purge your streets, O ye sons of men, and wash your houses clean; make yourselves holy, and put on righteousness. Cast out your old strumpets, and burn their clothes; abstain from the company of other women that are defiled, that are sluttish, and not so handsome and beautiful as I, and then will I come and dwell amongst you: and behold, I will bring forth children unto you, and they shall be the Sons of Comfort. I will open my garments, and stand naked before you, that your love may be more enflamed toward me."[19]

Compare this to a short excerpt from *Thunder, Perfect Mind*:

For I am the first and the last. I am the honored one and the scorned one. I am the whore and the holy one. I am the wife and the virgin. I am the mother and the daughter. I am the members of my mother. I am the barren one and many are her sons.

The parallel is very strong. Both texts are from the point of view of a feminine divine power. Both have a strong voice, both talk of an origin in the beginning, and both have multiple paradoxical statements. Dee's text speaks of being a "harlot... and a virgin", while *Thunder, Perfect Mind* speaks of being "the whore ... and the virgin". There is even the mention of many sons or children in both texts. The full Gnostic text makes many more paradoxical statements, all of which support the idea of this entity being a vehicle of passion.

A further correspondence can be seen in the infamous wife-swapping incident between Dee and Kelley, which Donald Tyson suggested was a form of Gnostic union:

There is a great deal of Gnostic imagery in the Enochian communications and Keys, and one of the features of Gnosticism is

the use of sexual energy to bring about a union with the divine in order to achieve a heightened spiritual awareness and an enlightened mind."[20]

The Valentinian tradition might offer some support to this argument with its most important sacrament, that of the Bridal Chamber. This ritual was intended as a spiritual marriage of the initiate with their angel, though it is not clear if there was ever an actual ritual enactment of this concept. There also does not appear to be any evidence to suggest that two people were involved in this ceremony, or that sex was involved, but some of the language used in Gnostic texts suggests the involvement of both a male and female, such as a passage in *The Gospel of Philip*, which reads: "a woman joins with her husband in the bridal chamber"[21].

Of course, it does not say that a woman joins with someone else's husband, as Dee and Kelley's wives eventually did, and even if it did say this, the wife-swapping would be a very literal enactment of what scholars generally believe to be a more symbolic sacrament within Gnostic tradition. Tyson suggests that the angels wanted Dee and Kelley to join in a mystical union, but that "since neither Dee nor Kelley would ever have agreed to a homosexual union to bind themselves together spiritually with the occult energies of sex, the angels chose the next best option and used the wives as surrogates."[22]

The Bridal Chamber also shares some interesting links with the Hermetic concept of the Knowledge and Conversation of the Holy Guardian Angel, made famous by the 15th Century grimoire *The Book of Abramelin*, which Dee may have had access to. Dee would also have likely been aware of the Qabalistic concept of *tiqqun*, the restoration of the world, which was often exemplified in the union of the Sephiroth of Malkuth and Tiphareth, which were traditionally called the *Kallah* (Bride) and the *Chatan* (Bridegroom) respectively.

Another link between Enochian magic and Gnosticism can be found in the Enochian angels' view of Wisdom. A female entity called Galvah relates her name to the Latin *Finis* ("the end"), but also speaks of the Wisdom associated with her and how such is always a feminine thing:

> I am Finis, I am a beam of that Wisdom which is the end of man's excellency. These also that are called [Daughters and Daughters of Daughters] are all comprehended in me, and do attend upon True Wisdom; which if Tritemius[22] mark, he shall perceive that true Wisdom is always painted with a woman's garment; For than the pureness of a Virgin, Nothing is more commendable."[23]

The Gnostics had a special admiration for the feminine aspect of the Divine, which they called *Sophia,* Greek for "wisdom", who fell from her original position and became trapped in the physical world. This is echoed in a vision of Galvah trapped in a field surrounded by a hedge, which can be seen to be symbolic of the world. Eventually Galvah breaks free with the help of another angel.

Galvah is widely believed to be the mother of the angels in Enochian tradition, with several references to her in this role. Interestingly, a passage from the Valentinian text *The Gospel of Philip* reads: "Wisdom, who is called 'barren,' is mother of the angels."[24]

Aaron Leitch argues that Galvah is not only Sophia, but that her mystical union with the Christos is symbolised in the Latin version of her name:

> It is my impression that the name Galvah is intended to represent the biblical *Omega* (The End), as we see it in the first and last chapters of Revelation: 'I Am the *Alpha,* and the *Omega.* The First, and the Last.' Therefore, Sophia—as Galvah/Omega—represents the passive and feminine aspects of Creation. Her bridegroom—the *Christos/Alpha*—represents the active and masculine aspect. (In Gnosticism, the union of *Sophia* and the *Christos* represents the Holy Spirit, symbolized by the white dove.)[25]

Another interesting tidbit is that the Qabalistic equivalent of Sophia is the Sephirah Binah, which translates as "understanding", a title which means little until we look at the earlier passage from the Daughter of Fortitude, where she describes herself as "Understanding". It is also intriguing to note that the pair of Binah is Chokmah, which means "wisdom", the traditional translation of Sophia, and both Sephiroth are seen as the divine feminine and divine masculine respectively. While the genders are reversed, this suggests a further link to the syzygies of the Gnostic Aeons.

The Gnostics valued women a lot more than many other groups at the time, and certainly more than the orthodox Christian Church. Not only was woman seen as the equal of man, possessing the same spark of the divine, and not only was the divine feminine recognised, heralded, and worshipped, but many women took prominent roles within Gnostic groups, including positions as priests, a practice that was strongly criticised by the infamous heresiologist Irenaeus, who, in his dismissal of Gnostic beliefs and practices, ended up preserving a lot of them to this day.

Indeed, there was even a Gnostic gospel attributed to a women, *The Gospel of Mary,* widely believed to be Mary Magdalene, which tells of how Jesus favoured Mary above the other disciples, giving her secret knowledge that they were not privy to. The text shows the negative attitude that others at the time had towards women:

> "[Peter] asked the others about the saviour, 'Did he really speak to a woman secretly, without our knowledge, and not openly? Are we to turn and all listen to her? Did he prefer her to us?"[26]

Levi, symbolic of the Gnostics themselves,

comes to Mary's defence, saying:

"Peter, you are always angry. Now I see you contending against this woman as if against an adversary. If the savior made her worthy, who are you to reject her? Surely the savior knows her very well. That is why he loved her more than us. We should be ashamed and put on the perfect person and be with him as he commanded us, and we should preach the gospel, without making any rule or law other than what the savior said."[27]

The Gospel of Philip also supports this view of Mary as the most favoured: "The companion is Mary of Magdala. Jesus loved her more than his students."[28]

Galvah tells Dee about the equality of women in a lengthy dismissal of Trithemius' view that no angel ever took the form of a woman, which caused Dee to doubt the veracity of Galvah. In her response she tells of the nature of angels and women in general:

Angels (I say) of themselves, neither are man nor woman; Therefore they do take forms not according to any proportion in imagination, but according to the discreet and appliable will both of him, and of the thing wherein they are Administrators: For we all are Spirits ministring the will of God. [...] But if Tritemius can say, That woman also hath not the Spirit of God, being formed and fashioned of the self same matter, notwithstanding in a contrary proportion by a degree; if Tritemius can separate the dignity of the Soul of woman from the excellency of man but according to the form of the matter, then might his Argument be good: But because that in man and woman there is proportion, preparation, of sanctification in eternity; Therefore may those that are the eternal Ministers of God in proportion to Santification

take unto them the bodies of them both. I mean in respect of the Form; For as in both you read Homo, so in both you find one and the self same dignity in internal matter all one. But Tritemius spake in respect of the filthiness (which indeed is no filthiness) wherewith all women are stained; and by reasons from the natural Philosophers: as a man tasting more of nature indeed then of him which is the Workman or a supernatural Master."[29]

Gnosticism was heavily influenced by a myriad of other traditions, including Neoplatonism, which, in turn, influenced other traditions like the Qabalah, which the magical explorations of the Renaissance period were intrinsically dependent on. These may have subtly influenced the form in which the angelic transmissions were delivered to Dee, or the angels themselves may explicitly express a Gnostic viewpoint of the world. Regardless of how one sees it, or even if one argues that Kelley deliberately employed Gnostic material in a constructed magical system, it is hard not to notice the parallels between Enochian magic and the traditions and teachings of the ancient Gnostics.

The above is an extract from Wilson's upcoming book *Enochian Magic In Theory*, which is a detailed and scholarly exploration of the Enochian system. The book is set for release by Kerubim Press in February, 2012. See www.kerubimpress.com for details.

NOTES

1 See *The Enochian Evocation of Dr. John Dee* by Geoffrey James, *Enochian Magic for Beginners* by Donald Tyson and *The Angelical Language, Volume I* by Aaron Leitch.

2 See *Rethinking "Gnosticism": An Argument for Dismantling a Dubious Category* by Michael Allen Williams.

3 *A True & Faithful Relation*, p. 164.

4 Ibid., p. 166.

5 Bentley Layton, *The Gnostic Scriptures*, p. 439.

6 Ibid., p. 49.

7 Ibid., p. 406.

8 Ibid., p. 311.

9 Willis Barnstone & Marvin Meyer, ed., *The Gnostic Bible*, pp. 307-324.

10 G.R.S. Mead, trans., *Pistis Sophia*, pp. 1-2.

11 Ibid., p. 16.

12 Geoffrey James, *The Enochian Evocation of Dr. John Dee*, p. xix.

13 James gives this as *Zacar Ca Zamran*, but this is an error. It is given as *Zacar Ca Od Zamran* in the First and Eleventh Calls and *Zacar Od Zamran* in other Calls, among several other variations.

14 Geoffrey James, *The Enochian Evocation of Dr. John Dee*, p. xix.

15 G.S.R. Mead, trans. *Pistis Sophia*, p. 12.

16 Ibid., p. 222.

17 Willis Barnstone & Marvin Meyer, ed., *The Gnostic Bible*, p. 480.

18 Enochian scholar Clay Holden suggests "Stone" should be "Sun".

19 *A True & Faithful Relation*, Actio Tertia, p. 25

20 Donald Tyson, *Enochian Magic for Beginners*, p. 34.

21 Bentley Layton, *The Gnostic Scriptures*, p. 343.

22 Donald Tyson, *Enochian Magic For Beginners*, p. 34.

23 Johannes Trithemius, cryptographer and occultist. Galvah criticises him for his derision of women as containing "filthinesse". See later for more on this. Dee's spelling omits the 'h' in Trithemius' name.

24 *A True & Faithful Relation*, p. 13.

25 Willis Barnstone & Marvin Meyer, ed., *The Gnostic Bible*, p. 273.

26 Aaron Leitch, *The Angelical Language Volume I*, p. 67.

27 Willis Barnstone & Marvin Meyer, ed., *The Gnostic Bible*, p. 481.

28 Ibid.

29 Ibid., p. 273.

30 *A True & Faithful Relation*, p. 13.

Petra Mundik

"This Luminosity in Beings so Endarkened":
Gnostic Soteriology in Cormac McCarthy's Blood Meridian

While the most memorable character within Cormac McCarthy's *Blood Meridian* is undoubtedly the enigmatic Judge Holden, the role of chief protagonist belongs to the inscrutable "kid," whose portentous birth and mysterious death mark the beginning and ending of the novel. The very first sentence of *Blood Meridian* literally draws the reader's attention to the protagonist, commanding us to "See the child" (3). The register of these words simultaneously evokes the simplicity of a child's storybook, as well as the sonorous language of the Bible. The kid, however, makes an unlikely protagonist; not only does he remain nameless throughout the novel, but the reader is never made privy to the character's interior life. Furthermore, the narrative does not unfold from the kid's perspective and the novel contains many scenes which could not have been witnessed by the protagonist. Insight into the kid's mysterious nature may only be gleaned through a close reading of his surrounding environment, namely, the comments of other characters, the symbolic qualities of the landscape, or the allegorical nature of certain scenes and vignettes.

The second clue which serves to establish the significance of the kid occurs when the narrative voice is suddenly interrupted by the words of the nameless child's equally nameless father: "Night of your birth. Thirty-three. The Leonids they were called. God how the stars did fall. I looked for blackness, holes in the heavens. The Dipper stove" (3). The Leonids are an annual meteor shower named after the constellation Leo, from which they appear to

originate. Every thirty-three years "the earth passes through a particularly dense section of the Leonid stream" producing a stunningly prolific display" (Reynolds 44). In *A Reader's Guide to Blood Meridian*, Shane Schimpf notes that the 1833 Leonid shower was so spectacular "that many interpreted them as a sign that the Apocalypse was at hand." Schimpf then argues that the "religious connection" of this celestial event "brings to mind the second coming of Jesus" (60). In other words, the portentous circumstances surrounding the kid's birth suggest the arrival of a messianic figure.

Other critics have also commented on the significance of the Leonid shower within *Blood Meridian*. Stacey Peebles refers to "a study entitled *Yuman Tribes of the Gila River*" in which "Leslie Spier notes that for some of the Yuman, the Leonid meteor shower of November 13, 1833, marks the beginning of recorded time." Peebles points out that "the kid, the novel's nominal if somewhat overshadowed protagonist, is born on the day the Quechan [Yuma] most likely began to keep time," arguing that this endows him with something akin to a "Christ-like significance" (238). The Native American Yumas, or Quechan, figure prominently in *Blood Meridian*, especially in Chapter XIX where they attack Glanton's gang of scalp hunters at the Yuma ferry crossing. Significantly, the kid is portrayed as one of the few survivors of this historically accurate massacre.

Further suggestions of a messianic birth are evoked when, in reference to the kid, the narrative voice proclaims: "All history present in that visage, the child the father of man" (3). The words are an allusion to William Wordsworth's short poem, "My Heart Leaps Up," which contains the lines: "The Child is the father of the Man; / And I could wish my days to be / Bound each to each by natural piety" (lines 7-9). The same three lines also appear as an epigraph to Wordsworth's "Ode: Intimations of Immortality from Recollections of Early Childhood." The lines are commonly interpreted as a reference to the inherent innocence and spiritual purity of childhood, as expressed in Christ's words: "Verily I say unto you, Except ye be converted, and become as little children, ye shall not enter into the kingdom of heaven" (Matt. 18:3). The implication is that children quite naturally possess the meekness, piety and goodness, which a grown man can attain only through spiritual discipline.

McCarthy's use of the allusion, however, is not without irony, for the Wordsworthian lines are immediately preceded by the observation: "He can neither read nor write and in him broods already a taste for mindless violence" (3). Edwin Arnold argues that "McCarthy's ironic play on Wordsworth is noteworthy, certainly, for it underscores not the child's 'natural piety' but the 'mindless violence' which overcomes it" ("Naming, Knowing and Nothingness" 62). This mindless violence hardly conjures up images of Christ-like meekness and forces the reader to revaluate the veracity of Wordsworth's rather sentimental recollection of the innocence of childhood. If McCarthy's "Child" already hungers for violence, what kind of "Man" will he be "father" to? This reading may at first appear to undermine the idea that the kid is a messianic figure; however the two readings are not incompatible. The contradiction may be resolved if we briefly consider the main tenets of the Gnosticism.

According to Gnostic theology, the entire manifest cosmos "is the creation not of God but of some inferior principle" (Jonas 327), known as the *demiurge* (William Blake's "Nobodaddy") and identified as Yahweh of the Old Testament. The demiurge rules over all that he has created,

sometimes with the assistance of evil angels known as *archons*, while the real or *alien* God remains wholly transcendent and removed from the created world. Humanity has a divided nature composed of a body and soul (*psyche*), which were created by and belong to the demiurge, but also a spirit (*pneuma*), which belongs to the alien God. The *pneuma* is actually a fragment, or "spark," of the divine substance which has fallen into, or in some cases, been maliciously trapped in the evil manifest cosmos. In other words, the *pneuma* "is not part of the world, of nature's creation and domain, but is, within that world, as totally transcendent and as unknown by all worldly categories as it its transmundane counterpart, the unknown God without" (ibid.). Thus people are composed of both mundane and extra-mundane principles and carry within them the potential for immanence as soul and flesh, or transcendence as pure spirit. The aim of Gnosticism is the attainment of *gnosis*, or spiritual insight akin to the Buddhist concept of enlightenment, which enables the *pneuma* to escape from the fetters of the manifest world and return to the original state of purity experienced before creation.

If we apply this doctrine to the messianic nature of the kid, it strongly suggests the concept of the descent of the *pneuma*, as symbolised by the falling stars which augur the kid's birth. Though the *pneuma* is a pure, incorruptible spark of the alien divine, its immersion in the filth of matter cause it to forget its true origins. Thus, even if the kid possesses something of the divine in him, his birth automatically causes him to become tainted by the evil that the Gnostics associated with the manifest world. In this sense, the kid resembles the Gnostic concept of the *Salvator Salvatus* or "Saved Saviour," who descends to the world with saving *gnosis*, only to fall under the spell of the world.

In *The Gnostic Religion*, Hans Jonas explains that although the *Salvator Salvatus* is "a definitive divine figure," this "does not prevent him from undergoing in his own person the full force of human destiny, even to the extent that he the saviour himself has to be saved" (127). Jonas explains that the Gnostic saviour's fall into the world is "an irremissible condition of his saving function" because "the parts of divinity lost to the darkness can be reached only down there in the depth in which they are swallowed up; and the power which holds them, that of the world, can be overcome only from within" (ibid.). Therefore, the Gnostic saviour "must assimilate himself to the forms of cosmic existence and thereby subject himself to its conditions" (ibid.). The Gnostic messiah must then undergo a process of spiritual introversion—"Know Thyself," as the Delphic Oracle advised—which enables him to wake up to his true nature. Only then can the saviour resume his soteriological function, which consists of imparting his wisdom to those still trapped in the mire of corporeal existence.

The Gnostic saviour's journey—from descend, to forgetting, to awakening, to ascend—also serves as a metaphor for the spirit of every living being. In other words, the path of every individual *pneuma* mirrors the path of the *Salvator Salvatus*; both fall into the darkness of the manifest cosmos and must awaken to their true in order to return to their divine source. The fact that the *Salvator Salvatus* and the *pneuma* are often interchangeable in Gnostic parables is compounded by the fact that the soteriological function of *gnosis* arises from within; hence the saviour must come to know himself, as must each individual human being. In this sense, everyone is responsible for one's own salvation. Thus, the paradoxical nature of the kid—namely his messianic birth coupled with his taste for violence—is a contradiction easily resolved in the light of Gnostic thought. In Gnosticism, the descending divine element—whether in the form of the *pneuma* or the saviour—finds itself so mired in the darkness of matter that it forgets its divine origins and takes on the unfavourable characteristics of those it has come to redeem. Only a flash of spiritual insight allows it to awaken to its true nature.

In Gnostic thought, the *Salvator Salvatus* is also known as the "Primal Man" or "Adam." Jonas draws attention to the fact in Gnostic theology the saviour "bears the name 'Man'" because the spirits "dispersed in this world are… part of his original substance, which he lost to the Darkness…so that he is actually present in every human soul, exiled, captive, stunned" (128). Indeed, the narrative voice within *Blood Meridian* subtly hints at such a situation by describing how, as the kid "walks through the narrow streets," "whores call to him from the dark like souls in want" (5). From a Gnostic perspective, the scene suggests that the divine fragments, imprisoned in the degraded flesh of whores, recognise the *Salvator Salvatus* and long to return to their source. Furthermore, if all men, and women, are a part of the saviour's "original substance" then one may well regard the saviour, or the original "Primal Man," as the "father of man"; a concept which resonates with McCarthy's description of the kid.

Though the kid finds himself among truly despicable characters when he joins the Glanton gang, he remains aloof and oddly disconnected from the frenzied violence which permeates the novel. Other critics have commented on the fact that the kid never really seems to be a part of the gang; Brian Evenson notes that within *Blood Meridian* "there is one who refuses to enter into the spirit of the pack itself—the kid, who seems to remain passive. In the most violent scenes and the most incessant wanderings, his character seems to vanish altogether" (46). Evenson suggests that this odd absence serves "as if to avoid implicating him in the violence, or as if to imply he is absent in spirit if not in body" (ibid.). A striking example of the kid's strange otherness can be found in a description of his observing a distant battle: "he saw from that high rimland the collision of armies remote and silent upon the plain below…He watched all this pass below him mute and ordered and senseless" (213). Not only does the kid take no part in the action, but the description of the violence as "remote" and "silent"—as well as the elevated vantage point—places the character into an almost godlike position of detachment.

Furthermore, the descriptions of the changing light serve to imbue the kid with a strange numinosity, while simultaneously plunging ordinary men into darkness: "the warring horsemen were gone in the sudden rush of dark that fell over the desert. All that land lay cold and blue and without definition and the sun shone solely on the high rocks where he stood" (213). Despite the fact that the sun is often portrayed as maleficent within the novel, light remains an ancient symbol of spiritual illumination and a common trope in various esoteric and writings. The seventeenth-century mystic, Jacob Boehme, whose influence on McCarthy is made evident in one of the epigraphs to *Blood Meridian*, uses a metaphor for spiritual development which is striking in its similarity to the aforementioned scene in *Blood Meridian*.[1] Boehme writes: "It is well known that the light of the sun does not shine upon the earth because we desire it to shine, neither can we attract the sunlight to us. All we do is to step out of the darkness, or climb to the top of the mountain which rises above the clouds" (Hartmann 46). Thus, the fact that the kid is the only one on whom the light shines, strongly suggests a degree of spiritual development higher than that of the other men fighting in the depths of the darkness below.

Significantly, *Blood Meridian* contains several scenes laden with esoteric symbolism in which the kid features as the focal point. Separated from the rest of the Glanton gang, the kid comes across "a lone tree burning on the desert. A heraldic tree that the passing storm had left afire" (215). This eerie image immediately calls to mind the burning bush out of which an angel spoke to Moses: "And the angel of the LORD appeared unto him in a flame of fire out of the midst of a bush: and he looked, and, behold, the bush burned with fire, and the bush was not consumed" (Exodus 3.3). Though no divine voice speaks forth from this strange phenomenon, the vision is not without significance. The description of the tree as "heraldic" (215) suggests the "action of announcing and ushering in with pomp and ceremony" (OED). Therefore, the tree serves as a dramatic messenger, or herald, of some important message.

The spiritual significance of the scene is compounded by the description of the kid as the "solitary pilgrim drawn up before it" who "had travelled so far to be here" (215). It is noteworthy that the kid is also referred to thusly right at the beginning of the novel, when he is described as "a pilgrim among others" (5). "Pilgrim" has two nuances of meaning, both of which evoke Gnostic concepts regarding the spirit's position in the manifest cosmos. In its earlier usage, the word "pilgrim" refers to "a foreigner, an alien…a stranger," or "a person who experiences life as a sojourn, exile, or period of estrangement" (OED). It is significant that the Gnostics often describe the fallen divine element, or *pneuma*, as "a stranger who does not know the ways of the foreign land" (Jonas 49). Later, the meaning of "pilgrim" took on a more specifically religious context, signifying "a person travelling through life, *esp.* one who undertakes a course of spiritual development" (OED). Both definitions place the kid in a distinctly Gnostic context of spiritual striving, exile and alienation.

The kid's experience of esoterically symbolic vignettes is not limited to the burning tree; his encounter with an old woman in Chapter XXII is one of the most spiritually momentous scenes in the novel. Wandering through the wilderness, the kid stumbles upon the site of a massacre of a "company of penitents" lying "hacked and butchered among the stones" (315). As he gazes "at this desolate scene," he sees "alone and upright in a small niche in the rocks an old woman kneeling in a faded rebozo with her eyes cast down" (315). Drawn towards the pious figure, the kid makes "his way among the corpses and [stands] before her," but she does "not look up" (315). The woman's posture suggests that she is lost in prayer; seeking solace in her faith amidst the terrible carnage of her slain kinsmen.

As the kid watches the praying woman, he notes that the "shawl that covered her head was much faded of its color yet it bore like a patent woven into the fabric the figures of stars and quartermoons and other insignia of a provenance unknown to him" (315). In *Notes*

on Blood Meridian, John Sepich points out that the "'stars and quartermoons' of her costume… resemble elements associated with Mary in Revelation 12:1 and in the painted depiction of Mary's appearance as Our Lady of Guadalupe" (*Notes* 123). The *Book of Revelation* features a mysterious "woman clothed with the sun, and the moon under her feet, and upon her head a crown of twelve stars" (12:1) whom theologians have identified as Mary. Moreover, the "woman" of *Revelation* is described as having "fled into the wilderness" (12:6), strengthening the connection between the Biblical figure and McCarthy's praying penitent. Furthermore, the very sub-heading of the chapter—"eldress in the rocks" (305)—calls to mind the two almost identical paintings by Leonardo da Vinci entitled "Virgin of the Rocks," depicting the baby Jesus, John the Baptist, the Madonna and the angel Gabriel in a barren and rocky wilderness, much like McCarthy's landscape in *Blood Meridian*.

The kid treats the kneeling woman with a due sense of sanctity, speaking "to her in a low voice" (315) such as one might use during confession. Indeed, the kid does confess, telling "her that he was an American and that he was a long way from the country of his birth and that he had no family and that he had traveled much and seen many things and had been at war and endured hardships" (315). Patrick Shaw similarly argues that the kid "impulsively confesses to the penitent in rhetoric reminiscent of a questing Christian knight in thrall to the Holy Virgin" (110). In fact, it is not only the kid's rhetoric, but also his posture which suggests a questing knight, for he kneels before the woman "on one knee" (315). Furthermore, he holds his "rifle before him like a staff" (315); a staff being a common accessory of pilgrims and travelers, thereby further emphasising the medieval quest motif already apparent in the kid's rhetoric.

As previously discussed, the kid is portrayed as somewhat of an outsider, remaining mysteriously aloof, detached or simply absent throughout the action of the novel. The kid's sense of alienation is also expressed in his words to the kneeling penitent: "He told her… that he was a long way from the country of his birth and that he had no family" (315). Given the allegorical nature of *Blood Meridian*, it is probable that this homesickness and loneliness reflect the kid's existential and spiritual positions. The position of outsider typical engenders a sense of alienation; a concept which resonates meaningfully with Gnostic ideas about the awakened man's position in the world. According to Gnostic thought, the alien divine—whether in the form of the Saved Saviour or the individual who has awakened to his true nature—

> …suffers the lot of the stranger who is lonely, unprotected, uncomprehended, and uncomprehending in a situation full of danger. Anguish and homesicknesses are a part of the stranger's lot. The stranger who does not know the ways of the foreign land wanders about lost. (Jonas 49)

Hans Jonas explains that this sense of alienation is the first step towards the attainment of *gnosis* and the subsequent escape from the prison of the created cosmos: "The recollection of his own alienness, the recognition of his place of exile for what it is, is the first step back; the awakened homesickness is the beginning of the return" (50). The kid's homesickness may well be interpreted as a desire for salvation; a thwarted longing clearly expressed in his words to the kneeling penitent.

After revealing who he is and what he has done, the kid attempts to redeem himself before the kneeling woman: "He told her that he would convey her to a safe place, some party of her countrypeople would welcome her and that she should join them for he could not leave her in this place or she would surely die" (315). When she fails to respond, the kid adopts an uncharacteristically gentle tone by referring to the old woman as "Abuelita" (315)—the affectionate, diminutive form of "Grandmother"—and asking, "No puedes escucharme?" (Can't you hear me?) (315). As though in mockery of the kid's gentleness and compassion, the grandmother reveals her devastating secret: "He reached into the little cove and touched her arm. She moved slightly, her whole body, light and rigid. She weighed nothing. She was just a dried shell and she had been dead in that place for years" (315). The allegorical meaning of this scene is almost over-determined; the symbols of exoteric religion have been revealed in all their emptiness and cannot redeem the seeker.

The rejection of Christian iconography and sacraments carries distinctly Gnostic overtones. The Gnostics believed that it was pointless to look to the church for salvation, for salvation could only come from within; that is, through the internal development of *gnosis* as opposed to the external blessings of organised religion. In *The Gnostic Gospels*, Elaine Pagels cites the unknown author of the *Gospel of Philip* who criticizes: "those who mistake religious language for a literal language, professing faith in God, in Christ, in the resurrection or the church, as if these were all 'things' external to themselves" (133). A genuine spiritual experience, on the other hand, must involve an "internal transformation" so that "whoever perceives divine reality becomes what he sees" (ibid. 134). In Gnostic terms, this means that one who acquires *gnosis* is simultaneously made aware that his true self is the divine *pneuma* and that this is identical to the divine principle of the alien God, or the Godhead. Much like the Buddhists, the Gnostics taught that only "those who come to recognize that they have been living in ignorance, and learn to release themselves by discovering who they are, experience enlightenment" (ibid. 111). Thus, the Gnostics rejected the idea that one could turn to a divine interlocutrix, like the Virgin Mary, for salvation. For them, such religious iconography was really nothing more than a "dried shell."

In *Blood Meridian*, the realization that the "Madonna" is a mummified husk serves as a kind of negative epiphany, which seems to have a profound impact on the kid' psyche. The laconic kid's uncharacteristically self-revelatory outpouring regarding the places he has been

and the things he has done serves a cathartic function; sins are purged by the act of confession. The spiritual cleansing is followed by a desire for redemption and the kid's eagerness to "convey" the kneeling woman "to a safe place" is born of this soteriological longing. The kneeling penitent, however, is revealed to be a symbol of death, not salvation. Consequently, the kid's hopes for salvation are cruelly dashed. Shaw argues that the "kid's epiphanic miscalculation vis-à-vis the penitent mummy is literally momentous beyond words, for immediately thereafter he disappears for seventeen years" (110). The novel gives no account of the kid's mysterious disappearance, with chapter XXII ending with the negative epiphany and chapter XXIII beginning: "In the late winter of eighteen seventy-eight..." (316). The kid's disappearance mirrors the seventeen year absence of the Biblical Jesus, whose childhood is depicted up to the age of thirteen, after which are given no account of his whereabouts until his thirtieth year. This analogy further strengthens the kid's position as a messianic figure within the novel, albeit a failed one.

The kid's spiritual yearning is also conveyed through the fact that throughout his lonely years of wandering, he "had a bible that he'd found at the mining camps and he carried this book with him no word of which he could read" (312). Commenting on this detail of the kid's life, Schimpf writes that: "if one accepts the Gnostic interpretation of the novel, it is significant that the Kid is not able to attain knowledge of the bible and this, in part, might explain his inability to achieve salvation and instead is subject to the vagaries of fate" (320). Similarly, Sepich draws a comparison between the fact that: "The 'provenance' of the 'stars and quartermoons' the old woman wears is said to be unknown to the kid. In this connection, it is noteworthy that the kid at this time carried a Bible with him, 'no word of which he could read'" (*Notes* 123). Both interpretations suggest that the kid's inability to interpret these words and symbols represents his inability to find salvation.

It is easy to see why both Sepich and Schimpf

regard the Bible, along with the celestial signs on the penitent's cloak, as symbols of spiritual insight. Such a view, however, is totally at odds with the very concept of *gnosis*. First of all, the Bible and the Virgin Mary represent the teachings of exoteric Christianity, which the Gnostic's regarded as utterly counterproductive in terms of spiritual development. The Gnostics believed that the Bible, in particular the Old Testament, was a collection of lies spun by the demiurge in order to keep the divine substance ignorant of its true nature and thus forever imprisoned in the created world. Birger Pearson explains that: "the main tendency in Gnosticism is to subject texts of the Hebrew Bible to critical scrutiny and offer interpretations that run counter to the traditional ones" (101). When the Gnostics did read the Bible, they used it largely to find evidence with which to condemn the creator of this world by pointing out his many hypocrisies and contradictions.

For the Gnostics, *gnosis* meant a direct experience of the divine, which could not be communicated through the second-hand accounts found in holy books. For example, according to Pagels, the Gnostic followers of Valentinus "argued that only one's own experience offers the ultimate criterion of truth, taking precedence over all second-hand testimony and all tradition—even gnostic tradition!" (25). As a result of this "insistence on the primacy of immediate experience" (ibid. 145), the Gnostics favoured the solitary path to spiritual development. Pagels explains that the Gnostics "could not accept on faith what others said, except as a provisional measure, until one found one's own path" (ibid.). The Gnostics' rejection of second-hand accounts is strikingly similar to the teachings of the Buddha, for whom "direct, personal experience was the final test for truth" and who taught that a "true disciple must know for himself" (H. Smith, *The Religions of Man* 108). Therefore, if the esoterically subversive religious imagery within *Blood Meridian* is indeed Gnostic, then the fact that the kid carries a Bible which he cannot read takes on a slightly different nuance of meaning.

As has already been established, the kid's attachment to the Bible signifies a longing for *gnosis* or enlightenment; however such insight has clearly not been attained. In fact, during his years of wandering through the world with an unreadable Bible, the kid appears to have drifted even further from his messianic role: "In his dark and frugal clothes some took him for a sort of preacher but he was no witness to them, neither of things at hand nor things to come, he least of any man" (312). The kid's failure lies not so much in his illiteracy, but in the fact that he is searching for the *gnosis* in the wrong places. Rather than adopting the solitary path of meditative introspection favoured by the Gnostics and the Buddhists, the kid wanders aimlessly from place to place; searching for answers in the book which is totally inaccessible, and therefore useless to him. The Bible offers the kid no more redemption that the empty shell of the kneeling Madonna figure.

A glimmer of hope remains, however, in the fact that the kid clearly longs for deliverance and that he is capable of compassion. The Gnostics valued and encouraged compassionate behaviour, placing an "emphasis on the fellowship of man," who was "united not only by the community of origin but also by the community of the situation of aliens in the world" (Jonas 264). Although the kid's concern regarding the wellbeing of the kneeling penitent may seem incongruous, especially if considered in light of the fact that he has spent his youth slaughtering the innocent with a band of vicious scalp-hunters, there is evidence to suggest that the protagonist has always had within him this potential for compassionate behaviour. This inclination to help others manifests itself during the Comanche attack on Captain White's army. Though struggling to refill his rifle in the heat of battle, the kid notices that a "man near him sat with an arrow hanging out of his neck" (53). The kid's natural instinct is to help the man by reaching for "the bloody hoop-iron point," but then he notices that is too late for the man has "another arrow in his breast to the fletching" and is already "dead" (53). It is noteworthy that the dead man is described as being "bent slightly as if in prayer" (53). Once again, a dead figure adopts the posture of a kneeling penitent; a detail which links this particular episode to the kid's future encounter with the "eldress in the rocks" (305).

The same urge towards compassion is evoked later when the kid joins the Glanton gang. The kid is the only member of the gang who volunteers to help the injured David Brown, who has "an arrow in his thigh, fletching and all, and none would touch it" (161). Brown pleads with the other gang members for assistance, asking "Will none of ye help a man?" (161), but receives no reply. After watching Brown make an excruciatingly futile attempt at removing the arrow from his own leg, the kid comes forward and says: "I'll try her" (162). The kid bears down on the arrow until the point comes "through the flesh of the man's thigh," then cuts "away the bloody point deftly" and withdraws "the shaft from the man's leg" (162). Brown praises the boy, calling him a "stout lad" and a "sawbones" (a slang term for "surgeon"). But later when the kid returns "to his own blanket," the ex priest calls him a "fool" (162), adding "God will not love ye forever… Don't you know he'd of took you with him? He'd of took you, boy. Like a bride to the altar" (162).[2] In other words, had the kid not been successful, Brown would certainly have would have killed him. Given, however, the kid's initial hesitance in offering to help Brown, coupled with the fact that he has been with the gang long enough to understand the nature of its members, it is obvious that he knew the risk that he was facing when he extracted the arrow. Thus, the kid's willingness to risk his own life in order to assist a suffering man suggests that he possesses an essentially compassionate nature; a character trait which comes to the fore despite his involvement with a depraved band of scalp hunters.

Similarly, after the gang attacks a peaceful settlement of Gileños and encounters some minor resistance, the Mexican Juan Miguel, or "McGill" as he is called, is "skewered through with a lance" (157). Seeing a fellow gang member

in trouble, the kid "approache[s] him," only to be held back by Glanton's command to "Get away from him" (157). Glanton then promptly shoots McGill "through the head" (157). Although Glanton's action can be read as a mercy killing, the kid's first instinct is to help, even if only by comforting the fatally wounded man. Scenes such as these establish the kid as somehow at odds with the other callous gang members, for whom such a mercy killing has more to do with convenience than actual compassion.

The kid displays further signs of these compassionate tendencies then the Glanton gang find themselves pursued by the army of General Elias and are forced to abandon four wounded members who can no longer ride. Four healthy men are selected by lottery to carry out the mercy killings, the kid among the chosen. Instead of shooting the man with a shattered hip named Shelby, the kid sits with him while the other members of the gang ride away. When the kid looks at the wounded man, he sees that "Shelby was crying" (207). "You wont thank me if I let you off," warns the kid, mindful of the approaching army, but he leaves the choice up to Shelby: "If you want me just to leave you I will….You'll have to say" (207-8). Though death at the kid's hands would be much easier than at the hands of his enemies, Shelby refuses to make the sensible choice. Consequently, the kid does not kill him. In a final act of compassion, the kid fills Shelby's water flask "from his own" (209)— though water is desperately scarce—then mounts his horse, looks "back at the wounded man" (209) and then rides away.

In *A Reader's Guide to Blood Meridian*, Shane Schimpf also comments on the kid's compassionate nature, arguing that: "He alone in the novel represents what is supposedly noble and good in man—our capacity to empathize with another person and show mercy" (3). Schimpf, however, argues that *Blood Meridian* is an allegorical novel concerned with the paradigm shift from a religious world view, to a scientific one and that the "paradigm that has become antiquated is the religious one—the paradigm embodied by the Kid" (ibid.). In other words, the kid is the embodiment of outmoded values, set against the ascending power of the terrifying Judge Holden. The kid and the judge are also diametrically opposed from a Gnostic perspective. If the kid's latent goodness can be identified as the divine element ensnared and confused by the manifest cosmos, then the judge, who seems to be the very embodiment of evil, can be thought of as a Gnostic archon responsible for keeping fragments of the divine enslaved within the prison of the material realm.

Whether one employs the contemporary dualism of science vs. religion, or the more traditional Manichean dualism of good vs. evil, it is clear that the kid and the judge are constantly portrayed in opposition to one another. This opposition is established in the strikingly inverse physical descriptions of the two antagonists. For example, the kid "is not big" but "has big wrists" and "big hands" (4), while the judge is "enormous" but his "hands [are] small" (6). More significantly, the kid's "face is curiously untouched behind the scars, the eyes oddly innocent" (4). Conversely, the judge's face is "serene strangely childlike" (6) and he possesses "small and lashless pig's eyes" (310). If the eyes are windows into the soul, then the kid's countenance suggests that beneath the scarred exterior he still possesses pure innocence, while the judge's appearance suggests the very opposite; although he has the face of a child, his eyes betray his swine-like nature.

There are several instances in the novel where the kid makes a point of standing up to the judge; even if only by demonstrating that he is not afraid of him. When the Glanton gang run out of food and need to slaughter a horse for its meat, the judge calls for someone to come hold the animal while he brains it with a rock. When no one responds to the judge's request, Tobin, the ex-priest, leans towards the kid and whispers: "Pay him no mind lad" (219). The kid ignores the warning, rises, spits into the fire, eyes the ex-priest and asks: "You think I'm afraid of him?" Then he turns and defiantly walks "out into the darkness where the judge waited" (219). The "dark beyond the fire," where the judge waits, is

both literal and metaphorical, symbolising the darkness of evil. The kid boldly walks into the judge's evil realm without fear of being devoured and, for the time being, survives to tell the tale. Similarly, in a symbolic gesture of defiance, the kid refuses to partake of the meat offered up the by the judge, despite the fact that he must be starving. As the kid, Tobin and Toadvine crouch "at the rim of the pit" (282) above a natural well, the judge calls for them to: "Come down and share this meat" (283). The very fact that the judge is calling them down into a "pit" has sinister, demonic connotations. Furthermore, the sharing of meat, as with the sharing of bread, suggests a form of communion, which the kid clearly rejects: "The kid had set one foot over the edge of the pit and now he drew it back" (284). Not only does the kid refuse to come forward, he actually draws further back from the judge.

Tobin once again warns the kid about the power of the judge when the three of them are alone in the dessert. Not being able to kill the judge, whose sinister intentions towards the kid are now obvious, the kid manages to at least shoot the judge's horses. Hiding under the "boardlike hide of a dead ox," Tobin and the kid listen "to the judge calling to them" (293). The judge first tries to come to a settlement over the dead horses using legalistic jargon:

> He called out points of jurisprudence, he cited cases. He expounded upon those laws pertaining to property rights in bests mansuete and he quoted from cases of attainder insofar as he reckoned them germane to the corruption of blood in the prior felonious owners of the horses now dead among the bones. Then he spoke of other things. (293)

The mysteriously unspecified "other things" fill the Tobin with horror. "Dont listen" (293), he tells the kid. The kid claims that he "aint listenin," but Tobin demands: "Stop your ears" (293). Tobin stops his own ears and then stares pleadingly at the kid: "His eyes were bright from the bloodloss and he was possessed of a great earnestness. Do it, he whispered. Do you think he speaks to me?" (293). Later, the judge will confirm Tobin's fears by condemning the kid with the words: "Hear me, man. I spoke in the desert for you and you only and you turned a deaf ear to me" (307). Clearly, whatever is being said by the judge is of a great seductive power; a classic scene of temptation by the devil. Tobin feels that he can only resist the evil if he blocks it out, but the kid is once again prepared to boldly expose himself to evil without letting it overcome him.

The most interesting aspect of this desert encounter is that the kid does not kill the judge when given the chance, even though his own life is clearly in danger as the judge has already shot and wounded Tobin. It seems odd that the kid, who has shown no prior hesitation to killing others in self defense, should endanger his own life and the life of a friend by refusing to kill a hostile enemy, especially when he has a clear shot of his target. A clue to this dilemma lies in the slightly surreal conversation between Tobin and the kid, which suggests that the judge is no ordinary human being and that killing such an entity is not a straightforward matter. When the kid states: "If I kill him we can take the horses," Tobin, who knows that the kid is a "deadeye" (281), replies: "You'll not kill him. Dont be a fool. Shoot the horses" (291). The gun-proud kid clearly feels that Tobin knows what he is talking about, as he does not offer a counter-argument in defense of his own marksmanship. Later, the kid tries to discuss the nature of the judge with Tobin, arguing "He aint nothin. You told me so yourself. Men are made of the dust of the earth. You said it was no...parable. That it was a naked fact and the judge was a man like all men" (297). Tobin simply replies: "Face him down then....Face him down if he is so" (297). Again, the kid's inexplicable reluctance to face down the judge indicates that he is takes Tobin's warnings seriously.

The judge is fully aware that the kid could have shot him, but didn't, and so calls for the young man to come out from his hiding place and join him: "The priest had led you to this, boy. I know you would not hide. I know that you've not the heart of a common assassin. I've passed before your gunsight twice this hour and will pass a third time. Why not show yourself?" (299). The fact that the judge gives the kid three opportunities to shoot endows the scene with mythical, specifically Biblical, overtones, reminiscent of Peter's denial of Jesus. "Before the cock crows thou shalt deny me thrice" (Matthew 26:34). In a sense, not shooting the judge is equivalent to denying him, for, as Robert Jarret argues, "the kid repudiates the use of violence to settle [his] quarrel with the judge. The judge interprets such acts as symbolic not of the kid's affiliation with but as his repudiation of the gang through his disavowal of its violence" (85). Indeed, when the kid refuses to respond, either by shooting or showing himself, the judge expresses his disappointment: "No assassin, called the judge. And no partisan either. There's a flawed place in the fabric of your heart. Do you think I could not know?" (299). Once again, the judge's words recall the Bible, specifically Jesus' words to the "lukewarm" souls who stand before him in Revelation: "I know your works: you are neither cold nor hot. Would that you were cold or hot! So, because you are lukewarm, and neither cold nor hot, I will spew you out of my mouth" (John 3:15-16). Desiring either a loyal disciple or a worthy adversary, but finding neither, the judge accuses the kid of the same sin of neutrality.

We may regard the kid's lack of action not as an act of cowardice or indecision, but as the most effective means of standing up to the judge. Were the kid to shoot, he would be complying with the judge's code of violence. Therefore, the judge would win whether the kid shot at, or joined him. Thus, much like Melville's Bartleby the Scrivener who opts out of the game of life, the kid replies to the judge's taunts with a silent "I would prefer not." It is interesting to note that Herman Melville, whose influence on McCarthy is profound, was a self-proclaimed Gnostic. Seen in this light, Bartleby becomes a Gnostic hero, refusing to participate in the demiurge's game of creation. Melville expresses this very concept in "Fragments of a Lost Gnostic Poem of the 12th Century" (1891), which contains the lines: "Indolence is heaven's ally here, / And energy the child of hell" (lines 6-7); meaning that to participate in the world is to cooperate with the demiurge, while complete withdrawal aids the spirit's return to the truly divine Godhead. Thus, the kid's refusal to play the archon-judge's game in the desert may be read as a form of Gnostic protest.

Though not strictly a Gnostic, Jacob Boehme placed such emphasis on the existence of evil within the cosmos that his writings are often mistaken for Gnosticism. Boehme argued along similar lines to Melville, claiming that the "more [evil] were resisted, the greater would be the fierceness; like a fire that is stirred, whereby it burns but the more" (*Six Theosophic Points* 100). Referring to this particular doctrine of Boehme's, Franz Hartmann explains that: "Therefore no man can successfully resist the devil by fighting him on the same level, nor can any one overcome temptations in the end except by rising above them" (109). According to Boehme, passive resistance is the best weapon against evil; for if one attempts to actively fight the devil, one will only end up playing according to the rules of his game and thereby falling under his influence. This is precisely the attitude adopted by the kid when he refuses to engage with the judge in the desert. Thus, the kid's refusal to shoot at the judge is a greater display of enmity than participating in an act of violent retribution.

This theory is confirmed by the fact that the judge seems to be disappointed by the fact that the kid refused to shoot. At their next meeting following the desert encounter, the judge acknowledges the enmity between them by speaking of it in typically sonorous terms: "Our animosities were formed and waiting before we two met. Yet even so you could have changed it all" (307). Similarly, at their final meeting, he tells the kid: "I recognized you when I first saw you and yet you were a disappointment to me. Then and now" (328). These words suggest that the kid

was destined to stand in opposition to the judge; a concept foreshadowed by the description of the messianic birth at the beginning of the novel. Nevertheless, the judge seems to believe that the kid could have forsaken his messianic role and become his disciple. "Dont you know that I'd have loved you like a son?" (306), he asks, revealing his thwarted desire to mould the kid in his own, twisted image.

The judge condemns the kid for his failure to become a true disciple: "You came forward, he said, to take part in a work. But you were a witness against yourself. You sat in judgement on your own deeds. You put your own allowances before the judgements of history and you broke with the body of which you were pledged a part and poisoned it in all its enterprise" (307). For the judge, it doesn't seem to matter that the kid collected scalps like the rest of the gang members, what matters is that he felt a twinge of compassion as he did so. "You alone were mutinous," claims the judge, "You alone reserved in your soul some corner of clemency for the heathen" (299). The judge doesn't condemn the kid for failing to participate in the violent actions of the Glanton gang; he accuses the kid simply of having a conscience.

In the words of the judge: "it was required of no man to give more than he possessed nor was any man's share compared to another's. Only each was called upon to empty out his heart into the common and one did not. Can you tell me what that one was?" (307). The kid refuses to accept the judge's accusations and, defiant as always, replies: "It was you…You were the one" (307). According to the judge, the kid fails the gang by refusing to participate whole-heartedly and by always withholding a part of himself. Peebles argues that the kid withholds the very part which makes him a messianic figure in the novel: "The small part of the kid that held back from complete, orgiastic, communal destruction with the Glanton gang—perhaps the same part that through Quechan mythology figures him as an icon of human history, or humanity—is odious and damning in the judge's eyes" (239). In Gnostic terms, this part corresponds to the *pneuma*, or the "immaterial divine spark imprisoned in a material body," which "is as alien to the world as is the transcendent God" (Pearson 13). Precisely because this fragment of the divine essence does not belong to the manifest world, it falls outside the jurisdiction of the archon-judge and thus cannot be manipulated by him.

It is worth mentioning that the concept of the divine "spark" constitutes a running theme throughout *Blood Meridian*. Even when the spark is depicted by its literal signifier, the writing still contains metaphysical overtones. Consider, for example, the following description of a dying fire: "the wind blew in the night and fanned the last smoldering billets and drove forth the last fragile race of sparks fugitive as flintstrikings in the unanimous dark of the world" (185). The description of the sparks as "fugitive" suggests that they are escaped prisoners; a concept strongly evocative of the Gnostic belief that the spirit is a divine spark imprisoned in matter, which can only be liberated through the cultivation of *gnosis*. Furthermore, the "unanimous dark" through which the sparks travel, evokes the "realm of darkness" which is the manifest cosmos, as opposed to "the divine realm of light" (Jonas 42), from whence the sparks originate. Divine sparks are again evoked when the men throw their lice-ridden clothes into a fire: "the filthy hides of which they'd divested themselves smoked and stank and blackened in the flames and the red sparks rose like the souls of the small life they'd harboured" (240). According to Manichean teachings, the imprisoned "particles of light are to be found" not only in human beings, but also in "plants," "animals" and even within "water" (Rudolph 338). The scene seems to be depicting the divine sparks leaving their material prison upon the death of the life-form.

Further analogies between the transcendent spirit and the visible spark are made when, undressing in the dark, the men find themselves surrounded by the eerie phenomena of St Elmo's Fire:

Then one by one they began to divest themselves of their outer clothes…and one by one they propagated about themselves a great crackling of sparks and each man was seen to wear a shroud of palest fire. Their arms aloft pulling at their clothes were luminous and each obscure soul was enveloped in audible shapes of light as if it had always been so. The mare at the far end of the stable snorted and shied at this luminosity in beings so endarkened and the little horse turned and hid his face in the web of his dam's flank. (222).

Once again, the words "spark" and "soul" appear in close proximity, alongside the mention of death evoked through the reference to a "shroud." The passage also suggests that the "luminosity" of the divine is present even in the most depraved human beings. According to Irenaeus' account of Gnostic beliefs, the divine spark in man was compared to "gold sunk in filth," which "will not lose its beauty but preserve its own nature, and the filth will be unable to impair the gold" (Jonas 271). In other words, even when the spark, or *pneuma*, is plunged into the darkness of material existence, it maintains its divine nature.

We find a similar reference to St Elmo's Fire as symbolic of divine fire in McCarthy's favourite novel, *Moby-Dick*. In "Chapter 119: The Candles," Captain Ahab addresses the eerie electrical phenomenon with the words: "Oh! thou clear spirit of clear fire, whom on these seas I as Persian once did worship…of thy fire thou madest me, and like a true child of fire, I breathe it back to thee" (476-7). Ahab not only refers to himself as a "Persian," which clearly identifies him as a Manichean, but acknowledges that his true self is made of the divine fire, or *pneuma*, which strives for reunion with the divine, hence the desire to "breathe it back" into its transcendent origins.

The idea that all men, no matter how depraved, contain the divine spark within them is reinforced yet again when the Glanton gang are depicted seated around the fire: "they watched the fire which does contain within it something of men themselves inasmuch as they are less without it and are divided from their origins and are exiles. For each fire is all fires, the first fire and the last ever to be" (244). Fire, here, seems to be symbolising the spirit; that uncreated fragment of the divine, otherwise known as the *pneuma*. As has already been established, Gnostic thought teaches that the spirit, trapped in the material realm, is "divided from" its divine "origins" and dwells in a state of "exile." Furthermore, because every *pneuma* is identical in essence to the divine source from whence it originates, it can be said that each spirit is all spirits. The passage above also bears a striking resemblance to the writings of Boehme: "Now all the qualities are made to burn by the kindled fire, and the fire is fed by them; but this fire is only one and not many. This fire is the true Son of God Himself, who is continuing to be born from eternity to eternity" (Hartmann 87). This rather esoteric quote comes from Boehme's *Aurora*[3], which contains an exposition on the nature of the universe as it manifests itself in God, or, "The Seven Properties or Qualities of Eternal Nature." According to Franz Hartmann, Boehme felt he could write about the "spiritual processes taking place in the universe" because "the spirit of man is one and universal, and he who knows his own divine self knows the whole of the universe" (71). We can see how Boehme's insistence on the fact that "the spirit of man is one" is echoed in the claim that "each fire is all fires."

In his Gnostic analysis of the novel, Leo Daugherty places far less emphasis on the importance of the kid as a character, regarding him neither as a failed messiah nor as a potential antithesis to the judge. Nevertheless, Daugherty concedes that the kid is significant to the extent that he "feels the 'spark of the alien divine' within him through the call of what seems to be conscience. He thus 'awakens' a bit, attaining in the process a will outside the will of his murdering…subculture and the archon who runs it" (164). Thus, the kid refuses to

give himself wholly to the judge and is able to maintain some semblance of resistance, if not so much in his actions, then at least in spirit. Daugherty argues that the kid cannot effectively defend himself against the judge because even though the "kid has 'awakened'…he is not progressed sufficiently in wisdom much beyond mere awakening and thus has no chance at survival" (ibid.). That is to say, that the kid is not a fully enlightened Gnostic and thus cannot escape the prison of the manifest cosmos, which is the judge's domain.

Other critics have also noted the kid's gradual development, whether moral or spiritual. Harold Bloom, for example, argues that the kid undergoes a "moral maturation" and that "McCarthy subtly shows us the long, slow development of the Kid from another mindless scalper of Indians to the courageous confronter of the Judge is their final debate in a saloon" (*How to Read and Why* 257). Steven Frye argues that the kid "stands apart, not because of his purity or separation from the judge's world, but because in the end he responds to circumstances with a moral rectitude and resists the judge's pronouncements even unto death" (87). Similarly, Diane Luce writes that: "the kid becomes by tiny increments more thoughtful about his violence as his experience with death and suffering grows, and he eventually attempts to break with the judge and atone for his deeds" ("Ambiguities, Dilemmas, and Double-Binds" 26). Luce, however, adds that "whether these attempts prove effective remains ambiguous even at the end of the novel" (ibid.). I believe that the fact that the judge singles the kid out from the other members of the gang suggests that his spiritual awakening is of enough significance to earn the judge's wrath.

In a typically Gnostic reinterpretation of a Biblical theme, the judge condemns the kid in the words of Yahweh; as Tim Parrish states, the judge "seems to be playing God…to the kid-as-supplicant" (37). Just before he takes the kid's life, he proclaims: "This night thy soul may be required of thee" (327), echoing God's words to the rich man in Luke 12:20: "Thou fool, this night

thy soul shall be required of thee: then whose shall these things be, which thou hast provided?" After voicing this sinister warning in the form of a Biblical allusion, and then stating that the kid has proven to be a "disappointment" (328), the judge seems to offer the kid one last chance to join him: "Even so at the last I find you here with me" (328). The kid, however, rejects the judge's offer stating: "I aint with you" (328). Later, he again rebuffs the judge with the words: "You aint nothin" (331); repeating his earlier insistence to the terrified Tobin that the judge "aint nothin" (297). The judge merely mocks the kid for his use of a double negative, replying: "You speak truer than you know" (331). The judge's words may also be read as an affirmation of his own evil nature, especially if one conceives of evil in St Augustine's orthodox Catholic fashion as a *privatio boni* (privation of good) conceived of as a mere absence rather than a force in its own right and therefore a "nothing."[4]

The kid pays with his life for this final denial of the judge. After taking leave of the judge, and visiting a whore, the kid steps outside and looks up at the night sky: "Stars were falling across the sky myriad and random, speeding along brief vectors from their origins in night to their destinies in dust and nothingness…. he looked again at the silent tracks of the stars where they died over the darkened hills" (333). The stars, which travel to their deaths along predetermined paths, foreshadow the kid's impending and inevitable death. It is significant that, like his birth, the kid's death is augured by stellar phenomena. Commenting on the significance of this synchronicity, Stacey Peebles once again draws attention to the kid's mythological significance within the novel: "Like his birth during the Leonids, a meteor shower of cultural significance to the Yuman Indians, here his death is also marked by falling stars, another important signifier for the Quechan. The kid's life is bookended and emphasized by these semiotic markers" (242). Peebles argues that although the kid may appear to be "an ignorant, aimless wandered," his birth and death are "resonant with [Quechan] beliefs and therefore representational" (ibid.). [5] Therefore, "the kid is a necessary and important component in this mythological and ideological standoff with the judge" (ibid.). In other words, the kid is a sufficiently significant player in the cosmic game that both his entry into and his departure from the world do not go unnoticed or unheralded.

The exact nature of the kid's death remains a disturbing mystery; as the kid walks towards the jakes, he finds that: "The judge was seated upon the closet. He was naked and he rose up smiling and gathered him in his arms against his immense and terrible flesh and shot the wooden barlatch home behind him" (333). This is the last we ever hear of the kid. When two men later walk down to the jakes, they encounter a third man urinating, who warns them: "I wouldnt go in there if I was you." When one of the men asks if there is "somebody in there?," the urinating man simply repeats: "I wouldn't go in" (334). The men ignore him and one of them opens the door, only to exclaim "Good God almighty" (334). When his companion asks: "What is it?" (334), the man doesn't answer. John Cant comments on the fact that "despite McCarthy's propensity for making us 'see' all the action and his complete lack of squeamishness in depicting the endless catalogue of outrage that constitutes the novel, we do not 'see' the kid's fate" (173). In a novel where the most horrific scenes of violence are depicted in unflinching detail, the fact that the kid's death is censored and left to the imagination makes it all the more horrific.

Cant also argues that "McCarthy does not wish to show us this event since its full meaning is metaphorical" (ibid.). While I agree with Cant's emphasis on the metaphorical nature of the event, I believe that we can still hazard a guess as to the kid's ultimate fate by extrapolating some of the novel's earlier events. The very fact that the hardened men of the so-called Wild West respond with such horror to what they see in the jakes suggests that the kid underwent a taboo-breaking ordeal that somehow exceeded the level of violence and depravity common to that society. Sodomy would certainly qualify as taboo-breaking, but the visual signifiers of the aftermath would not be immediately obvious to casual observers. I propose, instead, that the judge cannibalised the kid, to a lesser or greater extent, and then regurgitated his flesh, for the remains of such a scene would no doubt inspire disgust and horror in even the most jaded of outlaws, no matter how desensitised they had become to the sight of ordinary dismemberments and disfigurations.

There is much evidence to support what Sara Spurgeon calls the "cannibalistic perversions" (90) of the judge. When we are first introduced to the Glanton gang, they are described as "a visitation from some heathen land where they and others like them fed on human flesh" and that "(f)oremost among them," like the head cannibal, "rode the judge" (78-9). Later in the novel, the body of a "halfbreed boy" is discovered "lying face down naked in one of the cubicles. Scattered about on the clay were great numbers of old bones. As if he like others before him had stumbled upon a place where something inimical lived" (118). This "inimical" thing is no doubt the judge, who is seen "standing in the gently steaming quiet picking his teeth with a thorn as if he had just eaten" (118). Sara Spurgeon argues that in this instance, "the judge rapes and cannibalizes [the boy], absorbs his essence and emerges renewed" (95) and I believe that a similar fate befalls the kid. The very fact that the "halfbreed boy" is found in a "cubicle" links the setting of this particular scene of cannibalisation to the kid's similar fate in "the jakes."

Furthermore, there is reason to suspect that the judge did not merely devour the kid's flesh, but also proceeded to regurgitate the meal. The threat of such an act was foreshadowed by the judge's earlier condemnation of the kid for being "[n]o assassin…And no partisan either" (299); words which recalls Jesus' threatening promise to the "lukewarm" souls: "So, because you are lukewarm, and neither cold nor hot, I will spew you out of my mouth" (John 3:15-16). It is likely, then, that the judge similarly spewed the kid out of his mouth for being a lukewarm soul.

If the judge and the kid represent to antithetical positions within the novel, then it can be assumed that the hideous death of the kid signifies the triumph of the judge's paradigm. From a Gnostic perspective, this suggests the triumph of evil over the tiny fragment of divinity lying dormant within the kid. Many of the Gnostic sects, however, believed in reincarnation and taught that the pneuma was eternal and could never truly be destroyed.[6] For the fully enlightened Gnostics death meant a final release from the manifest cosmos, while those who were still plagued by ignorance were thrust back into the world, life after life, until they too attained gnosis and escaped from the prison of existence. Thus, from a Gnostic perspective, the kid's death does not necessarily signify an ultimate failure. In fact, the kid's death actually evokes a recurring trope in Gnostics, specifically Manichean, allegories; namely, that of the "Sacrifice and Adulteration of the Soul," (Jonas 219) which involves the Primal Man, or the Salvator Salvatus, being devoured by one of the evil entities that rules over the manifest world.

Jonas explains that the "devouring has also an effect on the devourer" because "the devoured substance acts like a soothing poison" (ibid.) which either satisfies or dulls the appetite of the devourer. It is noteworthy that "some versions [of the myth] make the Primal Man not so much be defeated, as in anticipation of the effect voluntarily give himself to be devoured by the Darkness" (ibid.). Jonas explains that: "By this sacrificial means the furor of the Darkness is actually 'appeased'" (120). In *Blood Meridian*, the kid's last moments suggest that he also meets his death with a certain resignation to his fate. Luce argues that: "Though he appears passive, he goes to embrace his fate as if to a suicide—for the [kid] clearly expects to die. As he approaches the saloon he turns in silent farewell to the world and his life" ("Ambiguities, Dilemmas, and Double-Binds" 41). Thus, the kid's death may be a form of sacrifice intended to temporarily appease the wrath of the judge. Steven Frye, for example, argues that the kid's death "becomes a measured victory that echoes Christ's death on the cross, at least insofar as he is destroyed but never internally defeated, and he stands as an example of moral rectitude and heroism in the face of omnipresent evil" (90). Such a sacrificial role would not only justify the portentous omens surrounding the kid's birth and death, but would also shed light on the judge's fascination with the kid, as well as the judge's claim that he "recognized" (328) the kid when he first saw him.

And yet, despite the kid's sacrifice, the judge seems entirely triumphant at the end of the novel: "His feet are light and nimble. He never sleeps. He says that he will never die. He dances in light and in shadow and he is a great favorite. He never sleeps, the judge. He is dancing, dancing. He says that he will never die" (335). Steven Frye argues that: "It appears then, that in spite of the kid's resistance, the world remains the judge's domain, a place in which heroic resolve and moral rectitude must inevitably end in death" (90). It seems that if the kid was a messiah, then he was indeed a failed one; for evil, in the form of the judge, continues its cosmic dance, with no respite and no terminus. Even though Gnostic thought teaches that the world is permeated by evil, a glimmer of hope can always be found within the sparks of the divine substance imprisoned here. I believe that even though the novel proper ends with the death of the kid, and the judge in celebratory dance, we must look to the epilogue for the final word on the Manichean struggle between good and evil.

The epilogue marks a change into a heightened, poetic register; signified not only by the italicized font, but also by the esoteric symbolism which abounds within the strange vignette: "In the dawn there is a man progressing over the plain by means of holes which he is making in the ground. He uses an implement with two handles and he chucks it into the hole and he enkindles the stone in the hole with steel hole by hole striking the fire out of the rock which God has put there" (337). On the surface level, this passage can be interpreted quite prosaically. For example, Sepich argues that "the novel's epilogue is literally a description of digging postholes using a throw-down tool"; a historically significant "step toward the fencing of open range" (Notes 66). Similarly, Christopher Campbell explains that: "Anyone who has ever labored with just such an 'implement' in moderately rocky soil will recognize the sparks which fly with each plunge of the tool" (40). Nevertheless, the densely symbolic quality of McCarthy's prose suggests that there is more to the epilogue than can be gleaned from a literal interpretation, no matter how factually accurate such an interpretation may be.

When interviewed on the subject of Blood Meridian, Harold Bloom rejects the literal reading of the passage as "a very bad interpretation" (Josyph 214). According to Bloom: "That two-handed implement is, as I say, doing one thing and one thing only: it is striking fire which has been put into the rock, clearly a Promethean motif" (ibid.). Jonas explains that the Gnostics favoured the Promethean motif for its antinomian themes; Prometheus, as Zeus' "challenger and victim," represented the Gnostic "'spiritual' man whose loyalty is not to the god of this world but to the transcendent one beyond" (Jonas 97). From a Gnostic perspective, the fact that the man in the epilogue is described as "striking the fire out of the rock which God has put there" suggests that he is freeing sparks of the divine "fire" trapped in matter—or "rock"—by the "God" of this world, the demiurge. While the Gnostics referred to the fragment of the divine as a "spark," rather than a "fire," Evelyn Underhill points out that: "fire imagery has seemed to many of the mystics a peculiarly exact and suggestive symbol of the transcendent state which they are struggling to describe" (421). For example, transcendentalist philosopher, Ralph Waldo Emerson, employs this imagery in "The Poet," where he writes: "We were put in our bodies, as fire is put into a pan to be carried about" (92). Similarly, Boehme writes of "the fire of the soul" which is "illuminated by the divine light" (Hartmann 18). Thus, the "fire" in Blood Meridian's epilogue seems to be "that uncreated and energizing Fire" (Underhill 421); symbolic of the spirit, as well as the Godhead, with which it is one in substance.[7]

Leo Daugherty writes that it was precisely Blood Meridian's epilogue which led to his first glimpses of "the novel's Gnostic, and perhaps even specifically Manichean, features" (168). Daugherty identifies the "man progressing over the plain" as "the revealer or 'revelator' of the divine, working to free spirit from matter – the pneumatic (albeit corporeal) messenger, in possession of gnosis, who is in service to the good, 'alien God'" (169). Fully awakened himself, the Salvator Salvatus "awakens the spirit [of his fellow man] from its earthly slumber, and imparts to it the saving knowledge" (Jonas 45). The task of the Gnostic saviour is reminiscent to that of the Bodhisattva in Buddhist thought: "who does not only set himself free, but who is also skilful in devising means for bringing out and maturing the latent seeds of enlightenment in others" (Conze, Buddhism 128). Even after attaining Enlightenment, the Bodhisattvas choose to remain in the world of manifest illusion, refusing to enter the state of Nirvana until every living entity has escaped from the cycle of birth and rebirth. Thus, the figure in the epilogue seems to be a Salvator Salvatus; one who, unlike the kid, has responded adequately to the call of gnosis and reached his soteriological potential. The presence of the enkindled fire as a symbol of spiritual awakening throws light on the judge's mysterious reference to the kid as "Young Blasarius" (94). According to Schimpf, the term appears in Black's Law Dictionary and refers to "an incendiary," (148) or one who starts fires. Thus, the kid's potential for "striking the fire out of the rock" is obliquely alluded to by the judge himself.

The epilogue continues with the words: "On the plain behind him are the wanderers in search of bones and those who do not search" (337). Sepich argues that the mysterious "wanderers" are merely bonepickers in search of buffalo bones, explaining that: "When the use of bone phosphorous for agricultural fertilizer was discovered in the nineteenth century, buffalo skeletons became significant commodities in the economy of the West" (67). Though historically valid, such an interpretation does not explain the presence of "those who do not search." Harold Bloom takes the argument against a literal interpretation even further, arguing in an interview that the lone figure is "clearly contrasted with creatures who are either ghoulish human beings, if they are human beings, or already are, in fact, shades, looking for bones for whatever nourishment that might bring about" and adds that he "cannot see that as any kind of allegory of anything that has happened to the American West" (Josyph 214).

If, however, one looks at the passage as a Gnostic allegory, rather than a historical one, one may go some way toward illuminating the meaning of those who are "in search of bones" and "those who do not search." The distinction drawn between the two different kinds of "wanderers," suggests that those who have not attained gnosis can be divided into those who search for answers in the wrong places and those who do not search at all. Those who wander the barren plain "in search of bones" are the followers of those exoteric religions that hinder spiritual progress by placing all the emphasis on the afterlife. Rather than seeking spiritual insight here and now, these wanderers look to the empty promise of death for salvation; worshipping the creator of this flawed world in their charnel houses, where they horde the relics of their dead saints.[8] According to the Gnostic Gospel of Thomas, Jesus rebuked his disciples for their preference for the "secondhand testimony" of dead prophets over the "primacy of immediate experience," stating: "You have ignored the one living in your presence and have spoken (only) of the dead" (Pagels 145). Conversely, "those who do not search" are the thoroughgoing materialists; tranquillising themselves with the trivialities of everyday life, content with the acquisition of material goods, and possessing no desire for spiritual insight. According to Gnostic thought, they are "the "unenlightened people" who believe they can "find fulfilment in family life, sexual relationships, business, politics, ordinary employment or leisure"; the true Gnostics "rejected this belief as illusion" (ibid.). Thus, "those who do not search" are even less awakened than those who seek for answers in dry bones.

As Bloom points out, the crowd of wanderers is "clearly contrasted" with the figure of the solitary man. While the man is depicted as "progressing over the plain" with the decisive determination of one who has a goal, the wanderers "move haltingly in the light like mechanisms whose movements are monitored with escapement and pallet" (337), their halting, mechanical movements suggesting a complete lack of personal agency. Furthermore, Schimpf argues that the "escapement and pallet" serve as "a reference to clocks and their mechanism," which is "a clear echoing of the idea of an orderly universe that can be fully described and controlled" (45).[9] From a Gnostic perspective, the difference between the lone man and the wanderers is that the former is no longer controlled by the machinations of universal fate (Greek, heimarmene) while the latter are still its hapless puppets. According to Gnostic teachings, heimarmene determines the motion of the entire cosmos, from the celestial spheres to the lowliest organism, thereby turning it into "a prison from which there is no escape" (Rudolph 58). Only the attainment of gnosis "opens up a way on which man (strictly only a small part of man, namely the divine spark) can escape" (ibid.). Buddhism also "distinguishes two classes of people," namely, the "saints" who "alone are truly alive" and the "common worldlings" who, much like McCarthy's wanderers, "just vegetate along in a sort of dull and aimless bewilderment" (Conze, Buddhist Wisdom Books 38). Similarly, the difference between the two types of people in Buddhism is a direct result of spiritual development, or lack thereof.

The halting movement of the wanderers makes them "appear" to be "restrained by a prudence or reflectiveness," but this is only an illusion and "has no inner reality" (337). "Reflectiveness" is synonymous with "thoughtfulness" or "contemplativeness" (OED) and therefore a state of mind associated with meditation and spiritual practice. The wanderers only appear to possess insight into their situation, when in reality they move like sleepwalkers. Buddhism teaches that: "Only the enlightened are awake to reality as it is; compared with their vision of true reality, our normal experience is that of a dream, unreal and not to be taken seriously" (Conze, Buddhist Wisdom Books 38). Similarly, the fully awakened Gnostic "comes to understand that the material world is a dream" (Wagner and Flannery-Dailey 282). From both a Buddhist and a Gnostic perspective, only the lone figure "progressing over the plain" can be said to be fully awakened, fully aware and thus in control of his destiny; the wanderers are mere cogs in the unrelentingly deterministic machine that is the manifest cosmos.

The wanderers "cross in their progress one by one that track of holes that runs to the rim of the visible ground" seemingly seeking "a validation of sequence and causality as if each round and perfect hole owed its existence to the one before it" (337). They cannot comprehend the mystery of the path that lies before them; misunderstanding its nature and its cause. What is essentially the work of the Saved Saviour, they mistake for a natural occurrence which has arisen quite simply and organically out of itself. The passage seems to be suggesting that the ordinary worldlings are incapable of recognizing the miracle of the saints, saviours and Bodhisattvas, even if their works lie right before their eyes. Nevertheless, the Salvator Salvatus does not abandon "that prairie upon which are the bones and the gatherers of bones and those who do not gather. He strikes fire in the hole and draws out his steel. Then they all move on again" (337). These are the words with which Blood Meridian concludes. We are not left with the judge's eternal dance, but rather with the unconquered solitary figure, slowly working towards his soteriological goal.

Many critics, however, feel that the epilogue offers no redemption whatsoever and see Blood Meridian as a wholly nihilistic novel. Michael

Carragher, for example, writes that "we look to the epilogue to find a bone-strewn plain a man apparently sowing war" and concludes: "No, there is no salvation; we are all damned to hell" (20). Similarly, Steven Shaviro writes that: "We are called to no responsibility, and we may lay claim to no transcendence. Blood Meridian is not a salvation narrative; we can be rescued neither by faith nor by works nor by grace", concluding that: "It is useless to look for ulterior, redemptive meanings" (148). Edwin Arnold, however, insists that there is "always the possibility of grace and redemption even in the darkest of [McCarthy's] tales" ("Naming, Knowing and Nothingness" 46) and I believe that Blood Meridian is no exception. Furthermore, Harold Bloom, along with Leo Daugherty, are among the few to argue that this "man striking fire in the rock at dawn is an opposing figure" who, to some extent, counteracts the evil of the judge. Bloom concludes that the "Judge never sleeps, and perhaps will never die, but a new Prometheus may be rising to go up against him" (Modern Critical Views 7). Like Bloom, I argue that despite the fact that the kid fails in his messianic role, and that the seemingly immortal judge continues his Shiva-like dance of destruction, the lone figure of the epilogue saves Blood Meridian from unrelenting nihilism. The judge may be immortal and terrible beyond imagining, but he cannot stop the lone figure "striking the fire out of the rock" (337); no amount of evil can extinguish the sparks of the divine.

NOTES

1 Boehme's influence on McCarthy is made evident through one of Blood Meridian's epigraphs – "It is not to be thought that the life of darkness is sunk in misery and lost as if in sorrowing. There is no sorrowing. For sorrow is a thing that is swallowed up in death, and death and dying are the very life of the darkness." Taken from Boehme's Six Theosophic Points, the quote describes the condition of the devils in hell, who have turned their back on the God's light so completely that they no longer even feel the pain of its absence; unlike man, who struggles between the two polarities of good and evil, heaven and hell.

2 Andersen points out that the wedding ceremony is again evoked when the judge finally takes the kid's life: "'Speak or forever,' says the barkeep, asking what he'll have, and this fragment of the wedding ceremony marks the consummation he's about to meet in death (he'll go like a 'bride to the altar' just as Tobin once predicted): when he turns and looks across the room he locks eyes with the judge" (108).

3 Schimpf argues that McCarthy's alternate title for Blood Meridian, namely "or the Evening Redness in the West" is "a clever reference" to Boehme's full title for Aurora, which is: "Aurora. That is The Day-Spring. Or Dawning of The Day in the Orient. Or Morning Redness in the Rising of the Sun. That is the Root or Mother of Philosphie, Astrologie and Theologie from the True Ground. Or A Description of Nature" (58).

4 Michael L. Peterson explains that: "Evil, then, from Augustine's perspective, is not a thing, not a being. Although evil in human experience can be very powerful and profound, evil does not, at least metaphysically speaking, represent the positive existence of anything….Evil is thus metaphysical deprivation, privation, or degradation. Augustine's term for evil is privatio boni (privation of good)" (90).

5 It is noteworthy that Peebles draws parallels between the Quechan belief system and Gnosticism: "Gnosticism can be seen not only in the basic thematics of the narrative, but also in these Quechan beliefs that parallel the narrative. Gnosticism teaches that the world was created

flawed, and thus is filled with suffering….Again, this is resonant not only with the narrative content of the novel, but also with the Quechan myths, with tales of godly antagonism and corresponding earthly suffering" (242-243).

6 Andrew Smith writes that: "Reincarnation or the transmigration of souls is implied in many Gnostic systems" (211). Similarly, Hoeller explains that: "Reincarnation seems to have been an important feature of the teachings of the school of Carpocrates," adding that "Some feel that reincarnation is implicit in the teachings of all Gnostic schools" (103).

7 McCarthy also uses "fire" to represent the divine spark in The Road. The father reminds the son throughout the journey through the apocalyptic wasteland that they are "the good guys" because they are "carrying the fire" (120). When the son asks, "Where is it? I don't know where it is", the father replies, "Yes you do. It's inside you. It was always there. I can see it" (279). Similarly, in No Country for Old Men, Sheriff Bell dreams of his father "carryin fire in a horn [. . .] And in the dream I knew that he was goin on ahead and that he was fixin to make a fire somewhere out there in all that dark and all that cold" (309). Here the fire stands in opposition to darkness, a concept frequently associated with spiritual ignorance, evil and death.

8 Julian II, the last pagan emperor of Rome, condemned the Galileans (Christians) for their obsession with death: "You have filled the whole world with tombs and sepulchres, and yet in your scriptures it is nowhere said that you must grovel among tombs and pay them honour" (Wright 414).

9 I do not agree with the rest of Schimpf's reading of the epilogue. Schimpf writes that: "Specifically, if one of McCarthy's intentions is to point out the triumph of science and technology over religion, it can be argued that the man in the epilogue is spreading science. Whether or not this man is the Judge is not that important, although I am inclined to think that it is….Man is altering the landscape to fit his needs via his tools. This is 'progress' but note where the progress takes place – in the barren landscape of the plain" (45). On the contrary, I believe that the figure in the epilogue is spreading spiritual insight, not scientific knowledge, and that he is in complete opposition to the judge.

WORKS CITED

Andersen, Elisabeth. *The Mythos of Cormac McCarthy: A String in the Maze.* Germany: VDM, 2008.

Arnold, Edwin T. "Naming, Knowing and Nothingness: McCarthy's Moral Parables." *Perspectives on Cormac McCarthy.* Revised Ed. Eds. Edwin T. Arnold and Dianne C. Luce. Jackson: UP of Mississippi, 1999. 45-70.

Bloom, Harold. *How to Read and Why.* New York: Scribner, 2000.

--- . *Bloom's Modern Critical Views: New Edition - Cormac McCarthy.* New York: Infobase. 2009.

Boehme, Jacob. *Six Theosophic Points: An Open Gate of all the Secrets of Life Wherein the Causes of all Beings Become Known; Six Mystical Points; On the Earthly and Heavenly Mystery; On the Divine Intuition.* Trans. John R. Earle. Montana: Kessinger, 1992.

Brading, D.A. *Mexican Phoenix: Our Lady of Guadalupe: Image and Tradition Across Five Centuries.* Cambridge: Cambridge UP, 2001.

Bramley, William. *The Gods of Eden.* New York: Avon, 1993.

Burton, Richard Francis. *The Book of the Thousand Nights and a Night.* Vol. 6. South Carolina: BiblioBazaar, 2009.

Campbell, Christopher D. "Walter De Maria's *Lightning Field* and McCarthy's Enigmatic Epilogue: Y qué clase de lugar es éste?" *The Cormac Journal 2* (Spring 2002): 40-55.

Cant, John. *Cormac McCarthy and the Myth of American Exceptionalism.* New York: Routledge, 2008.

Carragher, Michael. "I Tego Arcana Dei: Aspects of the Demonic in Cormac McCarthy's *Blood Meridian.*" *Publications of the Arkansas Philological Association* 23.1 (Spring 1997): 13-21.

Conze, Edward. *Buddhism: Its Essence and Development.* New York: Harper Torchbooks, 1959.

--- . *Buddhist Wisdom Books: The Diamond Sutra and the Heart Sutra.* London: George Allen, 1975.

Daugherty, Leo. "Gravers False and True: *Blood

Meridian as Gnostic Tragedy." *Perspectives on Cormac McCarthy*. Revised Ed. Eds. Edwin T. Arnold and Dianne C. Luce. Jackson: Mississippi UP, 1999. 159-174.

Eliade, Mircea. *The Sacred and the Profane: The Nature of Religion*. New York: Harcourt, 1959.

Emerson, Ralph Waldo. "The Poet." *The Complete Prose Works*. New York: Elibron Classics, 2006. 92-101.

Evenson, Brian. "McCarthy's Wanderers: Nomadology, Violence, and Open Country." *Sacred Violence: A Reader's Companion to Cormac McCarthy*. Eds. Wade Hall and Rick Wallach. El Paso: Texas UP, 1995. 41-48.

Frye, Steven. *Understanding Cormac McCarthy*. South Carolina: U of South Carolina P, 2009.

Girard, René. *Violence and the Sacred*. Trans. Patrick Gregory. Baltimore: The Johns Hopkins UP, 1979.

Grossman, Vasily *Life and Fate*. Trans. Robert Chandler. New York: Review, 1985.

Guénon, René. *Aperçus sur l'Initiation*. Paris: Éditions Traditionnelles, 1946.

--- . *The Reign of Quantity and the Signs of the Times*. Trans. Lord Northbourne. Baltimore: Penguin, 1972.

Guiley, Rosemary Ellen. *The Encyclopedia of Witches and Witchcraft*. New York: Facts on File, 1989.

Hartmann, Franz. *Jacob Boehme: Life and Doctrines*. New York: Steiner, 1977.

Hoeller, Stephen. *Gnosticism: New Light on the Ancient Tradition of Inner Knowing*. Illinois: Quest, 2002.

Jarret, Robert L. *Cormac McCarthy*. New York: Twayne, 1997.

Jonas, Hans. *The Gnostic Religion: The Message of the Alien God and the Beginnings of Christianity*. Boston: Beacon, 1958.

Josyph, Peter. "Tragic Ecstasy: A Conversation about McCarthy's *Blood Meridian*." *Sacred Violence: Volume 2, McCarthy's Western Novels*. Eds. Wade Hall and Rick Wallach. Texas: Texas Western P, 2002. 205-222.

Liddell, Henry George and Robert Scott. *A Greek-English Lexicon*. Oxford: Clarendon P, 1940.

Luce, Dianne C. "Ambiguities, Dilemmas, and Double-Binds in Cormac McCarthy's *Blood Meridian*." *Southwestern American Literature* 26.1 (Fall 2000): 21-46.

Melville, Herman. "Bartleby the Scrivener." *Billy Bud and Other Stories*. Hertfordshire: Wordsworth Classics, 1998.

--- . *Moby-Dick*. 1851. London: Penguin, 1994.

--- . "Fragments of a Lost Gnostic Poem of the 12th Century." *The New Oxford Book of American Verse*. Ed. Richard Ellmann. Oxford: Oxford UP, 1976.

McCarthy, Cormac. *All the Pretty Horses*. 1992. New York: Alfred A. Knopf, 1992.

--- . *Blood Meridian*. 1985. New York: Vintage Books, 1999.

--- . *Child of God*. 1973. New York: Vintage Books, 1993.

--- . *No Country For Old Men*. 2005. New York: Vintage Books, 2007.

--- . *Outer Dark*. 1968. New York: Vintage Books, 1993.

--- . *Suttree*. 1979. New York: Vintage Books, 1993.

--- . *The Crossing*. 1994. New York: Vintage Books, 1995.

--- . *The Orchard Keeper*. 1965. New York: Vintage Books, 1993.

--- . *The Road*. 2006. New York: Vintage Books, 2006.

Pagels, Elaine. *The Gnostic Gospels*. London: Weidenfeld, 1979.

Parrish, Tim. "The Killer Wears the Halo: Cormac McCarthy, Flannery O'Connor, and the American Religion." *Sacred Violence: A Reader's Companion to Cormac McCarthy*. Eds. Wade Hall and Rick Wallach. El Paso: Texas UP, 1995. 25-40.

Peach, Emily. *The Tarot Workbook: Understanding and Using Tarot Symbolism*. Somerset: Aquarian, 1984.

Pearson, Birger A. *Ancient Gnosticism: Traditions and Literature*. Minneapolis: Fortress, 2007.

Peebles, Stacey. "Yuman Belief Systems and Cormac McCarthy's *Blood Meridian*." *Texas Studies in Literature and Language* 45:2 (Summer 2003), 231-244.

Peterson, Michael L. *God and Evil: An Introduction*

to the Issues. Oxford: Westview P,
1998.

Reynolds, Michael D. *Falling Stars: A Guide to
Meteors and Meteorites* Pennsylvania:
Stackpole, 2001.

Rudolph, Kurt. *Gnosis: The Nature & History of
Gnosticism.* Trans. Robert McLachlan
Wilson. New York: Harper, 1987.

Sepich, John. *Notes on Blood Meridian.* Revised Ed.
Austin: U of Texas P, 2008.

-- -- . "The Dance of History in Cormac McCarthy's
Blood Meridian." *Southern Literary
Journal* 24.1 (Fall 1991), 16-31.

Schimpf, Shane. *A Reader's Guide to Blood Meridian.*
USA: Bon Mot, 2006.

Shaviro, Steven. "The Very Life of the Darkness: A
Reading of *Blood Meridian.*"
Perspectives on Cormac McCarthy. Revised Ed. Eds.
Edwin T. Arnold and Dianne C. Luce. Jackson:
Mississippi UP, 1999. 145-158.

Shaw, Patrick W. "The Kid's Fate, the Judge's Guilt:
Ramifications of Closure in
Cormac McCarthy's *Blood Meridian.*" *The Southern
Literary Journal* 30.1 (1997), 102-120.

Smith, Andrew Phillip. *A Dictionary of Gnosticism.*
Illinois: Theosophical, 2009.

Smith, Huston. *The Religions of Man.* New York:
Harper, 1965.

Spurgeon, Sara L. "Foundation of Empire: The
Sacred Hunter and the Eucharist of the
Wilderness in Cormac McCarthy's *Blood Meridian.*"
Bloom's Modern Critical Views: Cormac McCarthy.
Ed. Harold Bloom. New York: Infobase, 2009. 85-
106.

Underhill, Evelyn. Mysticism. New York: E.P.
Dutton, 1961.

Wagner, Rachel, and Frances Flannery-Dailey.
"Wake Up! Worlds of Illusion in Gnosticism,
Buddhism, and *The Matrix* Project." *Philosophers
Explore 'The Matrix.'* Ed. Christopher Grau. Oxford:
Oxford UP, 2005.

Wordsworth, William. *The Complete Poetical Works
of William Wordsworth.* London:
Macmillan, 1888.

Wright, Wilmer Cave. *The Works of the Emperor
Julian* Vol III. Massachusetts: Harvard UP, 1913.

A LITTLE WORLD MADE CUNNINGLY

SCOTT DAVID FINCH

A Little World Made Cunningly

This is an excerpt from a graphic novel I've recently finished called *A Little World Made Cunningly*. It is story about creativity disguised as a creation story. In this section a young soul goes out into the dark night mapped so well by Saint John of the Cross. In this lonely hour, she finds that a guiding light has been waiting to extend a gift. Unfortunately, she takes that "lilly", convinces herself it is her own creation, and gilds it.

Scott Finch

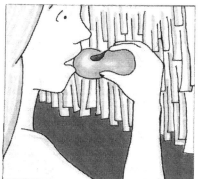

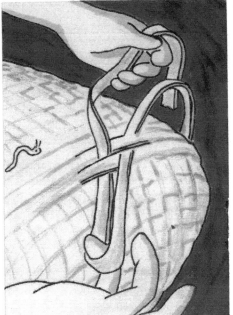

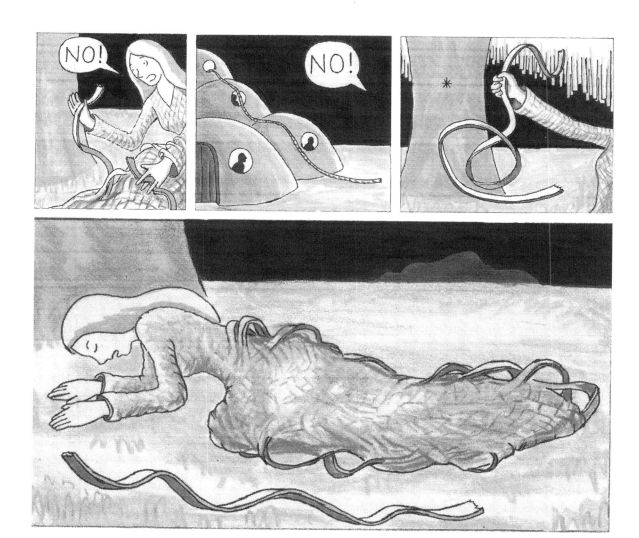

Andrew Phillip Smith

An Interview With Patrick Harpur

APS: The way you address the soul and related concepts doesn't really encourage any kind of systematic approach, so I won't ask you to define the soul—I'll spare you that—because that's not really how you look at it.

PH: Yes, that's not my favourite question.

APS: Perhaps you could just give us a general idea of what you mean by the soul, and the approach you take.

PH: I suppose my initiation into the soul was as a thing that is not very much mentioned in one's formal education and so on, except in a very poetic way. My initiation really, like so many people, was through reading Jung, where he of course prefers the term *psyche*, in the hope of sounding more scientific. But I prefer to move back from that again. It was through him that I began to understand the soul in the sense of the totality of the psyche, consisting of both consciousness and the unconscious. But he did me the great service of introducing me to the Greeks, and just as he realised that there was a collective unconscious that lay beneath our personal unconscious, which he identified with the Soul of the World, as described by Plato and elaborated by the Neoplatonists, especially Plotinus, it all began to make sense. I began to think less in terms of the Christian idea of a single, personal, immortal soul, and more in terms of the Soul of the World, in which the very stuff of the universe is soul stuff, as Plotinus would say. And if we, instead of being small individual souls, are individual manifestations of this much greater collective Soul of the World, so we are paradoxical; we are both individual souls, microcosms, but also we have access to—

we are drops in the ocean of—the collective World Soul. So I tended to talk less about these souls, as it were, as single entities, and about Soul, which is a kind of dynamic, oceanic stuff of which the universe is made, and which we temporarily incarnate a portion of in the course of our lives.

APS: Your other books haven't focused on the soul to quite such an extent, arguably.

PH: I would argue that they do, but perhaps not so directly. There is the central problem of reality, which is what my books attack from different perspectives, but the science of the soul *par excellence* is alchemy, so I deal with that in one book, and the faculty of the soul par excellence is the imagination, which I attack in *The Philosophers' Secret Fire*. The stuff of reality is Soul, or Imagination, or as Jung would say, it's psychic reality, and it's that psychic reality, that in-between reality, which I try to illustrate in *Daimonic Reality*. "Daimonic" is another word for imaginative in my vocabulary, or indeed of, approximately, Soul. So really I've been trying to develop different facets of the great diamond of Soul, but since you can't come at it directly without disappearing up your own bum, you have to come at it obliquely through the different ways in which Soul manifests, whether through works of art, or whether through alchemy, or whether through different kinds of religious experience—and I try to make distinctions. I'm always keen to distinguish between these different ways. My Soul book was slightly more polemical. I got really fed up with books with "soul" in the title, which were really about what I call "spirit", an entirely different perspective.

APS: Yes, I noticed in *A Complete guide to the Soul*, which has just been released in America as *The Secret Tradition of the Soul* (Evolver Editions, 2011), that the front cover blurb has "Who am I? What's my life's purpose? Where am I going when I die?" that you might characterise more as a spirit approach.

PH: I think those are legitimate Soul questions. But they're questions that I don't fully answer in the book. [laughter].

APS: Towards the end of the book you acknowledge *A Complete guide to the Soul* as a tricksy title, and I quite like that.

PH: A lie, in other words.

APS: I notice in the new book that you're quite hard on the spirit in the chapter "Soul and Spirit." Could you elucidate on that, and on what you mean by the spirit, and why most of these books on the soul are actually about the spirit?

PH: It's just that our model of what life's about tends to be based on the Enlightenment model, which comes under the aegis of Apollo, so it's all about ascending, and linear progress, or else it comes under the aegis of the Great Mother and is about growth and development. But these are *spiritual* categories. The idea that we ascend in a linear fashion towards truth, or else that we grow, mature and develop into some omega man or enlightened being. Whereas Soul isn't like that. It doesn't grow or develop. It is from the beginning complete in itself. Yet paradoxically it has to unfold itself and reach its potential, which isn't quite the same. It's a very moot point and extremely tricky, and I struggle to explain it in my book, never fully satisfactorily. But it has to unfold itself—as Jung would say, to individuate. But as Jung also says, this doesn't mean a linear progression. It's a kind of labyrinthine, meandering circling of the centre, gathering up all the facets of yourself, and expressing them in turn, which isn't quite the same as the psychotherapeutic model, which is more of a plant model—we start off as a seed and we grow into a fully fledged plant. It's that sort of distinction I'm trying to make. All the current models—which we take for granted

as being good and true—of personal growth, or of linear ascent into greater clarity, I think have to be counterbalanced. I attack that view in a polemical way, or seem to, I think, simply because it's been overemphasised in our culture. But I do concede later on in the book that it's also an essential part of our beliefs, because those beliefs that we grow or that we ascend are themselves archetypally determined. They have their own deities in charge of them. It's just they've been given too much emphasis, so I'm trying to emphasise the path of the soul, which is not upwards but downwards; not straight but circular, mazy, labyrinthine, and which doesn't so much grow as encircle. That's the sort of distinction I'm trying to make.

APS: But the ascent towards the One is very present in Neoplatonism, isn't it?

PH: It is. Neoplatonism, like Plato, contains different points of view. Just as Plato contains what I've called elsewhere a Logos Plato and a mythos Plato, and one gave birth to reason and the Enlightenment, logos. What the mythos gave was the imaginative, mythic view of reality, and Plato combines the two, and they could almost be regarded as opposites. So you can pick and choose from Plato. You can come out with completely different readings of him. But in fact he combines the two and that is what I try to do at the end of the Soul book, which is to show that the healthy psyche marries the perspective of spirit with the perspective of Soul. It's almost as if by marrying the straight line and the circular path you get a kind of spiral, which is Jung's preferred model. And indeed W.B. Yeats prefers that as well. His gyres are dynamic spirals which represent both history and our own personal psychic growth.

These are very arcane matters. Trying to come up with a geometrical, spatial model with how the psyche and its different perspectives can work in tension with each other, be reconciled with each other, is an age-old problem. All models in the end fail, and that's why I think the best metaphors for describing the marriage of spirit and soul, or the spirit perspective and the soul perspective, as I say, are either through music or through the metaphor of marriage itself. All fairy tales end in a marriage. More than that it's difficult to say. It's certainly true that Plotinus' flight from the alone to the Alone was an upwards journey towards the One, but he contradicts this throughout. Throughout he's very good on the soul. He's a masterful psychologist. People often read him as philosophy and are confused. But if you read him as psychology, much of the difficulty goes away, I think. That doesn't answer your question, does it Andrew?

APS: That's okay. It talks about my question. [laughter]

PH: The trouble is the question was too good. It's just a very difficult question. Yes, of course, I would argue that Plotinus subscribes to both perspectives, and *The Enneads* are full of what look like contradictions that in fact may turn out to be different emphases of the same thing.

APS: That distinction between soul and spirit was one of the things that attracted me to the Gnostics. Though there are some many different points of view. In some the soul is fashioned by the demiurge. I particularly like the *Exegesis of the Soul*, which ends with the soul and the bridegroom in the bridal chamber. But it has to be said that the experience of the soul when she falls down to Earth is very nasty. She's seduced by adulterers, she's made into a prostitute, consorts with thieves, and so on, until she repents and hears the call of the father and ends up in the bridal chamber. The Gnostic view of the soul is basically negative until the soul is reunited with the spirit. Could you comment on that?

PH: I couldn't really comment on that, Andrew, I'm not well enough versed in Gnostic literature. But I feel that it doesn't contradict my own view, because it's a bit like the myth of Eros and Psyche, which I cite. The idea that the soul's destiny is to suffer fully the pains of incarnation, the suffering of matter, to be embroiled in that, rather like the Christian incarnation. I'm not sure what the relationship of Gnosticism and Christianity is, but I know that Jesus appears in some Gnostic myths. I don't know whether it's an heretical branch of Christianity. I don't think

it is, I think Christians just called Gnosticism heretical because they couldn't accommodate it, but the Gnostic myths seem to me variations on the Christian myth. They're the variations that were subsequently outcast, and so they had to go underground. I would maintain that they re-emerged in the myths of science. The way of soul is not to declare anything heretical, but to dream the myth onward—that is, to allow all variations on the myth. But I digress. I'm very sympathetic to what little I know of the Gnostic universe, the idea of the soul suffering just as Psyche suffered. She had to suffer horribly before she could be reunited with Eros. Soul has to come to terms with the bitterness of death and mortality before it can be properly raised up again. Is that true of Gnosticism, do you think, of the Gnostic vision?

APS: Yes. Because the material world was created as a result of the fall of Sophia and the birth of the demiurge, there's often a feeling that this shouldn't have happened, and that the existence of the world is a bit of a problem. But in other views, for instance the Valentinian view, the whole process of God emanating and the fall is a process of God coming to know himself, though it's not stated very explicitly, the whole process of spirit becoming incarnated in matter, although it seems almost accidental, must be part of the whole divine process of God coming to know himself, and human beings doing the same. There has to be some purpose in incarnation which gives some possibility which doesn't exist when you're completely united with the godhead and everyone's in the pleroma and everything's happy. So, yes, I do agree with you there.

PH: It seems to me the best version of that myth is in fact the Christian version. Jung draws attention to the Book of Job. The Book of Job exemplifies how scandalous it is that God is removed from human experience, and that He's able to give Satan carte blanche to plague Job because Job is more righteous than he is. Jung says that it's a psychological necessity that after that He himself would have to appear on earth and suffer the full extent of human suffering and death, which he does through Jesus Christ.

That's the idea. If what you're saying about Gnosticism is the case, it seems to me that the Christian myth trumps it really. That's exactly what the incarnation of Christ is all about. It was about undergoing the full conditions of earthly existence so that there could no longer be any scandal about God being removed from his own creation. Do you see what I'm getting at?

APS: Yes, I do. In Gnostic myth Jesus is more of a revealer, an incarnated aeon who often doesn't have a genuinely physical body, from the docetic point of view, who is basically there to reveal the truth about the cosmic set-up and the myth and the condition of humanity. For instance, in the *Gospel of Judas* Jesus describes the whole Sethian myth to Judas, how there were the emanations and the luminaries and so on, and how the world came to be. While we're talking about Christianity and Gnosticism, I was quite struck by your admiration of the declaration of Jesus being both God and man. You find it admirably unliteral. I found that a very interesting view of it.

PH: All heresies, as Christians call them, all alternative myths, fall into two categories really. One says Christ is just only a man, and the other says that in fact he was a pure spirit who was not really a man. And the idea that you could come up with a creed that rejected both these solutions, and combined them in saying that he

was both absolute spirit, God himself, and also a man, is such an impossible paradox that it's very tempting to believe it. It's the impossibility of belief, or the absurdity as Tertullian put it—I believe it because it's so absurd—and indeed to the Greeks it was foolishness, and to the Jews it was blasphemy. I think that's the strength of Christianity, and hence I find that article of the creed very attractive. Having been very used to paradoxes of that kind through studying alchemy, and so on, it's the impossibility of ever attaining the red stone which is the Christian equivalent of the incarnation.

APS: Outside of actual Christian literature, Tertullian's statement and the dual nature of Christ are usually more or less ridiculed by commentators, so I enjoyed your point of view there.

PH: Exactly. It's impossible to believe. It is ridiculous, so that seems to be its strength, which requires something different from belief, which Christians call Faith. It's a kind of state of mind, a changing of your whole world view. That's what I like about it. I like impossible paradoxes. I'm very interested in Søren Kierkegaard, who always refers to Christ simply as "the paradox." He says, "Christ is the paradox which you can't think. He stymies all thought" So you have to be changed, you have to be transformed in some way, whereby you can embrace that paradox, and that change is what he called faith. I think that's an interesting way of defining faith, not as a kind of action that you perform, but a whole different world view that you have to embrace.

APS: You're working on a novel about Kierkegaard?

PH: I've been working on it for years. It's finished, but I have to find a publisher for it. I've got quite close, but it's more than people can follow. So I'm sitting there with this novel about Kierkegaard, but I can't find anyone to publish it, which is a shame. Kierkegaard is in a different category to people you read out of interest. You either change your life or you don't with Kierkegaard. I got very obsessed with him.

APS: I really enjoy your insight into myths, and your books have really some of my favourite interpretations of myths, You mentioned Cupid and Psyche, but there's also Sigurd, and Heracles. You do address a version of the Gnostic myth in *The Philosophers' Secret Fire*. It's actually a typical Valentinian myth. You relate it to the myth of scientisim, don't you?

PH: That's right. I was in two minds whether to put that in, because I realised I didn't know anything about Gnosticism

APS: It's an interesting comparison, anyway.

PH: I have read books on Gnosticism in the past, but I've been unable to retain much. The myth is so tortured and tortuous really, and so difficult, that I just find it so hard to get a handle on it. And also although there are elements of Christianity in there, and Neoplatonism, they're a right old mishmash, I do find them to be a bit Manichaean in their rejection of matter and this world. The whole burden of my thought really is that this world is absolutely essential. It is the earthly paradise. My vision would be much more Blakean. The question of seeing through the illusions of this world. The earthly paradise lies all around us, rather than elsewhere. We don't have to make the great astrological journey through space, confronting the star demons and so on. But nevertheless I put this myth in because I wanted to make the point that came to me in a flash. It's because I was obsessed with the

structural anthropologist Claude Lévi-Strauss. Reading Lévi-Strauss is like reading magic. You read myths that look completely different, and then he shows you how they are the same myth, but just with all the signs changed, as it were, and turned topsy-turvy. I suddenly realised that the Christian myth was just one variant of the ur-myth, of which the Gnostic myths were other variants. And that the Christian myth had completely broken the rules. Rather than allowing the imagination free play to riff on itself and to produce different variations of itself in a huge mythological loop, it had stopped the mythological process dead by insisting on the literal reality of itself, casting out all the Gnostic variations into outer darkness where they became merely heresy. And I thought, well if the repressed always returns in another guise, where have all these Gnostic myths gone? In what guise have they returned? And it seemed to me that they had returned in the myths of science. They were no longer wonderful imaginative extravaganzas about the cosmos, but as literalized versions of what the universe was like. That's why I put that Gnostic myth in and drew some fairly feeble parallels with modern scientific myths. I think modern science is an imaginative thing. It's an imaginative construct and shouldn't necessarily be taken literally. I'm fighting one long war against literalism really. And indeed, modern cosmology does sound like some sort of modern Gnostic myth, don't you think?

APS: Yes, I love all the strange ideas.

PH: Exactly. It's become fantastical. It seems very Gnostic to me, and I think that's where the Gnostic myths went. They went underground and re-emerged in science. But lo and behold, we take them all literally, as if they were the case. But I'm not sure that modern cosmology is any more the case than the old Gnostic myths are. That's to say they're true, but imaginatively, not literally.

APS: You have a fascinating critique of Darwinism too, as a myth, and the effect that it had on Darwin, who lost his early poetic appreciation of nature and whose mind ended up, in his own words as "a kind of machine for grinding laws out of large collections of facts."

PH: I got a lot of stick for that, yes. I did a short version of that chapter for *Fortean Times*. Do you know that magazine?

APS: Yes, I've written for it too.

PH: All the outraged Darwinists wrote in, saying I'd completely failed to understand Darwin. What I object to in Darwinism is: I don't object to the Darwinian account of creation as a myth but, as usual, I'm not sure it should be taken literally, and indeed, I find that there's not enough evidence for it, and I don't know why people keep insisting there is. I was watching David Attenborough talking us through the great chain of being that is Darwinism, and it comes to the moment when you've got somehow to describe how one genus turned into another genus. And of course the theory is that we have it with the archaeopteryx. And this is the moment, this is the great thing. And then he draws attention to some South American bird which has vestigial claws, and then he says, "And it's creatures like these that form the great chain between one genus and another." And I thought, hang about, these are only two examples and neither of them are at all good. They can both be explained in other ways. Darwinism, or the Darwinist view of the world, seems to me to rely on an act of faith. Because there just isn't enough evidence of transitional species. But whenever I say that people poo poo me and say, "Oh, there's masses of evidence." But I don't think there is. What you get is a lot of different species that are isolated in the fossil record, and Darwinists are constructing a chain out off them. But even so there isn't a very good chain. There ought to be masses of clearly defined chains of beasts turning from one thing into another, but there aren't really there's only the archaeopteryx, and as I point out, that has a very disreputable provenance. So I'm not convinced by Darwinism as a literal interpretation of how we come to be and, indeed, I point out that it is only a variant of a much older and more important myth where we have not risen up from animals but descended from divine beings. I think it's a literalization of the myth that our ancestors were all animals, which no one in the tribes who believe these myths takes literally. And I also see this clearly in Darwin's personal history. This episode I quoted in the rain forest, Darwin having an incredible imaginative vision of nature, which his Heraclean, Apollonian ego then panics in the face of, and he starts to try naming everything because the superabundance of it frightens him, like his own unconscious which continues to plague him all his life, causing him the most incredible emotional turmoil. He's clearly a tortured soul, and he's clearly a man who is repressing all sorts of things he can't face. Delightful and nice man though he was. So that was the burden of my attack. But it wasn't really an attack, it was more of a *jeu d'esprit*. I'm being asked to believe all these things, but what if I believe something else? That's why I say that it's not less reputable to believe in Darwinism than it is to say we're all descended from spacemen. I'm half joking, but I'm also trying to make the point that it's a myth. Should we be taking it as literally as we do?

APS: I don't know if you've ever read *Beelzebub's Tales to His Grandson* by Gurdjieff, but he has a chapter where he describes how every so often it becomes a burning issue to decide whether we're descended from the apes or the apes are descended from us. According to Beelzebub what actually happened is that at a time of worldwide disaster male and female humans were separated from each other. The men could satisfy themselves sexually by masturbating and having sex with each other, but this wasn't quite fulfilling enough for the women, so they took other animals as sexual partners. Because of the cosmic conditions of the time the women became pregnant and gave birth to apes. So apes are neither descended from humans not the ancestors of humans but are crossbreeds.

PH: That's very good, that's brilliant. I think it's just our resemblance to apes that has fooled everyone. It's just we look a bit like them. And they're always saying, well, we have nearly the same DNA, but we have nearly the same DNA as a flatworm. It doesn't really prove very much. So I'm sceptical.

APS: Your scepticism is noted. I find Darwinian evolution interesting, and I more-or-less go along with it, but it's one of these things that if you don't agree with it you're considered an intellectual pariah. So there is a lot of pressure to go along with it. It reminds me of the pressure to wear a poppy on Remembrance Day in Britain.

PH: Yes, exactly.

APS: Let's talk a little about your personal history. You said you were fascinated with Lévi-Strauss. Did you study anthropology? Was that your academic background?

PH: No. I read English.

APS: I was assuming that because Eileen in *Mercurius* read anthropology that actually you had.

PH: She did anthropology and archaeology at Cambridge, it turns out. But I did English. All the anthropology is just self-taught.

APS: I see. And your entry into this world of ideas that you've been exploring and experiencing was through Jung?

PH: Yes, absolutely.

APS: And James Hillman, the post-Jungian, seems to have been important to you. I see that he died recently.

PH: Yes, he died last week. I did meet him once, but only briefly. In *Mercurius* I was researching and reading about alchemy in order to make sense of it for about four years. One of the main things I was struggling with was the difference between soul and spirit. That was already an obsession for me in alchemy. And the day I sent off the manuscript of *Mercurius* I felt lovely and free and happy. I went into the local town in Salisbury where I was living and I went to the bookshop, and there was this shelf of books by a man named James Hillman, who I'd never heard of. It looked quite interesting, and I picked out one and I bought it and read it and then I went back and bought another and another and another. They seemed to stay on the shelves. And

a lot of things I'd been struggling with became clear to me, and he was much more articulate than I was. He had a great influence on me. I would say it was more in articulating things I was almost expressing myself. I suddenly came across the name Hillman and it suddenly seemed to be all there. He's cleverer than I am, and much more learned, so he was very important and he made certain distinctions which I'd been trying to make but hadn't quite managed to. He's been a great boon. I would say that Jung and Hillman and Kierkegaard are amongst my biggest influences. Along, of course, with the Neoplatonists and Plato. They're also huge. And of course all the alchemists. And romantic poets too. Blake has been a huge influence, and Yeats more than Blake. Gradually I managed to put all these people together. I realised there was a great golden chain of occult knowledge, that extended all the way from Plato to the Renaissance, the romantic poets, to Blake and then Yeats and then Jung, and then Hillman. And I'm very proud to think that I'm a tiny link in that golden chain. I haven't offered much that's original—well, there isn't anything original—but I've tried to articulate some of the truths of the golden chain in a modern way. Every generation has to try and articulate it in one way or another for themselves. So having been a tortured and tormented soul, completely unsure of what I should be doing in the world, the discovery of the golden chain, and realising that they were my people, where I belonged, my tribe, was a great happiness for me. So I know where I am now.

APS: You mentioned that you were involved in ufology?

PH: Yes. I was always interested in flying saucers as a boy. My Dad was interested in flying saucers. He had a lot of early books from the fifties. And I always used to wonder, what on earth were they, what's going on? And how come no one ever mentioned them, because I thought they were quite a challenge. Any vision of reality that one had, I thought, ought to include UFOs, otherwise it's not worth the candle. So *Daimonic Reality* was my attempt to include them in my worldview.

APS: I thought it worked really well. The similarities between that and fairy encounters, and all sorts of otherworldy apparitions

PH: It was an eye opener for me too. I realised you couldn't get rid of UFOs just by poopooing them or by having one theory about them. In a way, their absurdity is their strength, but the more you go into them the more you find not that they change, or that the mystery is solved, but that your worldview has changed. It forced me to consider all sorts of things that became crucial like: what's in the mind and what's out there? And what is reality? Does it lie somewhere between the psyche and the world? When I subsequently came across the Soul of the World and so on, which seemed to be both inside of us and outside of us simultaneously, this was a great blessing. I tussled with all these problems while considering what kind of reality UFOs represented. A lot of ufologists have found that. Some of them just get stuck on one hypothesis, such as they're all spacemen, or insist that they're all hallucinations, but there are a lot of enlightened ufologists who have followed where the UFOs lead, and the more you try and iron out the paradoxes, the more you're led into all sorts of strange realms. Esoteric philosophy, and so on. You end up like that fellow Andy Collins who started psychic questing and doing UFOs, and he was just a sales rep from Essex, and now he's an Egyptologist studying Babylonian fragments and subatomic physics. In fact, studying UFOs with an open mind is a really good initiation into a completely different visionary worldview, a more poetic one actually.

APS: And your father was Irish, was he? Anglo Irish?

PH: My Dad was Irish, yes. He came to England when he was a lad. He was the son of a Church of Ireland clergyman, as were his grandfather and great-grandfather. So they were what the English call Anglo-Irish, but what the Irish call English.

APS: It's like that Brendan Behan comment, an Anglo-Irishman is an Englishman with a horse.

There ought to be the reverse term for Irishmen living in England: Hiberno-English.

PH: Yes, there ought to be. So that was that, and my mother was English but was raised in France. Her mother was a very good medium, so my mother was very interested in spiritualism, which she imparted to us children. So I was always interested in spiritualism as well, and read a lot of spiritualist books in my teens, and that definitely fed into my work. Although I got rather disenchanted with spiritualist literature because it has so many shortcomings—it's either preachy or banal—at the same time I never doubted the existence of spirits and of an afterlife. So that would definitely be part of my background.

APS: You mentioned that the alchemists were a big influence on you, and I've just this week finished *Mercurius*, which was really wonderful. I can't resist being literal and asking you if you were ever involved in an attempt at the actual great work?

PH: I wasn't, no. No, I couldn't do the chemistry.

APS: Although your descriptions of what's happening inside the pelican apparatus are very allusive, because they're written in alchemical language, you really do give the feeling that there's something going on, something happening both physically and in the realm of soul. But you read the alchemists an awful lot when you were researching that?

PH: Yes, but it was his [the vicar John Smith] description not mine, remember? In order to arrange it properly and edit it, I had to read a lot of alchemy, yes.

APS: And I have your earlier two novels waiting on my shelves.

PH: Well, those are out of print. I did odd jobs for years so I could read people like Jung. And I wrote poetry. I wanted to be a poet but it turned out I was crap at it, which was a bit of a blow. So I got a job in publishing as a hack. It was a packaging company and they package books for publishers. That is to say, picture books for non-readers. So I packaged books for them and I dropped my standards,. But an agent contacted me, and she was a very cut-throat agent, and said that my father had sent her some short stories I had written. She was in fact a very remote relation. And she summoned me and said I could definitely write a book. You can have sex, violence or the supernatural, which do you want? And I said, well first of all I have no plans to write a book, secondly I don't know anything about sex or violence. So I chose the supernatural. So she said, well go away and write one and I'll sell it. So I put it out of my mind, but by this time I was so sick of doing hack work anyway that I thought, well I may as well do some hack work for myself. A plot came to me in the bath fully-fledged. It was the time when the Pope was visiting England, for the first time ever, and I had been reading *The Holy Blood and the Holy Grail*, and I thought, what if there's a bunch of Cathars in England posing as orthodox monks when the Pope comes to visit, and they do some awful thing to him in order to reinstate Catharism. So I sketched this plot down and I wrote a couple of chapters and she flogged it to the Americans. So I was in business. So I wrote this bloody book, and it's been easily my most successful. But after that of course I got delusions of grandeur, because it's not really a book, more of a film really, a thriller. A very good English editor said, well that's all very well, but why don't you write a proper book? So I got delusions of grandeur and my second book, *The Rapture*, was a much more serious attempt to write a proper novel, and of course it did commensurately much worse than the first. And then he commissioned me to write a third, and by this time I'd got hold of the *Mercurius* papers and disappeared for four years. By the time I presented them to him he was appalled, naturally. And that was the last book I published with Macmillan. I was cast into the outer darkness after that. I don't think it had any reviews, but the publishers sent it out to whole loads of people who I thought would be congenial to it, and they all wrote to me with little appreciative notes which I extracted and put on my website, so it looks as if I had a lot of good reviews. People like Colin Wilson and

Charles Nicholl and John Michell, who I was in touch with. But in terms of actual reviews in periodicals there were only two I think. Which is two more than I get now.

APS: You also do occasional courses.

PH: Yeah. Well, it started out with Jules Cashford, who's a Jungian analyst. She wrote a book with Ann Baring called *The Myth of the Goddess*, and also a book about the moon, called *The Moon: Myth and Image*, which is fantastic. Anyway, she's a mythographer, and I've known her ages. And we're always being asked to talk at places, and we hate talking, and we never get any money for it. So we thought, if we have to talk, why don't we set up our own course, and ask for money. And we've done quite a few now—we've done about ten, I suppose, and they're going quite well. We usually do them in the spring and the autumn, but we're not doing one this autumn because she's abroad. But we're doing one next Easter, from 6-8 April, details on the website. And it's about the daimonic really. We give talks,. She's more visual so she gives illustrated talks. Then we have jaunts into the Dorset countryside, looking at sacred sites and fonts and standing stones, and things like that. So it's two days of talks and outings. Mysteries. You can't really workshop my stuff. I suppose we could run initiation courses where we bury people in shallow graves in the woods. [laughter] The website is www.mysticimagination.info

APS: I wanted to ask you about your own otherworld experiences. Do you have many personal experiences that you may or may not be willing to relate?

PH: I'd be perfectly willing to, Andrew, but I'm not really what people would call psychic, though I have seen a couple of ghosts—but everyone has seen ghosts. My otherworld experiences have been of the imaginative sort. Very, very stirring, but completely internal and mundane. Finding insight into the nature of Mercurius, or something. But it wouldn't be considered an otherworldy experience. It would be considered quite a normal experience, but for me it was rather abnormal. But I haven't had any great visions. Well, I say that. I don't know, but when I was young, in my twenties, I did a lot of meditating, thinking I'm bloody well not going to get a job, I'm going to sit here till I get a vision of ultimate truth. I thought there's no good in getting a job, is there, till you've sorted out the nature of reality. I did a lot of meditating and I did have a lot of out of the body experience, but I think that's fairly usual too, but it was fairly interesting to me, and fairly illuminating, but not very generally interesting I think. But no, I've never seen a UFO, though I long to. Also, Dorset is chock-a-block with huge black panthers roaming the countryside. My sister has written a book about that. She's the world authority on mystery big cats. I've failed to see one of those, even though they're more often seen in Dorset than a pig even. Have you had any interesting experiences, Andrew, any unusual things, visions?

APS: In my childhood I sometimes had these experiences where I suddenly experienced unity and a very different feeling of self and a feeling that I knew my purpose in the world. I was involved in a version of the Gurdjieff-Ouspensky work for much of my adult life, and while I had many other experiences of various kinds I viewed them in the context of the Gurdjieff-Ouspensky system, so I won't really talk about those. When I was reading *Daimonic Reality* I was asking myself what other unusual experiences I could remember. One was when I was at university in Swansea. I was walking through some woods at dusk in Winter, on my way to deliver an essay or something, when I saw these faces of quite dark-skinned, long-faced men coming at me out the woods. But I had a very bad hangover and it's easily explained, at least on a literal level, as a case of the DTs! And I was living alone in Aberystwyth—I had a little room on the seafront—in the 1990s. I'd been reading a biography of the Welsh poet Alun Lewis, who had lived in Aberystwyth and had died in India in the Second World War. His death had been accounted for as an accident but it may have been suicide. At the end of this book they had a transcription of a séance in which Alun Lewis was brought through and he dictated a few lines which sounded very like his poetry. I had a strong reaction when I was reading this, that it shouldn't have been included in the book, which was otherwise an ordinary literary biography. Then I started to get the feeling that if I allowed him, Alun Lewis would dictate his poetry through me and all I had to do was accept him, take a pen and let him write through me. I was quite spooked out by this, so I went out for a walk and washed some dishes to dispel the feeling and ground myself. A few weeks later I was describing this to a friend who was visiting with me, and as I was talking about the experience there were knocks on a water pipe in the room, something that I had never heard before and didn't hear again.

PH: That's well spooky, yeah. Obviously you had a link with him, that's very interesting.

APS: Well, I really enjoyed talking to you, Patrick.

PH: Well, it's nice to speak to another truth seeker.

Sorita d'Este

Woman was the Altar
The Wiccan Great Rite: Sex, Tea and Religion

"Assist me to erect the ancient altar, at which in days past all worshipped, the great altar of all things. For in old times woman was the altar. Thus was the altar made and placed."

The Book of Shadows

Magic, religion and sex; potent words which, when combined, often evoke strong emotional feelings and reactions in the repressed, religiously indoctrinated, socially inhibited and close-minded. Even in these times of mass media, which has desensitised western society in so many ways, even just to mention sex magic often causes startling reactions fuelled by misapprehensions. Thus the idea of the 'Great Rite', a central mystery in traditions of initiatory Wicca, with its magical and religious overtones reaching their zenith in the act of sexual union, has been at the root of many debates and rumours. Misunderstandings exist not just in secular society, but also within the magical and pagan communities about this ceremony, and quite possibly rightly so.

Today there are many different traditions of practice which use the term 'Wicca' to describe themselves and within the context of this paper I am using the term to refer specifically to the esoteric traditions in which members can trace their initiatory lineage to Gerald Gardner, 'Gardnerian', or Alex and Maxine Sanders, 'Alexandrian', or who otherwise practice an initiatory form of the tradition which closely follows the practices, beliefs and liturgy taught in the Gardnerian and Alexandrian traditions. Within these traditions there are three initiations, each of which takes place after a period of study and practice, though there are significant differences in how the degrees are bestowed, as well as in regards to the requirements for a candidate to be deemed suitable or ready for advancement to the next degree, due to the decentralised nature of the tradition. The liturgies for each of the three initiations are contained in the *Book of Shadows*, which is a book of rituals and spells, copied by an initiate from their initiator. The origins of the majority of these rituals has been shown[1] to originate in the books of the medieval grimoire tradition, Christian liturgy and Freemasonry, embellished with generous helpings of the writings of the infamous British occultist Aleister Crowley and that of Charles Leland, an American anthropologist.

For the textual analysis of the Great Rite which follows I have used public domain versions[2] of the text based on original manuscript copies of Gerald Gardner's *Book of Shadows*. Of course minor textual differences between the handwritten copies of different initiates will exist, but for the purposes of this paper such differences are not relevant as we are concerned with the precedents and origins of the rituals, rather than its development in initiatory covens subsequently.

By its very nature the Great Rite is one of the most private ceremonies of the Wiccan tradition and it is usual for all members of the coven to turn their backs or leave the circle when it is being performed in 'actuality', that is as a sexual consummation, rather than in 'token', that is its symbolic form without sexual consummation. The Great Rite is performed by a High Priestess and High Priest who are performing it as part of their elevation to the Third Degree, or who have already attained the Third Degree and who are performing the ceremony for another purpose, such as celebration or consecration. As an act of sexual union it is performed only between two consenting adults and ordinarily such a couple will also be sexual partners outside of the context of magical work. Traditionally the ritual is designed for use between a man and a woman, rather than two people of the same sex. Arguments for and against the enactment of this ritual by two individuals of the same-sex abound and debate is likely to continue on the subject for some years.[3]

In preparation for the Great Rite the altar will be set up according to tradition, the magic circle will be cast, and the guardians of the Watchtowers will be evoked to guard and witness proceedings. All participants will be admitted to the circle and all other celebration, worship or work will be done and completed before the enactment of the Great Rite begins,

Magus: Ere we proceed with this sublime degree, I must beg purification at thy hands.

The High Priestess then proceeds to perform the purification, which traditionally involves binding the Magus and then tying him to the altar. She then scourges him, a total of forty strokes admitted in batteries of three, seven, nine and twenty-one, a sequence and total number given a number of rites in the *Book of Shadows* with the purpose of attaining purification. When she is done, he is untied and the process is repeated on her by the Magus, after which a eucharistic feast of wine and cakes are shared between all present.

Gerald Gardner, who is known by some as the 'Father of Wicca' provides the first published account of this method of scourging in his novel *High Magic's Aid*, "Thou first must be purified.

Taking the scourge from the Altar, she struck his buttocks, first three, then seven, then nine, then twenty one strokes with the scourge".[4] The use of flagellation for the purpose of purification seems to hark back to the medieval Christian flagellants who used self-inflicted pain to alter consciousness and purify their souls, though there are also recorded examples of where the initiates of a medieval witch coven was allegedly scourged by the Devil during ceremonies. It is however not completely clear from the accounts as to what the exact purpose of the scourging in these medieval covens was, other than the possibility that it might have been as punishment for disobedience. In one example from 1678, one Katherine Liddel of Scotland claimed, amongst other things, "that he (the devil) was cold to the touch, and his breath like a damp air, and that he scourged them oft, and was a most 'wicked and barbarous master.'"[5] Within the tradition different reasons are given for the relevance of the total number of forty strokes, the most common being that it corresponds to the number of knots on a traditional scourge, for example five knots each on the eight strands of the scourge, the eight representing a concept known as the 'eight paths to power' multiplied by five, five being the points of the pentagram.

An interesting precedent for the forty strokes with the scourge can be found in the Bible, when St Paul says, "Of the Jews five times received I forty stripes save one."[6] The canonical laws of the time prohibited the use of more than forty strokes and in an effort to avoid any violation of the law by mistake it was common practice to give one stroke less. It was furthermore customary for the person who was being punished to be tied to a low pillar for the duration of the scourging to ensure that they would be forced to lean forward, a practice echoed in Wicca. Cyprian, in his third-century work *The Life of Caesarius Arelatensis*, describes this practice. It is then, as an aside to note, that after Solomon, Cyprian was probably the most attributed author of magical grimoires including the black book *Clavis Inferni, Keys to Hell*, which provides instructions for the control of the demon princes of the four cardinal directions.

Clearly however, the use of bondage and flagellation also allows for parallels with erotic BDSM to be drawn, with the roles of dominance and submission being interchangeable. It has been suggested that the use of this technique could be credited to a sadomasochistic preference held by Gerald Gardner for its use to raise magical power. This popular notion can in part be supported by the fact that the use of the scourge, flagellation, bondage and sexual energies are central to many of the rituals presented in Gardner's *Book of Shadows*. It is also ironic that these practices, which are so central to the initiatory tradition taught by Gardner, have been whitewashed out of the public image of the initiatory traditions and are nearly non-existent in the exoteric traditions. In fact, adherents to the pop-culture Wiccan traditions are often surprised and appalled by the idea of any form of ritual nudity, bondage or scourging, being unaware of its importance in the traditional rites. Then the rite continues,

Magus: Now I must reveal to you a great Mystery.

The High Priestess assumes what is known as the 'Osiris Position', standing naked with her scourge and ritual wand, her arms crossed over her chest. The Magus kisses her on the lips. The Magus now declares the body of the High Priestess, who in this rite is the representative of the Goddess, as being the altar for the ritual,

Magus: Assist me to erect the Ancient Altar, at which in days past all worshipped, the Great Altar of all things. For in the old times a woman was the Altar. Thus was the altar made and placed.

The High Priestess now lies down in the centre of the circle, in the pentagram position.[7] If there is a coven present, an assistant may cover her with a veil.

There are some noteworthy parallels here between the practices in Wicca and those found in the Preliminary Mass of Gold, the first initiation ritual into the Brotherhood of the Golden Arrow,[8] a mystical sex magic order founded by Maria de Naglowska in 1931 in Paris. In the Preliminary Mass of Gold the Priestess lies down in a west-east orientation, the Priestess blesses the wine, which is held by a male and the cup is placed on her genitalia, all of which are echoed in the rites taught by Gerald Gardner two decades later. The Brotherhood of the Golden Arrow was a mystical Gnostic sex magic order, who amongst other things celebrated the mysteries of both the masculine and feminine divine in their rites, primarily as Lucifer and Satan as the masculine, and the Mother and Sophia as the feminine. Their focus on Lucifer and Satan, as well as explicit sex magic practices, gave rise to the popular suggestion that they were a Satanic order.

Contemporary to the public emergence of Wicca, this idea of woman as the altar is prominently found in the writings of Dion Fortune's novel *The Sea Priestess*, where the hero Wilfred Maxwell has a soliloquy about his fiancé Molly saying:

When the body of a woman is made an altar for the worship of the Goddess who is all beauty and magnetic life, and the man pours himself out in worship and sacrifice, keeping back no part of the price but giving his very self for love, seeing in his mate the priestess serving with him in the worship - then the Goddess enters the temple.[9]

Fortune was likely to have been inspired by earlier esoteric works in her writing and the same sources may have also influenced the flow of ideas which culminated in the Great Rite. One such influential text, *La Sorcière*, written by the French historian Jules Michelet in 1862, argued that witchcraft had been the original religion of Europe. Michelet, on describing the preparations undertaken by the witch, declared, "With equal solemnity she purifies her person. Henceforth she is the living altar of the shrine."[10] Michelet presented a model of a nature and fertility cult, which was led by priestesses and had managed to survive and flourish underground during the Middle Ages as a sanctuary for oppressed women. Michelet's work laid the groundwork for later writers and anthropologists, such as Charles Godfrey Leland and Margaret Murray, both of whose work would be highly influential on the emergence of Wicca. In addition to emphasising the character of the witch as a positive figure, Michelet also cited the idea of the naked body of the witch as the altar, writing that, "At the Witches' Sabbath woman fulfils every office. She is priest, and altar, and consecrated host."[11]

In doing so Michelet may in turn have been drawing on accounts from the witch trials and the famous case of 'La Voisin', a major French scandal of the seventeenth century. In 1679 one of King Louis XIV's mistresses, Madame de Mountespan, enlisted the aid of Catherine Monvoisin, known as *La Voisin*, an infamous sorceress and poisoner. Both the women played the part of altar for black masses performed by Abbé Guiborg, a renegade Catholic priest. Noteworthy in the descriptions of these events are that, "as often as the priest was to kiss the altar, he kissed the body,"[12] and "at the end of the Mass, the priest went into the woman."[13] As a side-note of interest here is that the women were described as holding black candles in their hands during the ceremony and that the chalice would be placed upon their naked bellies, a practiced echoed in the Great Rite when consecrations are performed, and it is interesting to consider these similarities in the light of constant denial on the part of Wicca that it has any associations with Satanism.

Magus: And the sacred place was the point within the centre of the circle, as we of old times have been taught, that the point within the centre is the origin of all things. Therefore should we adore it. [The Magus kisses the High Priestess on her pubic area]

Here the reference to 'the point within the centre of the circle' is most likely a reference to the sun, the symbol of which is a circle with a dot in the centre. This is then also a symbolic reference to the phallus of the male, who as the channel for the god of the tradition also represents the sun, which will join in an act of sexual union with the Priestess in the centre of the circle, their union being the 'origin of all things' as it is through sexual union that new life is created.

Therefore, whom we adore, we also invoke, by the power of the lifted lance. [Invokes], O circle of stars [kiss], whereof our Father is but the younger brother [kiss], Marvel beyond imagination, soul of infinite space, before whom time is ashamed, the mind bewildered and understanding dark, not unto thee may we attain unless thine image be of love [kiss].

This section of the liturgy is drawn directly from the Gnostic Mass by Aleister Crowley, where the original text reads:

"Thee therefore whom we adore we also invoke, by the power of the lifted lance."[14]

"O circle of stars whereof our Father is but the younger brother, marvel beyond imagination, soul of infinite space, before whom Time is ashamed, the mind bewildered, and the understanding dark, not unto Thee may we attain, unless Thine image be Love."[15]

Crowley wrote the Gnostic Mass, which is also known as *Liber XV*, whilst travelling in Moscow and would later write about it in his autobiography saying that,

> I wished therefore to construct a ritual through which people might enter into ecstasy as they have always done under the influence of appropriate ritual. In recent years, there has been an increasing failure to attain this object, because the established cults shock their intellectual convictions and outrage their common sense. Thus their minds criticize their enthusiasm; they are unable to consummate the union of their individual souls with the universal soul as a bridegroom would be to consummate his marriage if his love were constantly reminded that its assumptions were intellectually absurd.[16]

Much of the symbolism of the Gnostic Mass is sexual, and although it is not stated, a note to the Gnostic Mass by Crowley implies that the priest and priestess engage in sex magic after the rite is over and the congregation departed.[17] Crowley wrote, "Certain secret formulae of this Mass are taught to the Priest in his Ordination,"[18] which fits with his emphasis on the 9° heterosexual union of the Ordo Templi Orientis, also referred to as the O.T.O., and again parallels the practice in Wicca where the coven usually leaves the circle if there is to be sexual consummation.

> Therefore, by seed and root, and stem and bud and leaf and flower and fruit do we invoke thee.

This was also in part inspired by Crowley's Gnostic Mass, which contains the phrase, "By seed and root and stem and bud and leaf and flower and fruit do we invoke Thee."[19] Crowley in turn took his inspiration in writing this piece from the poem *Song of Proserpine* by the early nineteenth century poet Percy Bysshe Shelley,

> Sacred Goddess, Mother Earth,
> Thou from whose immortal bosom
> Gods and men and beasts have birth,
> Leaf and blade, and bud and blossom,
> Breathe thine influence most divine
> On thine own child, Proserpine.[20]

The ritual then continues,

> Magus: O, Queen of space, O dew of light, O continuous one of the Heavens [kiss]. Let it be ever thus, that men speak not of Thee as one, but as none, and let them not speak of thee at all, since thou art continuous, for thou art the point within the circle [kiss], which we adore [kiss], the fount of life without which we would not be [kiss].

Some of the wording here is again drawn from Aleister Crowley, this time from his channelled text the *Book of the Law*, where it relates to the Ancient Egyptian stellar goddess Nuit, "O Nuit, continuous one of heaven, let it be ever thus, that men speak not of Thee as one but as none; and let them not speak of Thee at all, since Thou art continuous!"[21]

The Magus now performs an eightfold kiss, which marks eight points which when joined together produces the symbol used to represent the Third Degree in Wicca, being that of an upright pentagram with a triangle on top of it on the body of the High Priestess, with the five points of the pentagram being the feet, knees and genitalia and that of the triangle, the breasts and lips. This is the same pattern followed during the fivefold kiss which is usually performed by the Magus on the High Priestess whilst she stands or sits on the altar in preparation for the ceremony of Drawing Down the Moon, in which she becomes a vessel for the Divine and for initiations.

Superimposing this symbol formed by the kisses on the Qabalistic Tree of Life provides us with one of the many layers of symbolism found in the Great Rite. The points of the upward pointing triangle correspond to the Supernal Triad on the Tree of Life, comprised of the Sephiroth of Kether at the top, Chokmah at the bottom right and Binah at the bottom left. These Sephiroth correspond to the pure divine source with Kether, meaning 'Crown', Chokmah, 'Wisdom', as the masculine divine, and Binah, 'Understanding', as the feminine divine. The five points of the pentagram correspond to more of the Sephiroth, these being Daath, 'Knowledge', at the top; Chesed, 'Mercy', at the upper right; Netzach, 'Victory', at the lower right; Hod, 'Splendour', at the lower left; and Geburah, 'Strength', at the upper left.

These Sephiroth have planetary attributions, but it is their elemental attributions which are particularly relevant here. Chesed corresponds to Water, Netzach to Earth, Hod to Air and Geburah to Fire, providing a complete balanced group of the four elements. Daath, which is a pseudo-sephira and has some of the properties of a sephira, equates to Spirit and also occupies the position of gateway on the Tree of Life between the supernal Triad and the seven lower Sephiroth, which represent increasingly tangible levels of divine manifestation. The three Sephiroth which are left out of this sequence are particularly significant in Wicca, being Tiphereth, 'Beauty', which is solar; Yesod, 'Foundation', which is lunar' and Malkuth, 'Kingdom', which represents the kingdom of the four elements, or in other words the earth. However, it could be argued that the Great Rite represents the union of the polarity of female and male, which in Wicca is equated to the moon and sun, and the act of union is one of manifestation equating to Malkuth. Thus the missing Sephiroth could be seen not as missing, but rather as the participants and the act of the Great Rite itself.

Following the symbol being marked by kisses, the ceremony continues,

Magus: And in this way truly are erected the Holy Twin Pillars Boaz and Joachim [kisses breasts]. In beauty and strength were they erected, to the wonder and glory of all men.

This line is heavy with qabalistic symbolism and could have been inspired by the work of any of the contemporary traditions and writers at the end of the nineteenth and beginning of the twentieth century. Occult authors, such as Levi, Papus, Mathers and Fortune, all wrote about the Qabalah and used a great deal of Qabalistic imagery in their work, but it is most likely that the inspiration came once again from Aleister Crowley and his Gnostic Mass. In this rite, the Priestess is seated naked on the altar, between the Black and White pillars. Boaz and Jachim are the two pillars in the porch of the temple of Solomon, which are equated to the black and white pillars of the Tree of Life. These are the Black Pillar of Severity, the Goddess, and White Pillar of Mercy, the God, of the Tree of Life. The Black Pillar of Severity is on the left and the White Pillar of Mercy is on the right. The Middle Pillar of Balance represents the gateway to the temple, the entranceway to the Mysteries. This symbolism is also clearly expressed in the High Priestess tarot card in the Rider Waite deck. This deck, which was first published in 1910, was illustrated by the magical artist Pamela Colman-Smith. In this trump card the High Priestess is seated on an altar between the two pillars, with the black pillar on the viewer's left and the white pillar on the viewer's right. The pillars are marked with the letters 'B' and 'J' respectively, representing Boaz and Jachim.

Qabalistic symbolism permeates Wiccan liturgy, practice and beliefs, though often practitioners today seem to be totally unaware of its omnipotent presence in their workings. It is, for example the symbolism of the Black and White Pillars as representing feminine and masculine that determines the placing of the symbols or statues of the Wiccan deities on the altar, with the Goddess on the left and the God being placed on the right. The unnamed Middle Pillar of Balance between the Black and White Pillars corresponds to the centre line of a person, with the Sephiroth equating to the crown, Kether and pure divinity; the heart, Tiphereth and the sun; the genitalia, Yesod and the moon; and the feet, Malkuth as the four elements.

Another significant reference, which can be seen in part of the ritual text, is to the Ethical Triad, which are the three Sephiroth of Chesed, Geburah and Tiphereth in the middle of the Tree of Life. The words 'Beauty', 'Strength' and 'Glory' refer to the Sephiroth which comprise this Triad. The name of the Sephira of Tiphereth means 'Beauty', Geburah means 'Strength', and the alternative name commonly used for Chesed is Gedulah, which means 'Glory'. This is not the upward pointing triangle of the Third Degree symbol, rather it is the downward pointing triangle of manifestation of divine power, reflecting the divine union of the Supernal Triad, comprised of the Sephiroth of Kether, Chokmah, which crowns the White Pillar and Binah which crowns the Black Pillar.

At this point in the ritual any members of the coven who are present will leave the circle if the ritual is to be consummated in sexual intercourse. The Magus then continues,

O Secrets of secrets that art hidden in the being of all lives. Not thee do we adore, for that which adoreth is also thou. Thou art that and That am I [kiss].

Again this line of the liturgy is taken from Crowley's Gnostic Mass, where the original reads, "O secret of secrets that art hidden in the being of all that lives, not Thee do we adore, for that which adoreth is also Thou. Thou art That, and That am I."[22] This statement affirms the presence of the Divine within the Magus and the High Priestess, expressing a view which is echoed in other rites in the *Book of Shadows*, such as the Charge of the Goddess,

I am the flame that burns in every man, and in the core of every star [kiss]. I am Life and the giver of Life, yet therefore is the knowledge of me the Knowledge of

Death [kiss]. I am alone, the Lord within ourselves whose name is Mystery of Mysteries [kiss].

The rite continues with these words, again taken from the work of Aleister Crowley, where the original text refers to Hadit, the male principle in the context of the original text. Here then the Magus is essentially declaring his own divinity by identifying himself with Hadit. The original text reads, "I am the flame that burns in every heart of man, and in the core of every star. I am life and the giver of life, yet therefore is the knowledge of me the knowledge of death…[23] I am alone: there is no god where I am."[24] The eighteenth century Masonic tract *The Grand Mystery Lodge* Laid Open, 1726, described the 'five points of fellowship' where bodies should touch during the ritual embrace, as "foot to foot, knee to knee, breast to breast, hand to back, cheek to cheek."[25] This is clearly the origin of the use of this term in the Great Rite ceremony, though it is not identical. Here we should however clarify that the five points of fellowship from a Masonic viewpoint are defined as part of the work undertaken by a Mason. In Masonry, as in Wicca, the five-points of fellowship are represented by the symbol of the pentagram. For the Mason, this may also represent the five wounds of Christ when he was crucified at Golgotha.

The reference of 'lance to grail' is undoubtedly, taking into consideration the sheer quantity of material borrowed from it, a reference to the use of a lance and cup in the Gnostic Mass. However, it can also be interpreted as being a reference to the lance and grail of Arthurian legend, perhaps in an effort to imply Celtic mysteries and myths on which many, including Gardner, were keen to associate themselves with. In doing so the emphasis is then superficially moved to the sexual symbolism of the union of the lance and grail, but becomes an issue for Wiccans who feel anger towards the Church and Christianity as the symbolism of the lance and grail is in reality a reference to the blood of Christ, with its origins in the legend where Joseph of Arimathea used the grail to collect Christ's blood after his side was pierced by the lance when he was hanging on the cross, and is therefore a symbol of the blood and flesh of the man-god of Christianity in this context.

Another point worth noting here is that in one of the early Books of Shadow texts written by Gerald Gardner, the text instead reads "genitalia to genitalia"[26] and it would seem therefore that the use of 'lance to grail' was a conscious decision on the part of Gerald Gardner or one of his colleagues in the early stages of the Gardnerian movement. This might have been in an effort to be inclusive of those who did not wish to, or for some reason could not, consummate the rite in actually, but who preferred celebrating it in a symbolic form instead. Alternatively, it might have been that at this stage there was a need to try and whitewash the practices in an effort to separate it from the other similar sex magic practices that were considered Satanic, which is just as likely when you take into consideration the level of media interaction which was sought by Gerald Gardner and some other early Gardnerians of the period who were trying to, and had some success in doing so, promote the idea that Wicca was a survival of a nature loving pagan religion, rather than the forgotten child of magical practices steeped in Judaic-Christian symbolism, or worse that of traditions considered to be Satanic!

The ritual union is then enacted by the Magus and High Priestess in the circle, who conclude the rite by declaring in unison,

Magus and High Priestess: Encourage our hearts, Let thy Light crystallize itself in our blood, fulfilling us of Resurrection, for there is no part of us that is not of the Gods.

Not surprisingly even this last part of the ritual text is taken from Crowley's Gnostic Mass, where the original reads, "Make open the path of creation and of intelligence between us and our minds. Enlighten our understanding. Encourage our hearts. Let Thy light crystallize itself in our blood, fulfilling us of Resurrection."[27]

Although Wiccans often try to present a clean-cut image of Wicca to the public and to other traditions within the wider magical community, it contains numerous practices which present causes for concern. Firstly, by its nature, as a Mystery tradition the practices, beliefs and rituals of a coven are considered oath-bound and private. The tradition also employs the use of both flagellation and bondage as part of its rituals, blindfolds are used during initiation rites and rituals are often performed skyclad. These things alone, before we enter into the realms of ritualised sex, are enough for comparisons to be made with BDSM and other fetish practices, with their leanings towards dominance and control.

The use of flagellation and bondage hints at something dangerous and forbidden, the idea of men and women dancing around skyclad, unashamed of their nudity, combined with ideas of horned gods and magic awakens a primal fear of losing control and being helpless within the minds of those who have been conditioned to the modern world, whilst also being visually stimulating and exciting. The combination of fear and titillation in turn transforming into to feelings of guilt and self-loathing, which provides the fuel for the attention given by the media for these aspects of the practices of Wicca. This has fuelled many misapprehensions through the media portrayals of Wicca, and understandably so. After all, there can't be many parents who would feel comfortable with the idea that their teenagers are running around naked in the woods with other naked men and women, worshipping phallic gods with horns, and moon goddesses who are unashamedly sensual, with the knowledge that they will also be blindfolded, tied up and scourged! No amount of reassurance that this is a 'religion' is likely to put their minds at ease.

So then it is only natural that initiates of the tradition, especially those who are keen on gaining a positive image of Wicca in the media and a wider acceptance of it as a religion within the wider community, have sought to exorcise the idea of sex magic from the public image of the tradition and instead focusing on the symbolic ideas of union, as well as drawing comparisons with the historical *Hieros Gamos*, 'Sacred Marriage', and also with Tantra, which they consider to be more acceptable to the general public from whom they seek acceptance.

The Great Rite is often described as *Hieros Gamos*, the sacred marriage of the Priestess and Priest, the Goddess and the God, and Wiccans take the view that this rite has its origins in sacred marriage rites, which they believed took place all over the ancient world. Controversially however, whilst there are some scholars who argue that the *Hieros Gamos* was a widespread phenomenon, others argue that the evidence for this claim is lacking and that it might not have existed at all, or that if it did it was a very rare and unique practice.

The oldest and best known historical example of *Hieros Gamos* is that celebrating the goddess Inanna in ancient Sumer. The second millennium B.C.E. text called *The Joy of Sumer*, describes a ritualised union between the queen, who acts as the priestess representing the goddess Inanna and the king as representative of the shepherd god Dumuzi. In it the people first prepare the bridal bed with sweet-smelling cedar oil, arranging rushes and spreading a sheet over the bed. We are then told that the queen, that is Inanna, bathes herself with soap in preparation for Dumuzi, the king, who then joins her thus,

> The king goes with lifted
> head to the holy loins,
> Dumuzi goes with lifted head
> to the holy loins of Inanna.
> He lies down beside her on the bed.
> Tenderly he caresses her,
> murmuring words of love:
> O my holy jewel! O my wondrous Inanna!

> After he enters her holy vulva,

> causing the queen to rejoice,
> After he enters her holy vulva,
> causing Inanna to rejoice,
> Inanna holds him to her and murmurs:
> O Dumuzi, you are truly my love.[28]

The people then make offerings, which include food and the burning of juniper resin as incense after which they perform rites. At this point the union of Inanna and Dumuzi culminates, as the narrative continues,

> The king embraces his beloved bride.
> Dumuzi embraces Inanna.
> Inanna, seated on the holy
> throne, shines like daylight.
> The king, like the sun, shines
> radiantly by her side.
> He arranges abundance, lushness,
> and plenty before her.
> He assembles the people of Sumer.[29]

The festivities and rites conclude with feasting and the honouring of Inanna as the 'First Daughter of the Moon', 'Lady of the Evening'[30] and the 'Joy of Sumer',[31] showing the emphasis placed here not only on the actual union between the priestess and king, but also the emphasis placed on honouring the goddess as being the bestower of joy and plenty through the feast. Some of the descriptions given of Inanna in this text are also later echoed in the descriptions given to other goddesses, including that of the Shekinah in Jewish mysticism, who is also implicated in acts of sacred sex in medieval Kabbalistic texts and commentaries.

Whilst superficially there are parallels between the sacred marriage of Inanna and Dumuzi and the Great Rite, the rituals have little in common other than the idea that the man embodies the god and the female the goddess, and that they then join in an act of sexual union. It is however possible to see how this ancient practice could have been a source of inspiration for some of the symbolism found in the Great

Rite. There is also a difference in purpose, as the Great Rite is used for different purposes and is not celebrating the mysteries or mythic cycle of particular historical deities, whereas the 'sacred marriage' is part of an established mythic cycle and cosmology.

There has been a move in recent years by initiates and scholars towards making comparisons between the Great Rite and the Tantric *Pancamakara* Rite, also known as the 'Rite of the Five M's'. These comparisons can only be ascribed to a lack of knowledge, understanding and appreciation of the Western Esoteric Tradition and its layers of symbolism which has been distilled from the mystical practices of many thousands of years. Even this paper only touches upon some of those layers contained within the Great Rite, so many more can be revealed by looking more deeply at the origins and through gnosis gained in practice. The *Pancamakara* Rite comparison, whilst allowing a student to learn more about the practices of an unrelated tradition, simply does not bear any relation to the practice or liturgy of the Great Rite. It is a complex and devotional process, with numerous steps, sexual consummation being one of the last ones in a very long process, which involves the memorisation of long lists of gods, goddesses, spiritual beings, myths and cosmologies, as well as practical workings, meditations and so on. The two rituals are so different that any attempt at a meaningful comparison can only become frustrated and will not be valid.

As it has already been illustrated, the Great Rite is replete with Qabalistic symbolism and to further understand why this is so it is necessary to examine ideas of sexual union as a form of spiritual practice in the Kabbalah (as the origin of the Qabalah). The sixteenth century Kabbalist, Rabbi Moses Cordovero, 1522-1570 C.E., who systemised the Kabbalah into the root of what it is now, wrote about the Shekinah and sexual union. His teachings are extremely clear, and perhaps surprisingly graphic in their instructions to husband and wife considering the period they date from. In a commentary on the *Zohar* he wrote, "Their desire, both his and hers, was to unite Shekinah. He focused on Tiphereth, and his wife on Malkuth. His union was to join Shekinah; she focused correspondingly on being Shekinah and uniting with her husband, Tiphereth."[32] Cordovero may have drawn inspiration from the fifteenth century writings of Ephraim Ben Gerson, who in his homily to a groom, gave very clear instructions for the magical process to be enacted during the sexual act,

> Thus do Kabbalists know that thoughts originate in the rational soul, which emanates from the supreme. And thought has the power to strip off and rise and reach its source, and when reaching its source it attains communication with the supernal light from which it came, and both become one. When thought once again stretches down from on high, all becomes one line in the imagination, and the supernal light comes down through the power of thought that draws it down, and the Shekinah is found down below. The clear light then spreads to the thinker's location. So did early priests reach communion with the supremes through thought in order to draw down the supreme light, and all beings would thus grow and multiply and be blessed in accordance with the power of thought.[33]

If we look particularly at the alchemical imagery from the sixteenth and seventeenth century of the union of the king and queen, we can see a strong case for a symbolic precursor of the Great Rite. In these images the empowered man and woman, or the king and queen, are united sexually in a sacred vessel, such as a sepulchre, The Rosary of the Philosophers, *La Bugia*, or flask, *Anatomia Auri*, which can be seen as representing the otherworldly space of the magic circle as a place of divine union.

Although there are many earlier precedents

of the *Hieros Gamos* and sacred sex, the Great Rite in Wicca is most likely to draw its practice from the Thelemic magical orders of the early twentieth century, like the Ordo Templi Orientis, Great Brotherhood of God and Fraternitas Saturni, which all used sex magic as part of their practices. By the 1930s, although an act of sexual magic might have seemed socially shocking, on an esoteric level there were several magical orders which performed sex magic in Europe and America, including the Czech Universalia, the French Fraternity of the Golden Arrow and the Thelemic orders mentioned previously.

The late nineteenth and early twentieth century saw a number of pioneers of the use of sex for magic and union with the divine manifested through the sexual partner, whose work would influence those who followed, and who are only now starting to receive the recognition their work deserves. Foremost amongst these were the American sex magician Pascal Randolph, 1825-1875, and the American sexual mystic Ira Craddock, 1857-1902. Not only did Randolph travel considerably, meeting a number of prominent European occultists such as Eliphas Levi, Hargrave Jennings, Kenneth Mackenzie and Edward Bulwer-Lytton, but he also founded the Hermetic Brotherhood of Luxor. This magical order included sex magic teachings and was the inspiration for its inclusion in the Ordo Templi Orientis. Indeed, Randolph's words in his last public speech would see expression through the Thelemic teachings of Aleister Crowley,[34] with Randolph declaring the 'omnipotence of will'. Randolph's writings covered a range of esoteric topics, including sex magic, with one of his best known works being publicised as *Magia Sexualis*. This work was nearly lost, as at one point only a French copy of this work existed, which was translated by the Russian sexual mystic Maria de Naglowska, founder of the Brotherhood of the Golden Arrow and herself a keen advocate of sexual magical practices. Maria de Naglowska's practices veered towards BDSM and were within a Luciferian and Satanic framework, peculiarly in keeping with her being based in Paris[35] during the 1930s when she

created the order and its rites and taught them to the surrealist and symbolist artists who lived there.

Craddock wrote on a number of key themes, including the importance of sustaining sexual pleasure and the retention of semen advising men that if they did ejaculate, that,

When he takes his thoughts away from the bodily sensation just before the last thrill comes which precedes ejaculation, to fix them, not upon something on the bodily plane, but to lift his thoughts to that which he considers the very highest and grandest power in all the universe, call it by what name he will--First Cause, Unconscious Energy, Primordial Substance, Jehovah, Brahma, Allah, God, the Ultimate Force, the Divine.[36]

Aleister Crowley wrote a review of some of Craddock's work in his *Equinox* Vol 3 No 1, saying of her 'sexual' writings,

I am very far from agreeing with all that this most talented woman sets forth in her paper, but she certainly obtained initiated knowledge of extraordinary depth. She seems to have had access to certain most concealed sanctuaries.... She has put down statements in plain English which are positively staggering. This book is of incalculable value to every student of occult matters. No Magick library is complete without it.[37]

The Great Rite contains many layers of symbolism, but there is no doubt that based on the evidence, it a child of Aleister Crowley's Gnostic Mass, and as such one of the Great Beast 666's hidden legacies. Whilst it is difficult for many Wiccans, especially those who have come to the tradition from a feminist and Goddess-spirituality perspective, to accept and acknowledge the influence Crowley had on this and other rituals within the tradition, others are finding deeper meaning in the texts by studying the source texts from which they have been borrowed, combined with practice. The Great Rite will probably remain the most controversial and easily misunderstood rites of Wicca, but maybe that is part of its mystery and appeal.

This paper only touches on the first layers of symbolism and history of this ritual, there is a great deal more to unveil. For now however, it seems appropriate to end with a quote from Pascal Randolph, whose work undoubtedly influenced many who would follow, including the magical orders previously mentioned, even though he is rarely credited. In writing on sexual magic Randolph said,

The union of the man with the woman must be innocent. Lust for pleasure must not be the main purpose. Transcending carnal pleasure, aim at the union of the spirits, if you want your prayer to be exhausted in ecstasy. If you conform to these principles, the sexual act will become a source of spiritual and material force for you and a fountainhead of wisdom, happiness and peace. In magic, you search for that which is called the fortune of spirit.[38]

BIBLIOGRAPHY

Cavendish, Richard, *The Satanic Mass*. London: Pan Books Ltd, 1977.

Chappell, Vere, *Sexual Outlaw, Erotic Mystic: The Essential Ira Craddock*. Maine: Red Wheel/Weiser, 2010.

Crowley, Aleister, *Liber AL vel Legis sub figura CCXX*. London: O.T.O. 1938.

Crowley, Aleister, *The Equinox*, Volume 3 No. 1. Maine: Red Wheel/Weiser, 1971.

Crowley, Aleister, *Magick*. Maine: Red Wheel/Weiser, 2000.

D'Este, Sorita and Rankine, David, *Wicca Magickal Beginnings*. London: Avalonia, 2008.

D'Este, Sorita and Rankine, David, *Practical Elemental Magick*. London: Avalonia, 2009.

D'Este, Sorita and Rankine, David, *The Cosmic Shekinah*. London: Avalonia, 2011.

Farrar, Janet and Farrar, Stuart, *The Witches Way: Principles, Rituals and Beliefs of Modern Witchcraft*. Washington: Phoenix Publishing, 1984.

Farrar, Janet and Farrar, Stewart, *A Witches Bible Complete*. New York: Magickal Childe Inc., 1991.

Fortune, Dion, *The Sea Priestess*. Maine: Red Wheel/Weiser, 2003.

Fries, Jan, *Kali Kaula: A Manual of Tantric Magick*. London: Avalonia, 2010.

Gardner, Gerald, *High Magic's Aid*. London: Michael Houghton, 1949.

Kramer, Samuel Noah and Wolkstein, Diane, *The Joy of Sumer, in Inanna Queen of Heaven and Earth: Her Stories and Hymns from Sumer*. London: Harper Perennial, 1984.

Linton, Lynn, *Witch Stories*. Montana: Kessinger Publishing, 2003.

Michelet, Jules, *Sorceress: A Study in Middle Age Superstition*. Charleston: Forgotten Books, 2010.

North, Robert, *The Grimoire of Maria de Naglowska*. USA: New Flesh Palladium, 2010.

Randolph, Pascal B., *Magia Sexualis*. Rome, Ediz Mediterranee, 1987 (first published in French as *Eulis!*, 1876).

Skinner, Stephen and Rankine, David, *The Veritable Key of Solomon*. Singapore: Golden Hoard Press, 2008.

Randolph, Pascal B., *Magia Sexualis*, 1987, Rome, Ediz Mediterranee: Rome.

Rhodes, H.T.F., *The Satanic Mass*, 1955, Citadel Press: New York.

Wolkstein, Diane and Kramer, Samuel Noah, *Inanna Queen of Heaven and Earth: Her Stories and Hymns from Sumer*, 1984, Harper Perennial.

December 2009, Wales

NOTES

1
See D'Este, Sorita and Rankine, David, Wicca Magickal Beginnings: A Study of the Possible Origins of the Rituals and Practices Found in This Modern Tradition of Pagan Witchcraft and Magick. London: Avalonia, 2008.
2 See http://www.sacred-texts.com/pag/gbos/gbos05.htm

3 See http://www.thewellhead.org.uk/GP/Gay2.htm
4 Gardner, High Magic's Aid, p. 183. London: Michael Houghton, 1949.
5 Linton, Witch Stories, p. 140. Montana: Kessinger Publishing, 2003.
6 Corinthians 11: 24-25.
7 Her arms and legs being outstretched in a west-east orientation.
8 North, Robert, The Grimoire of Maria de Naglowska. USA: New Flesh Palladium, 2010.

9 Fortune, The Sea Priestess, p. 220. Maine: Red Wheel/Weiser, 2003.
10 Michelet, Sorceress: A Study in Middle Age Superstition, p. 123. Charleston: Forgotten Books, 2010.
11 Michelet, Sorceress: A Study in Middle Age Superstition, p. 99. Charleston: Forgotten Books, 2010.
12 Cavendish, The Satanic Mass, p. 373. London: Pan Books Ltd, 1977.
13 Cavendish, The Satanic Mass, p. 373. London: Pan Books Ltd, 1977.
14 Aleister Crowley, Magick, p. 587 (first written in 1913). Maine, Samuel Weiser, 2000.
15 Aleister Crowley, Magick, p. 588. Maine, Samuel Weiser, 2000.
16 Aleister Crowley, The Confessions of Aleister Crowley: An Autohagiography, p. 714. London: Arkana, 1989.
17 As noted by Kenneth Grant in Aleister Crowley, Magick in Theory and Practice, p. 436. London: Routledge, 1986.
18 Aleister Crowley, Magick, p. 597. Maine, Samuel Weiser, 2000.
19 Aleister Crowley, Magick, p. 588. Maine,

Samuel Weiser, 2000.

20 Percy Blythe Shelley, Song of Proserpine, 1820.

21 Aleister Crowley, 'Chapter I', Liber AL vel Legis sub figura CCXX, 1904.

22 Aleister Crowley, Magick, p. 588. Maine, Samuel Weiser, 2000.

23 Aleister Crowley, 'Chapter II', Liber AL vel Legis sub figura CCXX, 1904.

24 Aleister Crowley, 'Chapter II', Liber AL vel Legis sub figura CCXX, 1904.

25 The Grand Mystery Laid Open, 1726. NP.

26 See Farrar, Janet and Farrar, Stuart, The Witches Way: Principles, Rituals and Beliefs of Modern Witchcraft. Washington: Phoenix Publishing, 1984.

27 Aleister Crowley, Magick, p. 589. Maine, Samuel Weiser, 2000.

28 Kramer and Wolkstein, The Joy of Sumer, in Inanna Queen of Heaven and Earth: Her Stories and Hymns from Sumer, p. 108. London: Harper Perennial, 1984.

29 Kramer and Wolkstein, The Joy of Sumer, in Inanna Queen of Heaven and Earth: Her Stories and Hymns from Sumer, p. 108. London: Harper Perennial, 1984.

30 Kramer and Wolkstein, The Joy of Sumer, in Inanna Queen of Heaven and Earth: Her Stories and Hymns from Sumer, p. 108. London: Harper Perennial, 1984.

31 Kramer and Wolkstein, The Joy of Sumer, in Inanna Queen of Heaven and Earth: Her Stories and Hymns from Sumer, p. 108. London: Harper Perennial, 1984.

32 Azulai, Or ha-Hayyim, seventeenth century C.E.

33 Gershon, Homilies, fifteenth century C.E.

34 Who was interestingly born in the same year of 1875.

35 Just over 250 years after Catherine 'La Voisin' and her Satanic sexual rites.

36 Chapell, Sexual Outlaw, Erotic Mystic: The Essential Ida Craddock, pp. 186-187. Maine: Red Wheel/Weiser, 2010.

37 Crowley, The Equinox Volume 3 No. 1, p. 280. Maine: Red Wheel/Weiser, 1971.

38 Randolph, Magia Sexualis, p. 45. Rome, Ediz Mediterrane. 1987.

Andrew Phillip Smith

Two Poems of Rainer Maria Rilke

ARCHAIC TORSO OF APOLLO

We cannot know how his unperceived head
Contained eyes like ripening apples.
  Though
His torso still shines with a street lamp's
  glow;
Its gaze, turned down to low but not quite
  dead,

Holds itself and gleams. Otherwise the flex
And curve of the chest would not blind you
  so,
Nor from the soft twist of loins a smile flow
Through to the centre that carries his sex.

Otherwise this stone would stand mispor-
  trayed
Beneath the shoulders' translucent cascade
And would not glisten like a wild beast's
  hide.

And would not burst through its borders in
  strife
Like a star does. For here there is no side
Which does not see you. You must change
  your life.

SONNETS TO ORPHEUS II 13

Be ahead of all parting, as if you were past
It, like the winter you just went though,
For these winters one endless winter will
  outlast,
So, overwintered, your heart can outweath-
  er them too.
Be forever dead in Eurydice. Singing
  ascend,
Praising ascend, back to where pure
  relations mattered.
Here, in this realm of decay, disappearance
  and end,
Be a ringing glass, which as it rang itself
  shattered.

Be—and know too of not-being, the
  foundation
In eternity of your innermost vibration
Which you only now fulfil to the total
  amount.
To all that is used up, and to the hollow and
  dumb
Contents of Nature's collection, the
  unspeakable sum,
Joyfully add yourself, and the cancel the
  account.

Jeffrey Kupperman

Marsilio Ficino and the Neoplatonic Roots of Modern Hermetism

"Hermetic" is a word with which to conjure. It brings to mind images of ancient knowledge and secret societies. The wisdom of Hermes Trismegistus rivaled that of Moses and his knowledge was that of the *philosophia perennis*. Since the writing of the Hermetica, Hermetism has caught the minds and imaginations of philosophers and esotericists for nearly two millennia.

The corpus of Hermetic writings is in fact quite old, far older than the revival to be discussed. The current mainstay of the Hermetica, the collection of tracts known as the *Corpus Hermeticum*, was compiled and edited between the first and fourth centuries CE. The important *Asclepius*, one of the few out right magical Hermetic writings, was composed in the second or third.[1] The *Tabula Smaragdina*, or Emerald Tablet, definitely appears in its complete form by the early 9th century CE,[2] and portions appear in Arabic as early as the 6th.[3]

The *Corpus Hermeticum*, and the frequently accompanying *Asclepius*, is characterized by Middle and Neoplatonism, with constant allusions to contemporary Greek and Egyptian paganisms as well as Judaism and Christianity religions. The overall tone of the Hermetica is both philosophical and esoteric, which was not uncommon in antiquity. These writings, and the figure of Hermes Thrice-Grand to which they are traditionally attributed, have spawned Hermetic traditions from the Middle Ages[4] to the present.

MARSILIO FICINO – HERMETIC MAGUS

The Renaissance Hermetic revival has lead to today's renewed interested in Hermetism and ceremonial magic. This most important of Hermetic revivals stems from the translation of the *Corpus Hermeticum* into Latin by priest, physician and magus Marsilio Ficino, and it is Ficino who is the focus of this paper. Ficino was not only the first to translate the *Corpus Hermetica* into Latin, but also the works of Plato under the auspices of Firenze's powerful Cosimo de' Medici. It was Ficino, through both his translations and his originals works such as the *Theologia Platonica de immortalitate animae* and especially *De vita libri tres*, who became the forefront of the Renaissance Hermetic revival. He would, directly and indirectly, influence esoteric thought from his student Giovanni Pico to the abbot Johannes Trithemius and his students Heinrich Cornelius Agrippa and Philippus Aureolus Theophrastus Bombastus von Hohenheim (AKA Paracelsus) to Tommaso Campanella, Johann Valentin Andreae, Francis Berrett, Samuel Liddell "MacGregor" Mathers and many, many more.[5]

Ficino translated the *Corpus Hermeticum* between 1460 and 1463, finally publishing it as the *Pimander* in 1471. It was Ficino, in his foreword to this publication, who popularized the already extent image of Hermes Trismegistus as being a near contemporary of Moses, and eventually his predecessor Ultimately, it would be Ficino who, in the eyes of many scholars, will become the arch-Hermetist.

Dame Frances Yates saw Ficino as a "Christian Hermetist" whose magic was not simply Hermetic in nature, but, examining his talismanic healing practices and astrological magic, was specifically derived from the talismanic/animated statue portion of the *Asclepius:*[7]

> But they discovered the art of making gods. To their discovery they added a conformable power arising from the nature of matter. Because they could not make souls, they mixed this power in and called up the souls of demons or angels and implanted them in likenesses through holy and divine mysteries, whence the idols could have the power to do good and evil.[8]

And

> It comes from a mixture of plants, stones and species, Asclepius, that have in them a natural power of divinity. And this is why those gods are entertained with constant sacrifices, with hymns, praises and sweet sounds in tune with heaven's harmony: so that the heavenly ingredient enticed into the idols by constant communication with heaven may gladly endure its long stay among humankind. Thus does man fashion his gods.[9]

Further, Ficino's use of the Picatrix, which he may have read before translating the *Corpus Hermetica*[10] and which Yates' describes as being under "Sabean", that is to say "Hermetic"[11] influence, further ties him into the Hermetic Tradition even beyond the *Pimander.*

For Yates, Ficino's translation and publication of the *Pimander* marked the "inaugural moment" of the Renaissance Hermetic tradition.[12] Since her seminal work on the subject, scholars have understood Ficino's thought, and the philosophy of early Modern magic, through the eyes of Hermetism.[13] For instance, some 40 years later Paola Zambelli[14] continues to

hold Ficino aloft as the father of Renaissance Hermetism and even undergraduate students examine Ficino's astrology through a Hermetic lens,[15] as have many others, such as Paul Oskar Kristeller, Eugenia Garin, A.J. Festugière, K.H. Dannenfeld[16] and Antoine Faivre.[17]

FICINO'S INFLUENCE

As supreme Hermetic Hierophant of the Renaissance, Ficino's role in influencing generations of Hermetists is astonishing. I will only briefly discuss two of the most important: the 15th century German occultist Heinrich Cornelius Agrippa and the 17th century magus Tommaso Campanella,[18] both of whom would influence modern esotericism in important ways.

As a later Hermetic magus, and model for Christopher Marlowe's Faustus, Heinrich Cornelius Agrippa's own influence on modern Hermetism is of the utmost import. Agrippa's exposure to Ficino was at least three-fold. First, he frequently quoted, without credit, Ficino's writing.[19] Indeed, Agrippa's magnum opus of occult theory and practice, *De occulta philosophia libri tres*, has been characterized as a "vulgarization of the ancient magic revived in the fifteenth century by Ficino,"[20] with its first book based on Ficino's *De vita coelitus comparanda.* Second, Agrippa lectured on the teachings of Johannes Reuchlin, who had travelled across the Alps especially to visit Ficino in 1490.[21] Further, Agrippa's teacher, Johannes Trithemius, though ultimately deviating from it, based his typology of magic on Ficino's.[22] According to Frances Yates, if Ficino was the founder of Renaissance Hermeticism, Agrippa is the key to understanding it.[23]

As important as Agrippa may or may not be for understanding Renaissance magic after Ficino, his influence on modern Hermetism is undeniable. For instance, many of the correspondences found in the magical practices of the *Hermetic* Order of the Golden Dawn[24] are derived from *De occulta philosophia*, albeit indirectly through Francis Barrett's heavily plagiarizing magical textbook *The Magus*.[25] Agrippa, along with Ficino, influenced John Dee's angelology in what is now commonly known as Enochian magic.[26] Enochian magic will become a cornerstone of the Golden Dawn advanced magical system. Further, both Tanya Luhrmann and Ronald Hutton have argued that most contemporary magical groups, as well as several forms of modern Paganism, are descended from the Golden Dawn.[27]

Though he experimented more with daemonic magic, Tomasso Campanella deviated far less from Ficino than Agrippa. Separated by the centuries as they were, Campanella was a close follower of Ficino's magical practices as well as his esoteric music theory. D.P. Walker has suggested that, in fact, Campanella took Ficino's spirit-music theory and astrological

practices to their ultimate conclusions, even fully summarizing Ficino in *Metaphysica*.[28]

Campanella was also the author of *Città del Sole*, the *City of the Sun,* a utopian piece featuring a city ruled by Hermetic priests. Two of Campanella's students, Tobias Adami and Wilhelm Wense, were friends of Johann Valentin Andreae. Andreae is thought to have been responsible for the writing of the two Rosicrucian manifestoes, which were published in Kassel, Germany, in 1614 and 1615. According to Christopher MacIntosh, Rosicrucian utopian societal ideals were in part derived from *Città del Sole* through Adami and Wense's influence.[29]

Along with this ideal, the hallmark of Rosicrucanism is that of healing. According to the *Fama Fraternitatis*, the first of the Rosicrucian manifestos: "Their agreement was this: First, That none of them should profess any other thing, then to cure the sick, and that gratis."[30] It must be remembered that Ficino's great astrological work, *De vita libri tres,* was an astrological medical treatise. Other elements of the *Fama Fraternitatis*, such as the description of Brother C.R.C's abode, including musical instruments and works of Mathematicks[31] are also reminiscent of Ficino. One wonders if the image of the man who would eventually be known as Christian Rosenkreutz is based, at least in part, on Campanella's inspiration, the philosopher, priest, healer and magus Marsilio Ficino. All of this fits in well with Agrippa's influence of the Order of the Golden Dawn: the Inner Order of the Golden Dawn claims a Rosicrucian origin, calling itself the Rosea Rubeae et Aureae Crucis, the Rose of Ruby and the Golden Cross.

We have, then, a picture of Marsilio Ficino

as not only Hermetic magus and hierophant, but as a man whose influence extended far into the future. He gave shape not only to a great deal of Renaissance esoteric thought, but also to early Modern philosophy and 19th, 20th, and 21st century occultism. Ficino's Hermetic revival has become the foundation from which all later Hermetisms sprung. It is still very much with us today.

There is one flaw in this shining mirror of Hermetic truth and glory: Ficino wasn't a Hermetist. Despite this popular and repeated depiction of his espousing a magical theory derived from the *Corpus Hermeticum*, and especially the *Asclepius*, Ficino's Hermetism is, in fact, much in doubt. Rather, those who have moved away from Yatesian theory have demonstrated that Ficino's theory and praxis were firmly Neoplatonic in nature.

FICINO'S NEOPLATONIC SOURCES

Though famous for his Latin translation of the *Pimander*, Ficino's translational work was far more extensive than that. And, though Lorenzo de' Medici insisted on completion of this translation before Ficino could finish his work with the Platonic dialogues, this was primarily due to the mistaken belief that Hermes Trismegistus was prior to Plato and a source of his philosophy. Besides the Hermetica and Plato, Ficino also translated and/or commented on the works of Plotinus, Porphyry, Iamblichus, Proclus and Pseudo-Dionysius; Neoplatonists one and all. All of these Neoplatonic sources can be found in the two kinds of magical practice, talismanic and theurgic, which Ficino prescribed.

Yates claimed that the talismanic magic of the monumentally influential *De vita libri tres* was derived from Hermetic sources. Rather, the portions of the Hermetica with which Ficino was familiar, including the *Asclepius*, offered little by way of magical theory for him to grasp onto. It seems clear that his definition of "natural magic," which he posits in opposition to daemonic magic,[32] is derived from Neoplatonic sources.

Specifically, Ficino drew upon the works of the Neoplatonists Plotinus and Proclus while using arguments from Thomas Aquinas to support his form of talismancy. For his theurgy, the *Reply of Abammon, the Teacher to the Letter of Porphyry to Anebo*, better known under Ficino's title of *De Mysteriis Ægyptiorum*, was of great import.

For his primary definition of natural magic Ficino relied on Plotinus' *Ennead* 4.3 rather than upon the *Asclepius* as per Yates. The first eleven of that *Ennead*'s 23 chapters are encapsulated in the first chapter of the third book of *De vita* entitled "On Obtaining Life from the Heavens."[33]

In addition, the World-soul possesses by divine power precisely as many seminal reasons of things as there are Ideas in the Divine Mind. By these seminal reasons she fashions the same number of species in matter. That is why every single species corresponds through its own seminal reason to its own Idea and oftentimes through this reason it can easily receive something from the Idea since indeed it was made through the reason from the Idea. This is why, if at any time the species degenerates from its proper form, it can be formed again with the reason as the proximate intermediary and, through the Idea as intermediary, can then be easily reformed. And if in the proper manner you bring to bear on a species, or on some individual in it, many things which are dispersed but which conform to the same Idea, into this material thus suitably adapted you will soon draw a particular gift from the Idea, through the seminal reason of the Soul.[34]

In short, Ficino describes a kind of image and astrological magic that allows for the reconstitution of any "species," such as a body in poor health, through the use of objects, scents, sounds, food, etc.; i.e. Neoplatonic *sunthēmata* or "tokens" that are ontologically connected to the Idea or Form from which the degenerated species is derived. Further, through the use of such tokens, typically in the physical form of a talisman, the magus can bring down celestial powers for his or her use.

Though the rationale for this magical practice is derived from Plotinus, it also appears to rely upon Iamblichus' spiritual hierarchies that differentiate between encosmic and hypercosmic beings, whether they be daimons, archons, gods or otherwise. Ficino, in order to save his talismancy from drawing upon or usurping divine power for earthly ends tells us:

And so let no one think that any divinities wholly separate from matter are being attracted by any given mundane materials, but that daemons rather are being attracted and gifts from the ensouled world and from the living stars. Again, let no man wonder that Soul can be allured as it were by material forms, since indeed she herself has created baits of this kind suitable to herself, to be allured thereby, and she always and willingly dwells in them. There is nothing to be found in this whole living world so deformed that Soul does not attend it, that a gift of the Soul is not in it.[35]

Compare this with Iamblichus:

Let us, therefore, posit once again that, among the gods, some are material, others immaterial. Those are material that embrace matter within themselves and impose order upon it, while immaterial are those that are exempt from matter and rise above it . . . The material gods, then, have a certain communion with matter inasmuch as they preside over it; it is they, therefore, that are responsible for those phenomena that arise in matter, such as divisions, impacts and resistance, and the alteration, generation and destruction of all material bodies.[36]

A second important source for Ficino's talismancy is a work by Proclus, translated by Ficino as *De sacrificio*. This text supplied Ficino with the method of manipulating matter to influence and direct celestial power. Proclus describes a hierarchy, similar to Iamblichus, whereby all things are connected from above to below. By understanding these connections, which function through sympathy and token, the magus can understand how the world of images around us is informed by the world of Forms and thus manipulate it.

This hieratic knowledge allows us to understand why "the lion shrinks from the cock," which is due to "the presence of heliacal symbols [being] more effective for the cock" than the lion. The lion is less solar in nature than the rooster and is thus inferior to it, even if the lion is physically more powerful.[37] Then "[f]rom this evidence of the eyes, the authorities on the priestly art have thus discovered how to gain the favor of powers above, mixing some things together and setting others apart in due order."[38] While the making of statues, the topic Yates connects to Ficino's talismancy, is mentioned by Proclus, it is Proclus and Plotinus, with echoes of Iamblichus throughout, who fully inform Ficino's actual methodology in *De vita*, something absent from the *Asclepius*.

The final book of *De via* does not focus entirely on talismancy, even though it consistently use the same ideology Ficino espouses for the making of talismans; i.e. the use of sympathy and tokens. Though the contributions of Plotinus and Proclus on Ficino's magic are well noted by scholars who see beyond the Yates hypothesis, it is Ficino who betrays his Iamblician theurgic agenda when he wrote "[t]his [the World-soul's spirit] is absorbed by man in particular through his own spirit which is by its own nature similar to it, especially if it is made more akin to it by art, that is, *if it becomes in the highest degree celestial."*[39]

The act of becoming celestial is related to Ficino's idea of "species," for like is close to like and in order for humanity to raise itself it must contain the heavens within itself as well. That we have exactly this, and that there is an internal, psychological (in the literal sense of the word, the reasoning of the psyche or soul) is clear in a letter from Ficino to Lorenzo di Pierfrancesco de' Medici which states that "[w]e must not look for these matters outside ourselves, for the whole of heaven is within us and the fiery vigour in us testifies to our heavenly origin."[40]

This agenda is furthered beginning in the twenty first of the twenty seven chapters that make up *De vita coelitus*: "On the Power of Words and Song for Capturing Celestial Benefits on the Seven Steps That Lead to Celestial Things." It is here that Ficino introduces his theory of the esoteric use of music. Importantly, in Ficino's astrological hierarchy of magical practice music and song are associated with the sun. In his commentary on Plotinus, Ficino recognized the sun (Apollo) as the only planet worshiped by the (Neo)Platonic philosophers, mentioning Iamblichus by name.[41] His musical theory, which may be modeled after Iamblichus' treatment of the life of Pythagoras,[42] was so important to him that he went as far as inserting it into his translation of Iamblichus' *De Mysteriis*.[43]

Ficino's astrological music relies on two facets: the music itself and the words, both of which he considered solar in nature. The use of solar imagery is important for Ficino, the sun being, in effect, *sunthēmata* of God,[44] which takes the place of the Platonic "One;" the transcendent, emanating reality also known as the Good. The astrological music attunes the magus to the sun and through the sun, God in an act of theurgy. This appears to be true in a general way, regardless as to whether the music is sung to a different planetary power, as all music is solar in nature. The act of playing music always attunes the musician to the sun as well as whatever planet specifically invoked.[45]

The verbal component of music is considered especially important as is, along with Zoroaster and Al-Kindi, Iamblichus's argument that the "barbarous words" should never be altered due to their innate divine power. When the proper music is played, the magus, through this act, attunes him or herself over time to the planetary power to receive its gifts. Of this Ficino writes:

> We strive to adapt ourselves to this multifarious and occult influence by the same studied methods we use every day to make ourselves fit to receive in a healthy manner the perceivable light and heat of the Sun.[46]

It is through this Neoplatonic theurgy, as with Iamblichus, that the movement of humans and the movement of God (or the gods) are united.[47]

FICINO'S NEOPLATONISM AND MODERN HERMETISM

Ficino's magical practice combines elements of Plotinus' and Proclus' natural magic, underscored by Iamblichus' theurgy. Rather than being Hermetic in nature, the content and intent of his work is Neoplatonic. It may be said that during the Renaissance, Hermetism was blended into Neoplatonism and made to serve it rather than the other way around.[48] The implications of this are important. Focusing on Agrippa, we may now qualify his work as being Neoplatonic rather than an ill-defined "Hermetic"[49] as asserted by those scholars noted above. Culminating in the third books of *De occulta philosophia*,[50] Agrippa combines Ficino's Neoplatonism with Pico's Christian cabala. Again, the content is ultimately rooted in Neoplatonism not the Hermetism of the *Asclepius* for, as discussed, there is almost no practical magic to be found there.

This theme is one we have now seen repeatedly: Neoplatonic *content* with Hermetic *inspiration*.[51] Until the time of Meric Casaubon, when he demonstrated the relative recentness of the Hermetic material, and even afterwards, Renaissance occultists assumed an extreme antiquity for the mythical Hermes Trismegistus. His paganism was redeemed by his proximity to Moses and the ability to read a nascent Christianity into those works written under his name. This is in contrast to the Neoplatonists who were known to live after the time of Christ, some of whom were quite antithetical to Christianity, and whose paganism could not be so easily be saved.

The use of the *idea* of Hermetism has continued into the current day. This is seen especially in the Hermetic Order of the Golden Dawn and its numerous descendants. Though in many cases espousing the title of "Hermetic,"[52] content and ideology connected to the Hermetica is slim. Rather, it may be argued that the Golden Dawn's magic, being based largely on Agrippa via Barrett, is itself Neoplatonic in content, or at least in origin. With the focus on Hermetic thought and qabalistic terminology, it may be argued a certain amount of the depth of Neoplatonic theory and cosmology have been lost from the practice of modern popular ceremonial magic. Where Ficino extolled a deeply Platonic and Neoplatonic methodology and where Agrippa recorded, albeit somewhat haphazardly, a variety of magical theory based on a tripartite Neoplatonic schema, modern occultism has reduced this to tables of correspondences to be memorized and employed. There is little in the Golden Dawn material, for instance, that *explains* the *sumthēmatic* nature of those correspondences. Ficino is at the heart of this, but he is deeply buried.

Further, one does not see an emphasis on living attuned to these *sumthēmata* outside of ritual and the moral and ethical consequences of such a life, as found in both Neoplatonic and kabbalistic literature, both of which are important sources of the Golden Dawn tradition. Instead we see the Early Modern cosmology replaced by a post-Enlightenment mechanistic model, and eventually Postmodern thought. Such a mode of thinking is largely incompatible with Ficino's soul-oriented theurgy.

This move has in turn given rise to the concept of "plug-and-play" or "open source" magic as espoused by Chaos magicians on the one hand and perhaps the Open Source Order of the Golden Dawn on the other, as well as a great deal of modern Pagandom.[53] Such an approach takes on the appearance of the magic of the Renaissance, with its lists modeled on Neoplatonic *sumthēmata*, but lacks its metaphysics or philosophical depth.

Still, not all of Ficino's Neoplatonic revival has faded. There is, outside of the magical practices popular today, a resurgence of traditional esotericism. Examples of this can be found in renewed interested in grimoiric magic, much of which has a deep Neoplatonic base. Further, magicians such as Christopher Warnock have worked to revive traditional, that is to say pre-Enlightenment, astrology and astrological magic. Organizations such as the Phoenix Rising Academy are teaching the works of Ficino and other Neoplatonists.

The magic preserved and expounded upon by Renaissance magus Marsilio Ficino has survived, though perhaps somewhat denuded, into modern times. Rather than presenting the world with a Hermetic system of magic and talismancy as popularly thought, Ficino gave the world the Neoplatonic heritage of Plotinus, Proclus and Iamblichus, amongst others. Though seeming to base his esotericism on the *Asclepius*, in fact there is little magical content there to work from. Having influenced such figures as Tomasso Campanella[54] and Heinrich Cornelius Agrippa, it is arguable that Ficino's Neoplatonism, natural magic and theurgy are at the roots of two of the most influential esotericisms of the day: Rosicrucianism and Hermetic, or should we say Neoplatonic, magic.

NOTES

1 Florian Ebeling, *The Secret History of Hermes Trismegistus: Hermeticism from Ancient to Modern Times*, trans. David Lorton (Ithica, NY: Cornell University Press, 2007), 10.

2 Jon Marshal, "The Emerald Tablet of Hermes," accessed August 28, 2011. http://www.levity.com/alchemy/emerald.html.

3 Karen-Claire Voss, "The Tabula Smaragdina Revisited," accessed May 24, 2011. http://www.istanbul-yes-istanbul.co.uk/alchemy/TSpaper.htm.

4 Ebeling, *Secret History*, Ibid.

5 C.f. Paola Zambelli, *White Magic, Black Magic in the European Renaissance: From Ficino, P ico, Della Porta to Trithemius, Agrippa, Bruno* (Boston: Brill, 2007), 13-17)

6 Ibid., 60-4.

7 Frances Yates, *Giordano Bruno and the Hermetic Tradition*, Chicago: University of Chicago Press: 1964), 66—8. Frances Yates, *The Art of Memory*, (Chicago: University of Chicago Press, 1974), 151, 3.

8 *Asclepius* 37. Brian P. Copenhaver, *Hermetica: The Greek Corpus Hermeticum and the Latin Asclepius in a new English Translation withNnotes andIintroduction*, (Cambridge, UK: Cambridge University Press, 1992), 90.

9 *Asclepius* 38, ibid.

10 Zambelli, *White Magic*, 9.

11 Yates, *Bruno*, 48.

12 Christopher I. Lehrich, *The Language of Demons and Angels: Cornelius Agrippa's Occult Philosophy*, (Boston: Brill, 2003), 47.

13 Brian P. Copenhaver, "Iamblichus, Synesius and the Chaldaean oracles in Marsilio Ficino's *De vita libri tres*: hermetic magic or neoplatonic magic?" *Supplementum Festivum: Studies in Honor of Paul Oskar Kristeller* (1987): 441.

14 Zambelli, *White Magic*, especially 45-6.

15 C.f. Nicholas Campion, "What were the main features of Marsilio Ficino's hermetic astrology, and what did this owe to Hellenistic astrology?" accessed May 24, 2011. http://www.kepler.edu/articles/student/2q2000birch.html.

16 See Schmitt, "Reappraisals," 200.

17 Antoine Faivre, *Access to Western Esotericism* (Albany, NY: SUNY Press, 1994), 33.

18 Both Zambelli and D.P. Walker examine Giovani Pico, Johannes Trithemius and Cornelius Agrippa as important thinkers influenced by Ficino.

19 D.P. Walker, *Spiritual and Demonic Magic: From Ficino to Campanella* (Notre Dame, IN: University of Notre Dame Press, 1975), 27.

20 Brian Copenhaver, "Magic," p. 3, Accessed May 26, 2011. http://www.cmrs.ucla.edu/brian/research/finished_research/finished_articles/i26_magic.pdf.

21 Frank L. Borchardt, "The Magus as Renaissance Man," *The Sixteenth Century Journal* 21.1 (1990): 62

22 Lehrich, *Language*, 54.

23 Lehrich, *Language*, 2.

24 Emphasis added.

25 Donald Tyson, "On the *Occult Philosophy*," in *Three Books of Occult Philosophy*, Henry Cornelius Agrippa, ed. Donald Tyson (St. Paul, MN: Llewellyn Publications, 2000), xli-xlii.

26 Yates, *Memory*, 262.

27 Alison Butler, "Making Magic Modern: Nineteenth-Century Adaptations," *The Pomegranate* 6.2 (2004): 217.

28 Walker, *Spiritual*, 29, 210-1.

29 Christopher MacIntosh, *The Rosicrucians: The History, Mythology, and Rituals of an Esoteric Order*, (York Beach, ME: Samuel Weiser, Inc., 1997), 21.

30 "Fama Fraternitatis," accessed May 24, 2011. http://levity.com/alchemy/fama.html.

31 Ibid.

32 More frequently "demonic" magic, but referring to magic employing spiritual beings, demonic, angelic or other.

33 Brian Copenhaver, "Renaissance Magic and Neoplatonic Philosophy: *Ennead* 4.3.5 in Ficino's *De Vita Coelitus Comparanda*," in *Marsilio Ficino e il ritorno di Platone*, ed. G. Garfagnini (Firenze, Italy: Olschki, 1986), 352-4.

34 Marsilio Ficino, *Three Books on Life: A Critical Edition and Translation with Introduction and Notes*, trans. Carol V. Kaske and John R. Clark, (Tempe, AZ: Medieval & Renaissance Texts & Studies, 1998), 243.

35 Ibid., 243-4.

36 Iamblichus, *De mysteriis*, trans. Emma C. Clarke, John M. Dillon, Jackson P. Hershbell, (Atlanta, GA: Society of Biblical Literature, 2003), 249 [V.14].

37 Cf. Proclus, "On the Priestly Art According to the Greeks," in "Hermes Trismegistus, Proclus, and the Question of a Philosophy of Magic in the

Renaissance," trans. Brian Copenhaver, *Hermeticism and the Renaissance: Intellectual History and the Occult in Early Modern Europe* (Washington, DC: Folger Books, 1988), 104. Cf. Ficino, *Three Books*, 245.

38 Ibid., 104-5.

39 Ibid., 259. Emphasis added.

40 In Melissa Meriam Bullard, "The Inward Zodiac: A Development of Ficino's Thought on Astrology," *Renaissance Quarterly* 43, 4 (1990): 698. Unfortunately, Bullard, who is otherwise interested in the context of Ficino's work, assumes a modern psychological interpretation of these passages, ignoring their Neoplatonic metaphysical background, which call to mind Iamblichus' idea of a dual soul, one of which is celestial and clothed in the bodies of spheres of the seven planets.

41 Walker, *Spiritual*, 18.

42 Iamblichus, "The Life of Pythagoras or On the Pythagorean Life," in Kennethy Sylvan Guthrie, *The Pythagorean Sourcebook and Library* (Grand Rapids, MI: Phanes Press, 1897), 84-8.

43 Walker, *Spiritual*, 6.

44 Cf. Marsilio Ficino, *The Book of the Sun (De Sole)*, trans. Geoffrey Cornelius, Darby Costello, Graeme Tobyn, Angela Voss & Vernon Wells (PDF file), 44

45 Ficino, *Three Books*, 361.

46 Ibid., 357.

47 Gregory Shaw, *Theurgy and the Soul: The Neoplatonism of Iamblichus* (University Park, PA: Pennsylvania State University Press, 1995), 153.

48 Charles B. Schmitt, "Reappraisals in Renaissance Science," *History of Science*, 16:33 (1978): 206.

49 Ibid.

50 These three books, on Natural Magic, Celestial Magic and Religious Magic mimic the Platonic division of creation: the created world (Images), the celestial world (Numbers) and the supercelestial world (Forms).

51 Cf. Schmitt, "Reappraisals," 207.

52 For instance the publication "Hermetic Virtues," which is loosely affiliated with the Hermetic Order of the Golden Dawn connected to Chic and Sandra Tabatha Cicero.

53 Cf. Douglas E. Cowan, *Cyberhenge: Modern Pagans on the Internet* (NY: Routledge, 2005), 30-3.

54 Whose *City of the Sun* describes a very Platonic priesthood, modeled after the philosophers of Plato's *Republic*, but not one that is Hermetic in any particular way.

Sean Martin

Sham World, Sublime Light:
Gnosticism in the works of David Lindsay

Gnostic themes have been claimed for a wide variety of texts, from the work of William Blake and Hermann Melville to Karl Marx and Franz Kafka, amongst many others. Ioan Culianu writes of the confusion around what exactly "gnostic" is:

> Once I believed that Gnosticism was a well-defined phenomenon belonging to the religious history of Late Antiquity. Of course, I was ready to accept the idea of different prolongations of ancient Gnosis, and even that of spontaneous generation of views of the world in which, at different times, the distinctive features of Gnosticism occur again.
>
> I was soon to learn however, that I was a naïf indeed. Not only Gnosis was gnostic, but the Catholic authors were gnostic, the Neoplatonic too, Reformation was gnostic, Communism was gnostic, Nazism was gnostic, liberalism, existentialism and psychoanalysis were gnostic too, modern biology was gnostic, Blake, Yeats, Kafka were gnostic.... I learned further that science is gnostic and superstition is gnostic... Hegel is gnostic and Marx is gnostic; all things and their opposite are equally gnostic.[1]

It is not my purpose in the present short paper to discuss any of the above, although it would seem fairly certain that Blake was consciously Gnostic (as opposed to being labelled one by later critics).[2] A writer about whom we can safely say was a "conscious" Gnostic was the Anglo-Scottish novelist David Lindsay (1876-1945). Most of Lindsay's work can be classified as fantasy,[3] and he has a fair claim to being fantasy literature's first great Gnostic of the 20th century.

Lindsay was born in Blackheath, South London to a Scottish father and an English mother. Through his father's side, he was later to trace his ancestors back to 'the main stem of the Lindsays, whose history is in any book of Scottish families. Ivar, Jarl of the Norse Uplanders, is said to have been the original ancestor.'[4] He was distantly related to his 16th century namesake, the playwright Sir David Lindsay. His father deserted the family when Lindsay was a boy, and, as a result, Lindsay was forced to get a job to support his mother, aunt and sister, with whom he lived, rather than go to university. This effectively delayed the start of his literary career by 20 years. Lindsay worked as an insurance broker from 1894-1916, quite successfully, until he was called up. He served in the Grenadier Guards during the 1st World War (he held an administrative post, confining him to office work in London; he saw no overseas action). After being demobbed in 1919, he refused a directorship of his insurance company, stunning family and friends by moving to Cornwall with his new young wife, intent on becoming a writer.

It was something he had always wanted to do, and his elder brother, Alexander, had set a precedent by writing a series of adventure novels under the name Alexander Crawford before the war. But David's novels were to be very different. He had little contact with the literary world – his only real writer friends being E.H. Visiak and L.H. Myers, while the publisher Victor Gollancz thought him 'an exceptional man'.[5]

Other influences can be discerned: notably James Hogg and George Macdonald. But Lindsay was to remain very much his own man, developing an essentially Gnostic philosophy from his reading of Schopenhauer and Nietzsche. Lindsay's biographer, Bernard Sellin, argues that

have no suspicion of the existence of this interior reality. The mystic, for his part, has learned to 'open the doors of perception'... Separated by four centuries, Boehme and Lindsay fought the same fight; the fight to preserve the human spirit ceaselessly threatened by a corrupting environment.[6]

Lindsay was to echo Boehme in one of his *Philosophical Notes*, stating that the world is a 'vast sham':[7]

the root cause of Lindsay's Gnosticism came from the 17th century visionary and Hermeticist, Jacob Boehme (1575-1624):

> Boehme, like Lindsay, was a rebel who sought, in mystical revelation, a solution to the ill of the world. For Boehme, and for Nietzsche after him, the tangible world was a fraud; it contained an interior, fascinating reality of which we were unaware. "The visible world is a manifestation of the interior, and spiritual, world", wrote Boehme. The majority of us are misled by external appearances, and

> One must not regard the world merely as a home of illusions; but as being *rotten* with illusion from top to bottom; not a sound piece anywhere, but all springs, glasses and traps throughout.[8]

Behind this sham world of appearances stood what Lindsay termed the Sublime. Unlike Schopenhauer, he did not regard this as an aesthetic term. Rather, it was 'a metaphysical fact; the experience of transcendence, at the moment when man lost his individuality to make himself part of the whole.'[9] For Lindsay, 'reality is the progress homeward of the fragments of spirit',[10] the journey back to the Sublime, 'which stands above and behind the world and governs all its manifestations.'[11] As Bernard Sellin comments,

> Any list of the analogies between Lindsay's ideology and the Gnostic cults would be a long one... it would be necessary to cite the importance attached to spirit, the systematic depreciation of the body and the flesh, man as a stranger in the world, the conception of an evil world, indeed an evil God, the cult of the Mother and the Eternal Female, and the condemnation of sexuality.[12]

Lindsay's first novel, *A Voyage to Arcturus* (1920), is effectively a Gnostic *Pilgrim's Progress*. The novel recounts a journey by two men, Maskull and Nightspore, to the planet Tormance, which orbits the binary star Arcturus, and whose deity is an entity known variously as Crystalman, Shaping or Surtur. Maskull learns that Krag, the man who has taken them to this strange new world, is said to be Crystalman's nemesis, effectively Tormance's devil. As the story progresses, however, it becomes clear that Crystalman is not all he seems, and neither is Krag.

Maskull wakes on a plain of red sand, naked, to find that his two fellow-travellers are nowhere in sight. He has also developed new sensory organs, including a tentacle that protrudes from his heart. The new world he is on is full of strange colours and life forms. Tormance's gravity means that he is not able to stand, only kneel. A beautiful young woman by the name of Joiwind appears, offering him both clothing and the means by which he can stand the planet's gravitational pull: a blood transfusion. She explains that the new organ he has developed on his forehead allows him to read other people's thoughts, while the tentacle enables him to love others. Claiming to be affected by a strange light in the sky, Joiwind explains that that must be the light from Tormance's second sun, Alppain, which can only be seen by heading north. Wanting to see this light, Maskull soon embarks

on a quest that takes him through Tormance's wildly differing landscapes, from the Ifdawn Marest – a mountainous region subject to frequent and hugely violent earthquakes – to the broad valley of Matterplay, whose rivers contain a suffocating preponderance of life forms, many of which are generated spontaneously from out of thin air.

Maskull comes to realise that there is more to his quest to see Alppain's light than he initially believed. (On a second reading, it strikes the reader as allegorical, as does the method by which the three men travel to Tormance: their ship is powered by 'back-rays' which Nightspore explains as 'light that goes back to its source.'[13])

Maskull soon encounters Surtur himself, who informs Maskull that Tormance is his world, and that Maskull must serve him. Surtur's image enlarges to fill the sky before suddenly vanishing. Maskull encounters further characters in his quest, and it becomes clear that many of them represent different ways of life and belief. Joiwind and her husband Panawe are lovers of their world, enthralled by its many pleasures but also aware of its dangers. Oceaxe is a strong, domineering woman whose willpower governs her life, while Sullenbode is sensual, 'a mass of pure sex'. The male characters, too, all seem to be driven by one main outlook. The ascetic Spadevil lives life according to a sense of duty, while Corpang and the androgynous – for want of a better word – Leehallfae are intensely religious, but deluded. Only the Zen-like fisherman, Polecrab, seems to be content, and it is with him that Maskull has one of the most significant conversations in the book:

> 'Since I've come out of that forest,' proceeded Maskull, talking to himself, 'a change has come over me, and I see things differently. Everything here looks much more solid and real in my eyes than in other places... so much so that I can't entertain the least doubt of its existence. It not only *looks* real, it *is* real-and on that I would stake my life... But at the same time

that it's real, it is *false*.'

'Like a dream?'

'No – not at all like a dream, and that's just what I want to explain. This world of yours – and perhaps mine too, for that matter – doesn't give me the slightest impression of a dream, or an illusion, or anything of that sort. I know it's really here at this moment, and it's exactly as we're seeing it, you and I. Yet it's false. It's false

fearful struggle seemed to begin. The spark endeavoured to escape through to the upper air, while the clouds concentrated around it, whichever way it darted, trying to create so dense a prison around it, that further movement would be impossible.[15]

Although most of the sparks escape, some don't, and sink slowly towards the ground again, where they become denser and darker, and ultimately become matter (in this case a strange

in this sense, Polecrab. Side by side with it another world exists, and that other world is the true one, and this one is all false and deceitful, to the very core. And so it occurs to me that reality and falseness are two words for the same thing.'[14]

The concept of two worlds, a higher and a lower, recur throughout the book. In Matterplay, Maskull has a vision in which he can see green sparks flying upwards from the brook:

Each one wavering up towards the clouds, but the moment they got within them, a

walking plant-animal hybrid). The optimism of Matterplay is counterbalanced by Nightspore's vision in the stone tower on the island of Muspel, which represents the sole bastion of the higher world, the Sublime, on Tormance: he looks out of the window to see Crystalman living off the energies (the green sparks are visible again) of all of Tormance's inhabitants. The lower, vulgar world is literally leeching its denizens to death.

The cold fury of this final vision was not something Lindsay adopted for this one book. Gnostic themes were to recur in much of his subsequent work as well. In Lindsay's second novel, *The Haunted Woman* (1922), the mysterious upper window at Runhill Court looks out onto a view of Anglo-Saxon England which, in the context of the book, stands for the Sublime. In *Sphinx* (1923), the Sublime is visible in dreams, which Nicholas Cabot attempts to capture with his recording apparatus. *The Violet Apple* (written 1924-6, but not published until 1976) is Lindsay's thoroughly Gnostic take on the book of Genesis: when Anthony Kerr and Haidee Croyland eat the apples said to be descendants of the fruit of the Tree in Eden, they can see people's true nature and the true nature of reality, which is 'a common coffin'.[16] Lindsay describes Adam's and Eve's eating of the fruit as the gaining of knowledge, 'an eternal symbol of the first resurrection from the dead – of the first rising of man and woman from a world of unconscious animals.'[17] (The theme of resurrection is further stressed in that the novel is set over Easter). This is in perfect accord with the Gnostics of classical antiquity, who regarded Eve as the first human to attain *gnosis* once she had eaten the fruit from the tree.[18] In Haidee, Lindsay introduces a powerful female character who, Sophia-like, is able to mediate spiritual truths, a theme taken up in his last two novels, *Devil's Tor* (1932) and *The Witch* (almost finished on his death in 1945, but not published until 1976).

Lindsay enjoyed little success in his lifetime, but, ironically, interest in his work began to grow almost as soon as he was dead. Gollancz republished *Arcturus* in 1946, and it has been in print more or less ever since; all his novels are now in print. Colin Wilson, while taking Lindsay to task over his prose style, has frequently hailed *A Voyage to Arcturus* as one of the greatest novels of the 20th century. Alan Moore makes a claim for Lindsay as belonging to a long line of British fantasists and shamanic visionaries:

He seems part of no community. Largely excluded from the listings of that period's fantastic authors, Lindsay is denied even a retroactive entry into the fraternity. It's only in the ledgers of the similarly marginalized, in the annals of the British revelatory tradition that he finds true

fellowship. The School of Night. Dee, Machen, Blake, Dunsany, Hodgson, Bunyan, the Duchess of Newcastle [Margaret Cavendish].Stenographers of the Apocalypse.[19]

The apocalypse Moore speaks of is surely the revelation that the sham world is fatal; a destroyer of souls the way Crystalman feeds off the life forms of Arcturus. There is only one task incumbent upon us, Lindsay's books remind us time and time again: to return to the Sublime.

NOTES

This article is based on material previously published in *The Gnostics: the First Christian Heretics* by Sean Martin (Pocket Essentials, 2010).

1 Ioan P. Culianu, "The Gnostic Revenge: Gnosticism and Romantic Literature," in *Gnosis und Politik*, Jacob Taubes, ed. (Munich: W. Fink, 1984), p. 290; quoted in Arthur Versluis, "'Gnosticism,' Ancient and Modern," in *Alexandria* 1 (1991), pp. 307-08.

2 On Blake's Gnosticism, see my *The Gnostics: The First Christian Heretics* (Harpenden: Oldcastle Books, 2010, p. 123)

3 The two major exceptions being his novel *The Adventures of Monsieur de Mailly* (London: Andrew Melrose, 1926), which is an historical romance in the mould of Dumas (it is set in early C 18th France), and the unpublished manuscript *Sketch Notes for a New System of Philosophy* (aka *Philosophical Notes*) a philosophical work set out in 545 aphorisms. Extracts have been published in various magazines, with all of these being collected in the Savoy edition of *A Voyage to Arcturus*. Bernard Sellin includes further selections from the *Sketch Notes* in his biography of Lindsay. The entire manuscript is held by the National Library of Scotland in Edinburgh.

4 David Lindsay, autobiographical piece written to accompany the publication of Devil's Tor in 1932. Quoted in J.B. Pick, "A Sketch of

Lindsay's Life as Man and Writer", in J.B. Pick, Colin Wilson & E.H. Visiak, *The Strange Genius of David Lindsay* (London: John Baker, 1970), p. 6

5 Bernard Sellin, *The Life and Works of David Lindsay* (Cambridge: Cambridge University Press, 2006), p.31. Sellin speculates (p. 42) that he may have, at various times, met Walter de la Mare and Olaf Stapledon, but if he did, no close ties were formed.

6 Sellin, p. 53

reiterated by Aldous Huxley, who observed that "The world is an illusion, but it is an illusion which we must take seriously... Our business is to wake up," from "Shakespeare and Religion," in Aldous Huxley, *Huxley and God: Essays*, edited by Jacqueline Hazard Bridgeman (San Francisco: HarperSanFrancisco, 1992), p. 279

15 *A Voyage to Arcturus*, pp. 195-196

16 David Lindsay, *The Violet Apple* (London: Sidgwick & Jackson, 1978), p. 189

7 Lindsay, *Sketch Notes*, note 534.

8 Lindsay, *Sketch Notes*, note 534.

9 Sellin, p. 53

10 David Power, *David Lindsay's Vision*, (Nottingham: Pauper's Press, 1991), p. 3.

11 Lindsay, *Sketch Notes*, note 337

12 Sellin, p. 227

13 David Lindsay, *A Voyage to Arcturus*, (London: Allison & Busby, 1986), p. 32

14 *A Voyage to Arcturus*, pp. 164-165. The concept that the lower, false world is still somehow real – 'not at all like a dream' – was

17 *The Violet Apple*, p. 193

18 See my *The Gnostics*, pp. 34-35

19 Alan Moore, "Prism and Pentecost: David Lindsay and the British Apocalypse", Introduction to *A Voyage to Arcturus* (Manchester: Savoy Books, 2002), p. xx

Andrew Phillip Smith

On the Manichaeans:
An Interview With Nicholas Baker-Brian

APS: You're a lecturer in the Religious Studies department at Cardiff University, teaching New Testament studies, and late antiquity.

NBB: Yeah, very broadly, although the extent to which undergraduates are aware of the whole idea of late antiquity is still a bit muted really, because we have an obligation to teach New Testament studies, for instance. So there are obvious points of crossover between the New Testament period and late antiquity but my main commitments are in teaching Greek, some Latin and synthetic courses. So I actually teach a course on ancient Gnosticism, which has been running for about two years.

APS: And that's how you got involved with Manichaean scholarship, is it?

NBB: In a sense. I did my doctorate on one of Augustine of Hippo's lesser known anti-Manichaean writings, because Augustine was a virulent critic, although he had been a Manichaean for many years previously, and he wrote a work called the Contra Adimantum, Against Adimantus, which is important for a whole variety of reasons, but hadn't actually been the subject of a detailed academic study. So I was working on that from a Latin Augustinian perspective and then I eventually realised that some of the more interesting things were the Manichaean bits, so I started to branch out and I looked at the history and the scholarship of the Manichaean religion, which is vast. That's really how I got into it, through research.

APS: Maybe you could give us a quick overview of Manichaeism, the sort of thing that you would give your class when introducing them, just to set the stage a bit.

NBB: The thing that we call Manichaeism was ostensibly not an independent tradition when it started out. It began with the teachings of a character called Mani. I think most people know about Mani being a Persian visionary of some sort in the early third century, and Mani taught a distinctive type of Christianity, fundamentally, although there are syncretistic elements in the early teaching. And he attracted lots of followers. The sources indicate that he was evidently a prolific and tireless missionary for his ideas, all of which seemed to be revelations that Mani received from a divine spirit. He died under persecution from the Sassanian Persian authorities in the late third century, and his followers continued to develop his teachings and found churches in the Sassanian Empire in the Far East towards central Asia, and principally in the Roman Empire. The Fourth century was a period of tremendous change with the arrival of Constantine and the dynasty of Constantine and the emergence of Christianity as an officially sanctioned religion. The Manichaeans fit nicely into that whole fourth century context, and really only begin to start being persecuted as a heresy towards the end of the fourth century. From that point on they're running from a number of authorities all the way into the sixth and seventh century. Justinian, who is a famous Byzantine Roman emperor in the sixth century targets the Manichaeans as being heretical and issues lots of legislation against them. They also fall foul of the Sassanian authorities in Persia because there are still many Manichaeans in Mesopotamia at this time. Interestingly, rather than apostasise they simply move on. So they move in the sixth and seventh centuries eastwards towards central Asia and stay there as a very strong presence up to—well, it's difficult to say really—but up to about the twelfth century, although there's evidence of the Manichaeans in the late fourteenth and early fifteenth centuries. It's quite an interesting religion from a whole variety of perspectives, and quite tricky to deal with because some of the primary sources give conflicting evidence, and certainly with a religion spread so widely you'd expect a degree of significant variation in their ideas in a whole variety of contexts.

APS: I presume Manichaeans were from a great variety of ethnic groups.

NBB: In the early period most Manichaeans would have been ethnically west Asian, meaning Persian or Mesopotamian. As they spread westwards into the Roman Empire you had ethnically Roman Manichaeans. Take, for example, the case of Augustine. He was a Roman but he was also a North African. But as you head further along the centuries, particularly to the seventh and eighth centuries, Manichaeans start appearing as Turks. The Manichaean religion is adopted in the eighth century by the ruling Turkish dynasty in certain central Asian regions, called the Uighurs. So there were Uighur Turkish Manichaeans. There's a whole range of ethnicities, or ethnic identities. I can become a complex problem.

APS: And the great variety of languages must be a problem.

NBB: Absolutely. The religion is—I want to avoid hyperbole—one of the most unique ancient religions on the basis of the fact that it is taken up by a variety of linguistic types. So we find Latin, Greek, Coptic, Persian, middle Iranian, Turkic, a whole range of ethnic groups speaking a whole variety of languages that at some point dabble with being Manichaean, or commit themselves to being Manichaean. So in that sense it's very unique.

APS: One of the standard lines that you often see repeated in accounts of Manichaean religion is that it deserves to be counted as one of the world religion, and that it extended as far east

as China and as far west as Spain. But I've never seen any real concrete evidence concerning Manichaeism in Spain. I presume that's because it was part of the Roman Empire, but do you know anything about that?

NBB: In terms of Hispania, which would have been the province at the time, which includes Spain and Portugal, you're quite right. One of the principle problems with thinking about the Manichaeans in the antique period is under pressure from the imperial authorities who are working closely with the catholic (small 'c') church, in the fourth and fifth centuries, the Manichaeans are evidently not liked by the authorities for a whole variety of reasons. But what happens towards the end of the fourth century is that Manichaean as a term becomes a label of abuse, and the term is codified in a whole series of imperial laws which prohibit Manichaeans gathering and worshipping, and it becomes a label of convenience that can be put onto other people that the authorities didn't like. The best example of that in relation to what you're talking about is Priscillian, who was a charismatic Christian bishop in Roman Spain at this time, who was not a Manichaean. He appears to have eaten meat, for instance, so that would have been a no-no for a genuine Manichaean. But he did certain things. For example, he read apocryphal Christian texts that had fallen out of favour, and he was branded a Manichaean. So the sources will call him a Manichaean, and presumably that's what people are grasping at when they want to talk about the geographical profundity of the Manichaeans in this period, they include people like Priscillian, who was labelled as a Manichaean really as a term on convenience, as a way of getting him, and prosecuting him. But in no respects was he a Manichaean. There's very little material evidence. We have a few inscriptions denoting that certain people were Manichaeans, but we have no remains of Manichaean churches, we have no remains of Manichaean monasteries in the Roman Empire. Egypt is a special case in that regard. It's problematic to suggest such wide geographical breadth, but it's one way of selling the importance of the religion which I don't think many Manichaean scholars would necessarily object to.

APS: Yes, we can talk about Egypt. There was the publication of the material from Kellis. Maybe you could tell us about that. I don't think it's all that well known tot he interested public.

NBB: The Kellis material is a special case in point, really. It's been known for a considerable period of time, stretching back to the late nineteenth century that the Manichaeans had a very strong presence in Egypt. Alexandria is often cited in both Manichaean and anti-Manichaean sources as being a hotbed of Manichaean activity. And then in the 1920s and 1930s there was a significant collection of Manichaean texts that came to light from Narmusis? Which is the delta area of Egypt, all written in Coptic. But then in the late 1980s and early 1990s there was an ongoing excavation of a late-fourth-century Roman village in the Dakhlah Oasis down towards the bottom end of Egypt, central Egypt rather, which in its day was known as Kellis. There was a particular house there, known technically as house 3, which contained a significant number of what turned out to be after much painstaking work by a number of extremely talented scholars, people like Iain Gardner, for instance, who is based in Australia, turned out to be Manichaean liturgical texts written on papyrus and written on wooden boards, most of them in Coptic, although there were bilingual Manichaean texts, written in Syriac and Coptic, with some Greek. Most recently—there's been an edition in the last four years—of personal letters and correspondences between what appears to be a family of Manichaeans based around Kellis. It's quite interesting in terms of understanding social dynamics and family dynamics in this period, as there is evidently a Manichaean woman, a mother, based in Kellis, who is writing to her husband and a number of sons who are seemingly peripatetic Manichaean missionaries, maybe elects, maybe just hearers, who are going around Egyptian countryside and the urban centres of Egypt, spreading the Manichaean

message. Most recently there's been an edition of what appear to be extracts, excerpts from letters written by Mani himself, and translated into Coptic. Some of those have been found in Kellis and those have been published, I think it was in 2007 by Iain Gardner. The work on Kellis is still ongoing and I think there's still material to be edited and published. In understanding a very early Manichaean community in an area like Egypt which, in the fourth century, very many areas of Egypt were incredibly important for the development of a Christian monastic or ascetic ethos, and it seems that the Manichaeans were at the forefront of influencing the development of distinctive Christian monasticism. So the Kellis material has the potential of being the Nag Hammadi moment for Manichaean scholars.

APS: Fascinating.

NBB: Yes, most of the Kellis material is reasonably easily accessible. A significant proportion of it has been published, edited with facing English translations, so they are very accessible and I would encourage people to pick them up and have a look at them.

APS: Are they affordable as well, for those to don't have access to good university libraries?

NBB: They're reasonably affordable. They're published by Oxbow, and the most recent edition, which contains the excerpts from a couple of Mani's own letters, they're about £30. So in terms of scholarly editions I suppose they are affordable. Although most academic libraries will house copies of them. There's a really good reader of Manichaean texts from the later Roman Empire, edited by Iain Gardner, and that has a number of translations into English of Kellis material. So it's accessible stuff.

APS: I think that Jason BeDuhn speculated that in Egypt that the Gnostics—obviously there were Gnostic groups up and down the Nile because we have the Nag Hammadi material—they perhaps became absorbed into Manichaeism as the Sethian or Valentinian or whatever composite groups became less attractive and less powerful. Do you think that's a possibility?

NBB: I'm certainly aware of that idea. I certainly

think there are very strong correspondences between Christian Gnostic ideas as evidenced in the Nag Hammadi material, and Mani's own teachings, but also the writings and ideas of his later followers. I have reservations about calling the Manichaeans squarely Gnostic, but there were certainly very strong correspondences between Gnostic theology and Manichaean theology. Certainly in relation to the fluidity of religious allegiances in this period in the third, fourth, fifth century, in late antiquity, people could swap and change religious allegiance quite easily. It only becomes problematic in the mid- to late-fourth century when the imperial authorities are evidently clamping down on Gnostics and Manichaeans and other unsavoury parties from their perspective. It would be questionable the extent to which a Gnostic Christian would want to join a Manichaean group of Christians in this period because it would be jumping out of the frying pan and into the fire really. Certainly there are very strong correspondences between the two traditions.

APS: Do you think that Manichaeism, particularly early Manichaeism, should be categorised as a form of Christianity? I know that Mani called himself an apostle of Jesus Christ. Did they self-identify as Christians?

NBB: Not explicitly in the early period. From my perspective, in relation to the source material that I've looked at, there isn't a lot, particularly in relation to the early Manichaean period when Mani's alive, as a whole variety of sources, both hostile and sympathetic to the Manichaeans tell us, he was evidently a prolific author, writing letters, writing his own gospel, writing "Gnostic speculative" ideas about cosmology and cosmogony and theogony. And if you look at what's left of those texts, because they're all heavily excerpted, there's something Christian about them. Mani is evidently using existing Jewish and Christian texts to formulate his own ideas. In some instances, particularly in the letters that came to light in Kellis, we see Mani as effectively a Christian exegete who is using the gospels—and I mean canonical but also possibly apocryphal gospels—he's borrowing from them,

he's citing them, he's referencing them, he's paraphrasing them, in order to communicate his own sense of religious vocation. What it means to be a Christian in that period, and I think this is one of the big topics at the moment among early Christian scholars, is the extent to which there are a whole variety of Christianities in this period. Mani certainly qualifies as Christian, although what type of a Christian is a moot point really. He's certainly a Mesopotamian Christian, and that's a type of Christianity that is evidently going to be very different from the Mediterranean Christianity of somebody like Cyprian of Carthage at roughly the same period. So there's different types of Christianity in different geographical areas. I don't think I would necessarily have a problem with calling Mani a Christian. As you rightly point out, he self-designates as an apostle of Jesus Christ. He calls himself the paraclete, or the comforter that's promised in John's gospel, John 14. He's definitely working from a Christian position from what he says in his theology.

APS: In terns of Mani's origins, he was part of a baptismal group which much earlier scholarship tentatively identified as the Mandaeans but with the new material coming to light seems rather to be the Elkasites. Can you tell us a little about them?

NBB: Much about Mani's early life is very shadowy, and the Elkasites seem to have been a group based just south of the twin cities of Seleucia-Carpethothon, in Mesopotamia. They seem to have followed a monastic rule, for want of an expression, of a character called Elkasai who is a semi-divine legendary figure that appears in a whole variety of early Christian sources including Origen. He seems to have been a prophet and the author of a very important revelatory text, and scholars have linked this Elkasai with this group that Mani grew up in, this baptismal sect. They ostensibly were Jewish-Christians who abided by certain aspects of Torah, but nevertheless accepted the revelation of Jesus as messiah. So it was a hybridised form of Christianity whereby they most famously, in a possibly late-fifth-century Greek biography of

Mani known today as the Cologne Mani Codex, that text sets out Mani's early life within that baptismal sect and his separation from them, rather like Jesus in the gospels in relation to the Jewish authorities, he doesn't accept their interpretation of the law. The Elkasites seem to have been ritual washers, so they abluted on a daily basis, and Mani objected to this. In terms of what we know about the Elkasites we have to be a bit careful. We know about them largely through the Cologne Mani Codex, which is far from sympathetic to the Elkasites. The Elkasites in that text are effectively a stooge for the appearance of Mani on the world stage, the final great prophet. So what we know about them is quite limited. Some recent work has been done on this, particularly in relation to the problems raised by the sources, by a whole range of scholars

APS: Although this group turned out not to be the Mandaeans, there do seem to be some overlaps between Mandaean texts and Manichaean scripture, don't there?

NBB: Very much so. This was really before the appearance of the Cologne Mani Codex for the first time in the late 1960s but was published in the early 1970s in a series of articles. What we thought knew about Mani's early period was very much aligned with existing ideas in Mandaean texts, for example the Ginza. Some key ideas there about God and about revelation seem to tie in very neatly with what Mani himself was saying. As I understand it, this literature and scholarship on the Mandaeans has really been picking up pace from the 1920s onwards and reached a point where there's a Swedish scholar called Geo Widingren, who wrote a very important book on Mani. He was first and foremost a Mandaean scholar and he was primarily the person who advanced this relationship or apparent relationship between the baptists that Mani seems to have grown up with and Mandaean ideas and practices. He was looking at correspondences in Mandaean texts, but he was also looking at what late Islamic sources, which prior to the arrival of the Cologne Mani Codex had been the principle

sources of evidence really for Mani's early period. There's a very interesting text called the Fihrist By a character called al-Nadim, who's an Islamic writer in the tenth century. And this is effectively a kind of proto-wikipedia. It's an encyclopedia of all human knowledge and all human activity. Al-Nadim actually had an entry on Mani in there, so Widingren was looking at those entries in Arabic and making correspondences with what he was finding as he was editing the Mandaean texts, so certainly that idea that the baptists of Mani's early period were the Mandaeans has fallen out of favour really. Nevertheless, there still appears to be something in the water, the theological water. There are very strong correspondences between these baptists and the Mandaeans.

APS: Perhaps we could talk about some of the Manichaean ideas like the column of light.

NBB: All these ideas are drawn from a whole range of sources really. There's no one stable account of Mani's myth. The principle source detailing some of Mani's mythological ideas, a famous text written by Mani himself, a book for Shapur, Shapur I who was the monarch at the time that Mani was alive in Persia. Mani wrote an educational text for his benefit called the Shabuhragan, a book for Shapur, and he outlined aspects of the myth in there, mostly to do with the eschaton [the end times] and the punishment of sinners, who interestingly are people who aren't sympathetic to the Manichaeans. The whole cosmological outline of Mani's myth is really drawn from much later sources, may of which are actually lampooning the myth, as being a sort of fable or a joke. The interesting thing with regards to the myth is that opponents of the Manichaeans seem to suggest that the Manichaeans are doing themselves a service by abiding by this myth so faithfully. But really if you start to look at what's happening in Mesopotamia in this period, the third century and fourth century, myth appears to be one of the principle ways in which religious truth is communicated. Guy Stroumsa, who's based in Oxford, has done a lot of work on this, particularly on the relationship between Gnostic and Manichaean myth. Mani's myth is quite distinctive in the sense that he articulates quite neatly a whole range of divine personalities and divine characters. The Manichaean myth is extremely theatrical. I guess it's an attempt to situate human sin and human suffering in a cosmic context. It offers an explanation for suffering but it also offers a map of salvation. So the Manichaean believer would be able to imagine themselves as an aspect of this huge divine cosmic mechanism whereby at the point of death they are released from the confines of the material body that causes enormous physical suffering that really can't be controlled by the soul in any way. So the soul is alien to the experiences of the body. The soul ascends, literally—and I think Mani was very aware of spatial ideas—towards the heavens and along the column of glory and is processed in the astral bodies, primarily the sun and the moon, which contain the ships of light, which carry the purified soul heavenwards, towards heaven where they are received by a whole range of astral bodies, but primarily by the ultimate God, God the Father, and they are returned home safely. What should be [pointed out is that doesn't apply to everybody. The Manichaeans were very keen on linking the complexities of their myth to the internal hierarchies of the church. They had what is in effect a twofold structure in their church—I'm sure many people know about this. They have a group of elect, very senior Manichaeans who are revered for their asceticism and their religiosity, and they have a body of people called the hearers whose primary religious duty is to serve the needs of the elect. Fundamentally that amounts to supply alms, food and clothing. One of the duties of the elect was to consume a daily ritual meal whereby particular types of food, primarily vegetables, were consumed and metabolised in such a way that the light which was locked within the vegetable, within the foodstuff, was released in their metabolic processes of the body.

APS: This is the cucumbers and watermelons?

NBB: This is the famous cucumbers and watermelons that cry when plucked, as

Augustine says. Only the souls of the elect are considered fir for immediate salvation and for involvement or entanglement in this cosmic mechanism. The souls of hearers have to wait for another one or two stages of reincarnation to reach the point where they are freed like members of the elect. Everybody else, of course, had to wait much longer. The interesting thing about Mani's mythology is its detail, and it evidently draws on a whole range of sources and influences, foremost amongst them being some of the ideas contained in the Gnostic myth, though that as you know is a fairly broad thing and to pin it down to one gnostic text would be problematic. But there's also evidence of Mani using Jewish material, most famously the book of Enoch 1 Enoch. Some of the ideas in there about the presence and generation of sin and suffering. So it's really a very complex representation of the universe. One of the things that often gets lost is the weight of polemicizing against the myth, which people reading about Mani now carry with them unconsciously. Most of the students I teach say, well how can anyone really have believed this stuff? And that holds really for aspects of Gnostic mythology in general. I always tell them that the world in the second and third and fourth centuries was a very different place, and people had very different intellectual conceits in the period and Mani was offering, as far as he was concerned, a scientific understanding of the universe. So the myth is, in a sense, the thing that Mani revealed to humanity, the complexity of the work of the universe with all these different astral bodies influencing human thought and behaviour and determining human fate, was very much something that was received as an explanation for life.

APS: I find some aspects of it quite charming, the concrete aspects of it. That there really is more light in cucumbers and watermelons, or that you can look up at the milky way and see the liberated light on its way to the Father.

NBB: Jason BeDuhn, who you mentioned earlier, wrote a book that came out in 2000, called The Manichaean Body, which looked to reconstruct the lived experiences of antique Manichaens and the extent to which we could begin to understand the way they thought about the world. A Manichaean elect and a Manichaean hearer would have had a very animistic understanding of the universe. Although these characterisations come from people like Augustine, you can imagine that a Manichaean elect would be very upset at the thought of a plant undergoing suffering as it was plucked from the ground. There was a confessional prayer that was said by both the elect and the hearers prior to the consumption of food because eating food caused food harm because it was being gnashed by teeth, so in order to exonerate themselves from this sin there was a confessional prayer that was said before each meal. Every aspect of the universe was alive for Manichaeans.

APS: Which puts the lie to the general image of the Manichaean religion as something world-hating and negative.

NBB: That's one of the great tricks that people like Augustine pulled. He was able in a whole range of works to make the Manichaean religion to seem as unpleasant as possible, and as pointless as possible, which is obviously spurious considering he was a Manichaean for ten years of his life. It was just a PR stunt on his part. I think these simple dichotomies of body-soul are problematic in understanding how late antique Manichaeans understood their own embodiment. They probably didn't have such a straightforward understanding of the soul being out of place in the body. Certainly the body was a problem for Manichaeans, but it was something that had to be controlled and conditioned and turned into something that could be useful. So in other words, as far as the elect were considered, the body has to be efficacious, metabolising food in order to affect its successful release. So there are very complex relationships really. The dichotomies between body and soul are extremely complex. We're on really now beginning to appreciate some of these problems and starting to develop a clearer understanding of late ancient ideas of the body

particularly with regard to the Manichaeans..

APS: Is there any hint of mystical practice in any of the sources that we have? The spark of light gets liberated at death if you're one of the elect, but is there any hint of doing something like this within this life, apart from the bodily disciple and various ritual practices? Anything like a mystical ascent of the soul?

NBB: You're talking about theurgic ideas?

APS: Yes.

NBB: There's no specific evidence of mystical practices particularly within late antique Manichaeism, but there was evidently detailed meditation on the nature of the soul and on the fate of the soul, both in the body and after release. This is one of the interesting things about the Manichaeans particularly as they came to be settled in Egypt. A whole range of liturgical texts—psalms, effectively—came to light in the late 1920s, early 1930s, mostly written in Coptic, where there's evidently some sort of psalmic tradition of meditation on the fate of the soul and on the relation of the soul to the universe. But there's no explicit theurgic practice described in any of the sources, but clearly Manichaeans were thinking and liturgicising about these things. We don't know really what the contexts of these psalms really were because we don't really know anything about the physical space in which they were chanted or sung, There is evidence in some of the texts that came to light in the Kellis cache of Manichaeans involved in binding spells and incantations. A guy called Paul Mirecki has done some work on those, but again I wouldn't really want to speculate too far.

APS: When we read about Mani having a vision of his divine twin at 12 and 24 years old, I was wondering if there was anything corresponding to that for Manichaeans, or whether that was unique to Mani himself.

NBB: Well, it appears to have been unique. The source for that is this fairly late life of Mani, the Cologne Mani Codex.

APS: The first time I read of that episode I immediately thought, well, that's very suspect, it doesn't sound like a historical-biographical episode, but it was more symbolic. The 12 made me think of Jesus going to Jerusalem at the age of 12 in the Gospel of Luke.

NBB: Certainly the author of that text was following a tried and tested model of representing credible religious experiences. Key periods like the age of 12 and 24 are very accentuated in the text. There's a body of material that I don't know much about, because linguistically it's not my competency. But in the late nineteenth, early twentieth century there was this scramble for central Asian religious relics, in placing around, for example, Turfan, some of the early discoveries there by German and British archaeologists were Manichaean texts created by Manichaean monks at some point between the eighth and tenth centuries—the dating is debatable. Again there are psalmic liturgical texts relating to the fate of the soul. There's nothing explicit in terms of mystical experiences. Most of the mystical experiences pertain to Mani himself, and they're actually in texts that are quite clearly intended to situate Mani's authority as a figure who has experienced some level of divine revelation.

APS: We've spoken of Christian influence on Manichaeism and that it's arguably a form of Christianity, and then we have Augustine being a Manichaean before he becomes such an influential figure in the church, but do you think there was a backwash from Manichaeism back into catholic Christianity? I'm thinking of things like confession, celibacy, musical liturgy. Those have been listed as possible examples of Manichaean influence on mainstream Christianity.

NBB: Yeah, this is another area that people are working on at the moment. It's difficult to believe that there wouldn't be some very strong influence of Manichaean Christianity on an emerging catholic Christianity of this period simply because a lot of literature produced in the fourth century is effectively an exchange of ideas between catholic Christianity and Manichaean Christianity, and I would say that the flow of influences is stronger in terms of what the catholics are drawing from the Manichaeans

than what the Manichaeans are drawing from the catholics. Certainly in relation to some of the personalised details that you find, for example, in the Coptic psalm book, where some of the theology is very intimate and relates to the fate of the soul. The soul is speaking at points in these psalms. That sort of personalised—and I use the expression very guardedly—spirituality is very strongly pronounced in the writings of Augustine. So Augustine's most famous text the Confession, Augustine's prayer or plea to God, the contours of that personal appeal to God, I would argue, are Manichaean. And that's evidence of Augustine's Manichaean background coming through very strongly, although probably completely unconsciously to him. The extent to which fourth century desert monasticism borrowed from the Manichaeans is very strong but not necessarily always quantifiable. Some of the extremes of fasting, for instance, that you read about in the Apothemata, this collection of lives of Egyptian monks, they're things that the Manichaeans were doing, and perhaps doing much earlier. In relation to the theology as well, another aspect that may come out in Augustine's work is the models of determinism that the Manichaeans seem to have held, and the extent to which some people were likely to be saved and some people were likely to be damned, that comes through very clearly in Augustine's work the City of God, where there's a body of elect who will be received, then there's a body of the masses who will perhaps endure sin and suffering.

APS: Is there a secondary salvation for the mass of people in Manichaeism?

NBB: It's an area that's disputed. This is one of the great unspoken questions really. The Manichaeans aren't too explicit about this. You do find characterisations of the sorts of dilemmas that this issue raises in anti-Manichaean works. This is one of the popular conceptions about the Manichaeans. Lots of people say, well how could this religion have possibly have caught on if ti excludes large numbers of people from any personal sense of salvation? Whether or not it was actually an issue for the Manichaeans of the time, I don't think it necessarily was, and it's never explicitly addressed in any Manichaean text that I'm aware of. Certainly in the work by Mani detailing the eschaton, the opponents of the Manichaeans are being taunted by the Manichaeans who are obviously safe in the heavenly abode, and that seems to imply the mass of people who have failed to assist the Manichaeans. Really that's a reflection of the social experience of those Manichaeans, I would say. In other words, they probably were a reasonably small number of people who by and large fell foul of people and groups and societies and governments who weren't necessarily supportive of their religion, outside of their own church. So it's never really explicitly detailed.

APS: I wanted to ask you about Manichaeism and Islam, because they were in similar regions of the world and Mani has sometimes been compared to Muhammad in intentionally founding a religion and including figures from previous religions, though Mani's range of figures was much broader. They have been compared sometimes, haven't they?

NBB: Certainly this idea that Mani is a seal, the seal of previous prophets, that is explicit in Quranic and hadith representations of Muhammad, so there are definite correspondences there. When you think about the time and the proximity of Manichaeism in relation to early Islam, it's unbelievable really that there's not going to be some sort of correspondence and influence between Manichaeans and early followers of Muhammad. Early Islamic writers are obviously very intrigued by the Manichaeans, because they see correspondences, although rather like catholic Christians in the fourth and fifth centuries, the correspondences perhaps need to be exaggerated a little bit. So eventually the Manichaeans fall foul of Islamic writers and eventually of the Islamic authorities by being classified as heretics. There's certainly work that needs to be done on understanding how, for instance, Manichaean texts, particularly the very famous text that came to light in the late third century called the Kephalaia, which is a Greek word that literally means "Chapters",

the representation of Mani in there as a great teacher, as a great authority, and the way that this authority is communicated by a chain of recognised teachers and authorities, is very similar to the way that hadith develops in Islam, and there are accepted, recognised authorities for passing on the teachings of the prophet. So there are all sorts of correspondences that need to be teased out with more work.

APS: And were they treated as people of the book?

NBB: Not explicitly as people of the book, but they were certainly afforded a degree of protection by the early caliphate.

APS: Then we have Manichaeism lasting up until the fourteenth century, is that right?

NBB: There are sightings, or attested sightings, of Manichaeans into the fourteenth century, yeah.

APS: And then these odd survivals, such as Mani as Buddha in remote Buddhist temples into contemporary times. Could you talk a bit about what we know about the last phases of Manichaeism, and then the possibility of any direct or indirect influence on Catharism or the Bogomils?

NBB: I certainly think that's feasible, but the problem is, as you head down the centuries, the influence of the Manichaeans becomes very remote really, and very distant. You're quite right in saying there's evidence there, of a Mani Buddha. As I understand it, and some people wouldn't agree with me, there was a tendency in earlier scholarship, and I'm thinking of Runciman's book on the Medieval Manichee, of suggesting there was a direct genealogical association made between ancient Manichaeans and Cathars or Albigensians. But I don't know how stable that relationship actually would be. I think there are two problems. First of all, such groups are called . . . the name Cathar means "purifier" and actually the Catharistai, the purifiers are actually first noted as far as I'm aware in an early fourth century text by Augustine named the De Heresicus, On Heresies, and he's dealing with a group of Manichaeans who are being subject to judicial inquiry, and he's actually relating, and he's actually relating the details of the inquiry for his audience, and he talks about a schismatic group called the Catharistai, who take the purification process one stage further and actually eat human semen. This is obviously bunkum, it's heresiological invective that Augustine is picking up on and disseminating. But there's an early tenth century writer called Eckbert of Schönau, who you may have come across, who in a series of sermons actually lends this group of dualistic Christians in and around the area of Cologne an identity by calling them the Catharistai, and citing this text from the De Hereticus, and the characteristics of this group that Eckbert is talking about, these dualist Christian heretics, he draws directly from Augustine's writings. Their identity is drawn from earlier Christian writings. So the extent to which there are evident correspondences is arguable. Dualism is a characteristic of many religions. Extreme asceticism is a characteristic of very many religions. I wouldn't rule out some sort of influence between the Cathars and Albigensians and the Manichaeans, but where would they be getting the information? There were probably no Manichaean texts available to them. They were being characterised by their opponents as Manichaeans, so Manichaean was a very effective term of abuse. It basically meant "son of a bitch." So that kind of link is being revised now, but that's not to say that it's inappropriate. I always think of Stoyanov's book *The Other God* and the way in which Stoyanov doesn't necessarily tie himself down to very rigid forms of historical influence between different religious groupings between different periods, but the way he paints a very broad comparative canvas of influence. I don't think that's inappropriate and I think it has its place in understanding an alternative tradition, fundamentally. But I'm a little sceptical about direct links between the Manichaeans and the Cathars.

APS: In his interview with Miguel Conner in our book Voices of Gnosticism, Jason BeDuhn suggested that the Cathars may have emerged as the result of a Manichaean cell that had gone underground, I suppose as a family affair, and they may have almost forgotten who they were and resurfaced. It's just speculative but it's a possibility.

NBB: It's speculative, but I think we simply don't know. I don't know whether you know Tardieu's book *Manichaeism*, that's recently translated from the French, one of the most useful things in that book, which isn't very long, about 100 pages, is the thematic chronology in the back of the book. Most people know about the Manichaeans in the fourth century, a lot of people know about the Manichaeans in the fifth century, there's evidence of the Manichaeans in the sixth century and seventh century, and later, but really from the tenth century onwards they start to fall off the historical record, although their identity becomes confused with other groups who are being labelled Manichaean. We can't really say with any certainty whether or not they're actually Manichaean. Tardieu picks out references from really obscure texts to indicate that he Manichaeans were still around from the eleventh century, and that they were actually still active and doing Manichaean things. So I don't think this idea is so crazy really. The Manichaeans were evidently a sect who were continually persecuted by various authorities for very long periods of time, and even in the very early fourth-century Coptic material that came to light in Narmouthis, there's still in that early period a strong identity of being the church of the persecuted, so this is obviously an aspect of their corporate identity that forms very early on in their history. I don't see why they couldn't have endured persecution stretching all the way up into the twelfth and thirteenth centuries. So it's highly possible that there was some link and the Cathars were Manichaeans, but lie you said it speculation, but there's a possibility that that's the case.

APS: Well, I think that's a good place to end the interview. Thanks very much, Nicholas.

Andrew Phillip Smith

Into the Bridal Chamber:
A Face in the Crowd

If you ask anyone with a slight knowledge of the subject what some of the basic objections to Gnosticism might be, she or he is likely to reply, without necessarily knowing why, that Gnosticism is elitist. Elitism is seen by many as unfair, controlling, deluded, paranoid, outdated, at odds with modern egalitarian values. Gnosticism is seen as elitist because salvation or saving gnosis is supposedly not available to all, only to a select few.

What is an elite? The elite, as the Oxford English Dictionary puts it, with seeming approval, is "the choice part, or flower of society." What makes a person part of an elite in general society? Intelligence, wealth, spiritual desire or attainment, physical strength, a dominating character, being born into or elected into an elite social group are all options. The English word elite is cognate with 'elect', both as noun and verb. The elite are the elect, are the chosen. But to be chosen means that someone must pick you out. Though elites may supposedly be elected democratically, or may be designated by a higher authority, whether temporal or spiritual, many elites are self-selected. This is particular true of so-called elites in small or alternative religious groups.

Who in Gnosticism could constitute this elite? Since Gnosticism is a religion of salvation, the elite are the saved. Most obviously these are the pneumatics, those of the spirit, in Valentinian Gnosticism, who are distinct from the psychics, those merely of soul, and the hylics, those of matter. Here we have a category that, at least on the surface, may be rightly called elitist. There are similar categories in other Gnostic or related religions.

Perhaps it is the notion of salvation itself that is at fault. However there are many other religions of salvation, which may or may not be truly classed as elitist. Christianity comes to mind as a familiar example. Most of its adherents would deny that they are elitist. In the Hellenistic world the mystery cults also offered salvation through the god. The mysteries were open to all who qualified, but the prerequisites often selected only the wealthy, free and educated. Most, if not all, religions have some equivalent outlook even if they cannot be properly classified as soteriological or salvationist. There must be something essentially wrong, missing or incomplete in an individual human being, either in his or her natural state or in the current position imposed by human culture outside of the religion. If a human is in an adequate state without religion then there is no need for it. Even in paganism it is necessary for a human to have some right relationship with the gods or with nature to function properly and fully. So, all religion divides people into two groups, those who are saved, on the way to enlightenment, free from sin, who live rightly, and those who are not or do not. Without this distinction, religion and spirituality would be merely lifestyle options, as in some of the more superficial forms of the New Age movement.

Every spiritual approach has its pluses and minuses. If you believe that your approach merely is something that feels good to you, then while there is a certain honesty to that, there isn't any incentive towards any substantial transformation. Spirituality becomes a personal interest on the level of a hobby. If you believe that everyone on earth should be doing what you do then you are bound to proselytizer and attempt to convert everyone else. If you are an elitist then you are denying salvation to the bulk of humanity.

But a religion is only truly elitist if it proposes that only a limited group of people are to be saved. A religion that has as its aim the eventual conversion of the whole of humanity isn't really elitist, although it of course has other problems. Further, an elite can be temporary. A religion may acknowledge that though at present only a few may be worthy, the cosmic design may require all of humanity to eventually qualify so that creation can fulfil itself. This is the case with the Manichaeans who certainly had an elite group, known as the elect, but who saw their mission as liberating every last particle of light that is mixed with darkness, whether in humanity or in the material world as a whole. This is also implicit or explicit in many versions

of Gnosticism: in order for the process that began with the One or the Father emanating out into the Pleroma, and that reached crisis in the fall of Sophia and the birth of Yaldabaoth and the creation of the world and humanity, to be completed, all of humanity must be saved.

Of course there are nuances to each point of view. A secondary salvation may be allowed to those who don't have your own good fortune to be on the path but whose hearts are in the right place. Or, as with ecumenical Christianity, those who don't have the right religion but whose faith is respectable and mainstream enough— Islam, Buddhism, Judaism—may be granted a valid yet inferior salvation. The predestination of Calvinism is an odd sort of elitism, a pre-selection from the beginning. An effective elite may just claim to be part of a hierarchy, as with the high-and-mighty of most forms of Christianity, who may deny in their dogma that their salvation is any greater than that of the laity, though their actions, privilege and wealth may speak otherwise.

Even elitist spirituality may in turn proffer a deferred salvation to those who may be in on the right path. This may easily be shuffled off into another lifetime, as with the Cathars for whom salvation was a result of an individual dying with the status of a Perfect, the Cathar elect. Cathar Believers, the rank and file who were not under such strict obligations, would be reincarnated as Perfects in the next life. Reincarnation is indeed one of the most flexible systems for granting deferred salvation to the rest of humanity while allowing only an elite to qualify in the current world or age.

In the Apocryphon of John the realms of the four luminaries of the Pleroma are assigned to Adamas, Seth, the children of Seth and the finally saved. Adamas is the prototypical perfect human, Seth his son, and the model of the next stage in humanity. The children of Seth are the Gnostics, who as the souls of the saints, or the immovable race, will inhabit the third luminary in the Pleroma. The final luminary is for those who will eventually be saved, who are ignorant of the Pleroma and do not repent at once, but will do so eventually. In a question-and-answer sequence between John and the Saviour we are later told that souls that go astray will be cast into a body, into prison and chains, again and again until they become perfect and are saved. Ominously it is only those who achieved truly knowledge but turned away will be tortured and subjected to punishment continually.

What then are the real problems with elitism? It may not be fair but, hey!, life isn't fair. Perhaps my most basic objection is that elitism isn't a good way of relating to others. It also focuses on a specific human attribute or set of attributes. The most intelligent are not necessarily the kindest or most generous pr the most morally responsible. Ditto the strongest. Or the most spiritually developed. Altered or higher states of consciousness, or esoteric knowledge, does not necessarily make you aware of the needs of others. Those who look inwards do not necessarily look outwards. The focus of an elite is narrower than that of general humanity, as is the means of qualification. Various contenders for the elite do not concede equal validity to other self-designated elites.

What's the way out of this? One possibility is to consider elitism as pone particular mode of being. At root we are all similar, with similar capacities and needs. Those who are spiritually advanced, or on the road to it have in many ways fewer freedoms. Cathar Perfects, Manichaean elect and many many other considered spiritually advanced, including monks of various types, were subject to strictures of diet, daily activities, celibacy and other intimacy. Few readers or writers of *The Gnostic* would be willing to take these on board for extended periods!

I've always liked the comment by Mme Ouspensky on Gurdjieff's practice of self-remembering, that "when you remember yourself you are just another person in the room." Gurdjieff taught that one's spiritual evolution depended on the possibility of developing higher bodies that would survive the death of the planetary or physical body through 'conscious labour and voluntary suffering'. Apart from a handful of special individuals like Jesus, Muhammad, Buddha or Moses, Gurdjieff seems to have considered that at birth everyone's possibilities were more or less identical, and that right conditions of existence would result in everyone being able to follow conscience and evolve. Yet some of the consequences of his view of human possibilities are unappetizing. He once described humanity as acorns. Only a few of them would grow into oaks, yet those acorns that did not were not wasted as they decayed into fertiliser that enabled future oaks to grow. Gurdjieff's approach is a kind of spiritual meritocracy, dependent not on birth or religion or spiritual election but on the right use of one's personal energy and right action. He classified genuine "ways" of religion and spirituality as evolutionary fast tracks, but also said that these might be called subjective ways, as opposed to the objective way of the householder, in which people who followed their consciences would progress without requiring all the paraphernalia of spiritual disciplines, esoteric knowledge, a teacher, and so on. Nevertheless, Gurdjieff wasn't very specific about the future of those who weren't able to develop completely in this lifetime and in the hands of less scrupulous teachers his meritocracy has become a stark division into the elite and the masses, even if those particular terms are not used.

I would certainly classify myself as an egalitarian, yet I have a nagging feeling that there is something to the concept of a spiritual elite, and perhaps even to limited forms of meritocratic elitism in education and social life, though even typing this makes me uneasy. Of course, if a truly benevolent elite did exist, they would be concerned with improving the general good and helping others to better themselves, until an elite was no longer necessary. As stated, the problem is that those who presume this status to themselves are often the least suitable to assume it. In his book Politics and the Occult, Gary Lachmann pointed out that there may be something to be said for the concept of a spiritual elite proposed by, for example, the Traditionalist René Guénon. "The idea of some Sovereign Pontiff and his agents masterminding society for our own good is chilling, yet it is arguable that many of us do avoid the responsibility of governing ourselves. . . [Guénon's] advocacy of [an elite] isn't necessarily prompted by some nefarious appetite for political power. It may be rooted in an unflattering yet accurate assessment of human psychology."[1]

On the other hand, an elite may exist and yet be illegitimate. Possibly the most popular current view of a hidden elect is the paranoid and popular notion of the Illuminati. Here we have an elite that is supposed to have existed for centuries, if not millennia, influencing humanity behind the scenes, yet is concerned with controlling and limiting humankind for its own selfish motives. Here we have David Icke's reptiloids and his pink wrinkly old men and other brands of aliens, disguised as Queen Elizabeth II, George W Bush and all the other world leaders (presumably Obama too, but I can't be bothered to check), Or the Priory of Sion in its more nefarious manifestations. Or whatever odds and sods of secret societies from various countries and aeons can be daisy chained together to produce a conspiracy theory that will convince someone, somewhere that someone else, somewhere else, is controlling our lives. In Gnosticism we have the archons, and the great archon himself, lurking behind the scenery, chiefly in human minds, pulling strings and nudging the course of history in order to frustrate the escape plan mounted from the Pleroma.

The spiritual elite is often a paradigm, a pattern to be followed rather than an existing entity. Plato's ideal republic existing more in the world of forms or ideas than in ours. The ascended masters, the conscious circle of humanity, secret chiefs, Great White Brotherhood, Agartha, Shambhala, Atlantis, always an age or a continent away from us.

Yet who of us can really claim to be part of the spiritual elite? I felt that I was, for a while, a long time ago, when I was part of an esoteric group. but the feeling soon evaporated in the heat of all the hypocrisy and contradictions that were generated.

Perhaps in the end it is more important to feel one's common humanity, to have experiences in which one is the same as everyone else, as in a sports match at which you are just another supporter, a march at which you are just another protester, a birthday party at which you are just another member of the family, a city street in which you are just another passerby, a face in the crowd.

NOTES

1. *Politics and the Occult* (Quest Books, 2008), p. 180-181.

Edward Gibbon

On the Gnostics

Embedded in Chapter XV, 'On the Progress of the Christian religion' in The History of the Decline and Fall of the Roman empire, Edward Gibbon's (1737-1794) summary of the Gnostics was for a long time the fullest popular description of them in English. Gibbon's persistent dislike of Christianity, and his pinning of it as one of the causes of the decline of the Roman Empire led to a curiously schizoid assessment of the Gnostics. On the one hand he sees them as representing, along with the other heretics, examples of an extreme reaction to Judaism that mainstream Christianity avoided, and castigates the "vain science," by which he probably means the cosmological systems. On the other, he states, seemingly as his own imaginative opinion, that they were "distinguished as the most polite, the most learned, and the most wealthy of the Christian name"

Richard Smith, in his essay "The Modern Relevance of Gnosticism." included as a postscript to the revised edition of The Nag Hammadi Library in English, labels Gibbon's statement as "a mischievous lie" but acknowledges that Gibbon's statement "becomes, if not an advertisement for heresy, then at least a subversion of orthodoxy." [p.533. Stephan Hoeller, in turn, commented "(Admittedly Gibbon did not share the low esteem in which the Church Fathers held Gnostics, but does this make him a liar?)"[Gnosticism: New Light on the Ancient Tradition of Inner Knowing, p.185]

Perhaps the last word on Gibbon should be given to William Blake, who detested Gibbon's sceptical, Enlightenment sensibility. "

'Gibbon plied his lash of steel,
Voltaire turned his wracking wheel,
Charlemaine & his barons bold
Stood by, and mocked in iron & gold.'

[from the Rossetti MS]

While the orthodox church preserved a just medium between excessive veneration and improper contempt for the law of Moses, the various heretics deviated into equal but opposite extremes of error and extravagance. From the acknowledged truth of the Jewish religion, the Ebionites had concluded that it could never be abolished. From its supposed imperfections, the Gnostics as hastily inferred that it never was instituted by the wisdom of the Deity. There are some objections against the authority of Moses and the prophets, which too readily present themselves to the sceptical mind; though they can only be derived from our ignorance of remote antiquity, and from our incapacity to form an adequate judgment of the divine economy. These objections were eagerly embraced and as petulantly urged by the vain science of the Gnostics. As those heretics were, for the most part, averse to the pleasures of sense, they morosely arraigned the polygamy of the patriarchs, the gallantries of David, and the seraglio of Solomon. The conquest of the land of Canaan, and the extirpation of the unsuspecting natives, they were at a loss how to reconcile with the common notions of humanity and justice. * But when they recollected the sanguinary list of murders, of executions, and of massacres, which stain almost every page of the Jewish annals, they acknowledged that the barbarians of Palestine had exercised as much compassion towards their idolatrous enemies, as they had ever shown to their friends or countrymen. Passing from the sectaries of the law to the law itself, they asserted that it was impossible that a religion which consisted only of bloody sacrifices and trifling ceremonies, and whose rewards as well as punishments were all of a carnal and temporal nature, could inspire the love of virtue, or restrain the impetuosity of passion. The Mosaic account of the creation and fall of man was treated with profane derision by the Gnostics, who would not listen with patience to the repose of the Deity after six days' labor, to the rib of Adam, the garden of Eden, the trees of life and of knowledge, the speaking serpent, the forbidden fruit, and the condemnation pronounced against human kind for the venial offence of their first progenitors. The God of Israel was impiously represented by the Gnostics as a being liable to passion and to error, capricious in his favor, implacable in his resentment, meanly jealous of his superstitious worship, and confining his partial providence to a single people, and to this transitory life. In such a character they could discover none of the features of the wise and omnipotent Father of the universe. They allowed that the religion of the Jews was somewhat less criminal than the idolatry of the Gentiles; but it was their fundamental doctrine, that the Christ whom they adored as the first and brightest emanation of the Deity appeared upon earth to rescue mankind from their various errors, and to reveal a new system of truth and perfection. The most learned of the fathers, by a very singular condescension, have imprudently admitted the sophistry of the Gnostics. Acknowledging that the literal sense is repugnant to every principle of faith as well as reason, they deem themselves secure and invulnerable behind the ample veil of allegory, which they carefully spread over every tender part of the Mosaic dispensation.

It has been remarked with more ingenuity than truth, that the virgin purity of the church was never violated by schism or heresy before the reign of Trajan or Hadrian, about one hundred years after the death of Christ. We may observe with much more propriety, that, during that period, the disciples of the Messiah were indulged in a freer latitude, both of faith and practice, than has ever been allowed in succeeding ages. As the terms of communion were insensibly narrowed, and the spiritual authority of the prevailing party was exercised with increasing severity, many of its most respectable adherents, who were called upon to renounce, were provoked to assert their private opinions, to pursue the consequences of their mistaken principles, and openly to erect the standard of rebellion against the unity of the church. The Gnostics were distinguished as the most polite, the most learned, and the most wealthy of the Christian name; and that general appellation, which expressed a superiority of knowledge, was either assumed by their own pride, or ironically bestowed by the envy of their adversaries. They were almost without exception of the race of the Gentiles, and their principal founders seem to have been natives of Syria or Egypt, where the warmth of the climate disposes both the mind and the body to indolent and contemplative devotion. The Gnostics blended with the faith of Christ many sublime but obscure tenets, which they derived from oriental philosophy, and even from the religion of Zoroaster, concerning the eternity of matter, the existence of two principles, and the mysterious hierarchy of the invisible world. As soon as they launched out into that vast abyss, they delivered themselves to the guidance of a disordered imagination; and as the paths of error are various and infinite, the Gnostics were imperceptibly divided into more than fifty particular sects, of whom the most celebrated appear to have been the Basilidians, the Valentinians, the Marcionites, and, in a still later period, the Manichaeans. Each of these sects could boast of its bishops and congregations, of its doctors and martyrs; and, instead of the Four Gospels adopted by the church, the heretics produced a multitude of histories, in which the actions and discourses of Christ and of his apostles were adapted to their respective tenets. The success of the Gnostics was rapid and extensive. They covered Asia and Egypt, established themselves in Rome, and sometimes penetrated into the provinces of the West. For the most part they arose in the second century, flourished during the third, and were suppressed in the fourth or fifth, by the prevalence of more fashionable controversies, and by the superior ascendant of the reigning power. Though they constantly disturbed the peace, and frequently disgraced the name, of religion, they contributed to assist rather than to retard the progress of Christianity. The Gentile converts, whose strongest objections and prejudices were directed against the law of Moses, could find admission into many Christian societies, which required not from their untutored mind any belief of an antecedent revelation. Their faith was insensibly fortified and enlarged, and the church was ultimately benefited by the conquests of its most inveterate enemies.

But whatever difference of opinion might subsist between the Orthodox, the Ebionites, and the Gnostics, concerning the divinity or the obligation of the Mosaic law, they were all equally animated by the same exclusive zeal; and by the same abhorrence for idolatry, which had distinguished the Jews from the other nations of the ancient world. The philosopher, who considered the system of polytheism as a composition of human fraud and error, could disguise a smile of contempt under the mask of devotion, without apprehending that either the mockery, or the compliance, would expose him to the resentment of any invisible, or, as he conceived them, imaginary powers. But the established religions of Paganism were seen by the primitive Christians in a much more odious and formidable light. It was the universal sentiment both of the church and of heretics, that the daemons were the authors, the patrons, and the objects of idolatry. Those rebellious spirits who had been degraded from the rank of angels, and cast down into the infernal pit, were still permitted to roam upon earth, to torment the bodies, and to seduce the minds, of sinful men. The daemons soon discovered and abused

the natural propensity of the human heart towards devotion, and artfully withdrawing the adoration of mankind from their Creator, they usurped the place and honours of the Supreme Deity. By the success of their malicious contrivances, they at once gratified their own vanity and revenge, and obtained the only comfort of which they were yet susceptible, the hope of involving the human species in the participation of their guilt and misery. It was confessed, or at least it was imagined, that they had distributed among themselves the most important characters of polytheism, one daemon assuming the name and attributes of Jupiter, another of Aesculapius, a third of Venus, and a fourth perhaps of Apollo; and that, by the advantage of their long experience and aerial nature, they were enabled to execute, with sufficient skill and dignity, the parts which they had undertaken. They lurked in the temples, instituted festivals and sacrifices, invented fables, pronounced oracles, and were frequently allowed to perform miracles. The Christians, who, by the interposition of evil spirits, could so readily explain every preternatural appearance, were disposed and even desirous to admit the most extravagant fictions of the Pagan mythology. But the belief of the Christian was accompanied with horror. The most trifling mark of respect to the national worship he considered as a direct homage yielded to the daemon, and as an act of rebellion against the majesty of God.

Andrew Phillip Smith

Ignorant Design

Intelligent design has long been seen by its proponents as a more intellectually respectable alternative to creationism. Where we might not be able to swallow the literal creation of a human being on a single day, nor be able to clasp wholeheartedly to our bosoms the ultimate meaningless of neo-Darwinian evolution, with its more-than-glacially slow mutation of genes, the fittest for their environments of which happen to survive and so pass on their genes to the next generation, many religious people are more willing to accept a compromise between the two, known as Intelligent Design, or ID.

To the new atheists this is barely more scientifically respectable than creationism, but for others Intelligent Design has the advantage of not ignoring the fossil record or the existence of DNA or the genetic makeup of living creatures, or of not insisting that Adam rode a dinosaur in the Garden of Eden. (Surely there must be an atheist campaign somewhere to eliminate the use of the word creature: in a scientific context: a *creature* is made by a *creator*.) The argument by design proposes that certain aspects of the universe and living beings are better explained as being designed with intelligence rather than emerging as the result of fluke specifics of physical laws and the stress of environment. Ultimately the designer and director of evolution is God.

Science has responded to the argument by design with many strong objections, among them an argument from poor design. The world is like a garden, therefore there must be a gardener, says the theist. But parts of the world are desert. What then? Many specifics of human biology are sub-optimal. Apart from the famously useless (in adults at least) appendix, humans can't synthesise vitamin C, have inside out retinas, and have faces which are too flat, leading to crowded teeth and poor sinus drainage, which explains my teenage visits to the orthodontist and my constant catarrh.

Awkward as these defects are for ID-loving Christians, they pose no problem for Gnostics. According to Gnostics, human bodies are indeed designed, but by an ignorant demiurge who incompetently tries to imitate the pattern of the heavenly *anthropos*. We and the world were indeed designed, but it's an incompetent design made by an ignorant designer. A Gnostic creation museum is already under construction. Did he who made the lamb make thee?

Book Reviews

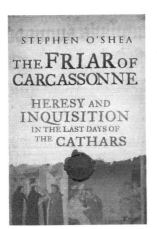

The Friar of Carcassonne Revolt against the Inquisition in the Last Days of the Cathars. **Stephen O'Shea. Hardcover, Walker and Company/ Profile Books, 340pp. $28/£17.99.**

Stephen O'Shea is capable of great history writing; his *The Perfect Heresy: the Life and Death of the Cathars* is witness to that. He's able to cover a complicated story efficiently and use his narrative talents to help the reader through a complex web of events (and an unfortunately confusing tendency for the same names to repeat- why did so many people have to be named Raymond or Bernard?). In *The Friar of Carcassonne: Revolt against the Inquisition in the last days of the Cathars* he returns to a story that he had covered in brief in the previous book, the story of Bernard Délicieux, which is indeed a fascinating story.

Bernard Délicieux, the eponymous friar of Carcassone, was a Franciscan who- amazingly -for a period of time succeeded in resisting the force of the inquisition in the Languedoc; protesting at the questionable testimonies won through interrogations and the divisive effect

on the small towns and villages of mutual fear and suspicion when people did not know if others had condemned them. His success didn't last, of course, and we know a lot of detail of the story precisely because it is recorded in the inquisition records when he was arrested and after prolonged trial (for obstructing the Holy Office, treason and killing the Pope), eventually died in prison in 1320, unfrocked and broken, physically and in spirit.

However, for a great part of the beginning of the book I kept wondering what had happened to O'Shea's narrative gift. Granted it's a harder book to structure than the Perfect Heresy, he needs to keep introducing "flashbacks" in the story to explain the background for the unfamiliar reader and the moving backwards and forwards is frankly confusing.

Another odd thing about the book is that the title leads you to believe that it is about the Cathars (and a lot of background about the Cathars is necessary to understand the situation) but the real fascination here has nothing to do with Cathar religion or people – it's all about Bernard Délicieux. The strangely modern sounding story of a man who, while apparently a convinced Franciscan monk, was able to sympathise with and come to the defence of his neighbours (even heretic Cathars) from the barrage of endless accusations that the inquisition had become and who also unbelievably succeeded in organising a popular movement for a while against the major massed forces of papacy and states due, seemingly, to the force of his personality combined with a gift for politics.

The decades of persecution of the Cathars had taken a tremendous toll on the spirit of the Languedoc region. The wars and slaughter had been followed by inquisition where careful techniques were used to encourage citizens to condemn others, leading to fear and suspicion of each other. This was what Bernard was struggling against. A sermon of Bernard's is said to have finished with a fable concerning a group of rams who over time had seen one by one of their number disappear; eventually one of them says "have we not horns?" and they realise they can band together to defend themselves, which they then do. Bernard went so far as to say "I am Jesus Christ" in that he had been sent to save the people of Carcassone from the outsiders who had come to destroy their community

Bernard's 'heresy' was not Catharism; it was his adherence to the Spiritual Franciscans, the revolutionary half of a spiritual schism in the Franciscan order that was ongoing in his period. The original Franciscan adherence to poverty (surely the only alternative at the time for those repulsed by the church's avarice) had already become muddied in the decades after his death in 1226 as the order attracted vast wealth and power. The Spirituals were a movement to return to that original purity, and had alternately been favoured and persecuted in the intervening time. There was a fear that the Spirituals and their lay followers, the Beguins, were dangerously close in spirit to the Cathars and could similarly divide the populace.

Bernard was, it seems, a great orator; as O'Shea describes him "a firebrand, imbued with profound spirituality and possessed of exceptional intelligence, at odds with the persecuting reflex of his time and the cruelty and spiritual corruption of the inquisition." *Le rage carcassonnaise*, Carcassonne madness, had been brewing since the turn of the century-anger against the damage done by the inquisitors- Bernard managed to lead the mob effectively in having prisoners released (for a time)from the hated Wall, the prison in Carcassone. He was persuasive in meetings with King Phillip IV, when that connection failed he tried to enlist the help of the Catalan prince Ferran of Majorca to annex Languedoc. (If he'd succeeded there, the shape of Southern Europe could have been completely different). His campaigns and machinations succeeded for years – how did he do it? When Pope Benedict XI (namesake of our current Pope) ordered his arrest and then suddenly died it was remembered that Bernard had predicted his death, and he was suspected of poisoning or worse.

And so it is that as the book progresses, one is more and more drawn in by the story- how easy it is to imagine a novel made from this theme! But the novelist would have to decide on where he stood on the uncertainties and it would lose out on subtleties: here we have just the equivocal evidence and its possible interpretations. Was Bernard overwhelmed by his own ability to move a crowd? How far did he go as a political wheeler-dealer? Was there any truth in the accusations of interest in magic or of poisoning the Pope?

In the afterword, O'Shea discusses the seductive urge to judge Friar Bernard anachronistically as a patriot of the Languedoc or a champion of freethinking or whatever suits our mindset. He was a man of his time; no saint but a remarkable man, nonetheless.

In the end he did succeed in casting doubt on the two registers (X and XI), enough doubt that they were no longer used as evidence and it was really with this issue he started his campaign. But his lingering legacy is the amazing story of his success (and failure) and the light it throws on the society of his time.

Tessa Finn

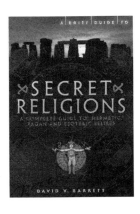

A Brief Guide to Secret Religions: A Complete Guide to Hermetic, Pagan and Esoteric Beliefs. David V. Barrett. Robinson. 320pp. £8.99.

David V. Barrett is a regular feature writer and reviewer for Fortean Times and specialises in obscure religious movements. A Brief Guide to Secret Religions homes in on the more marginal spiritual and religious groups, focusing on those that have their origin from or a significant presence in the UK. An appendix deals with Scientology which, the author maintains, does not quite fall into any of his main three categories. Perhaps there is the usual fear of litigation lurking here.

This chapter is tentative (perhaps because the Scientologists are notoriously litigious), "not suggesting that the Church of Scientology is in any way an occult religion . . . " but that "it may be instructive to consider very briefly the Church of Scientology in the context of some aspects of both New Age movements and Hermetic movements." (p.357-358.) God forbid that anyone should say so, let alone call Scientology a cult.

The survey is divided into three categories: New Age, Hermetic, Occult or High Magic groups, and Neo-paganism. Occasional double page spreads are headed "What I Believe" and contain excerpts from interviews with group leaders and ordinary practitioners on their personal opinions on a wide range of topics, from their reasons for following their particular paths to their views on life after death.

Barrett's approach is scholarly, balanced and neutral. While he rarely pokes fun at the many absurd claims and bizarre beliefs of the groups, neither does he gloss over the wishful thinking, alleged abuses, schisms and power struggles that inevitably emerge.

The New Age section is the most loosely defined, including extensive material on Theosophy and anthroposophy and associated personages and groups, on Gurdjieff, Subud, independent apostolic churches, as well as New Age proper, including Findhorn (which receives a particularly sympathetic treatment), UFO groups and alternative history.

The Hermetic section takes in the Golden Dawn and its various offshoots, along with Crowley, chaos magic, Satanism, and the issue of supposed ritual satanic abuse, primarily a fiction that occupied UK newspaper headlines in the 1980s and 90s and which Barrett sees as a modern equivalent of the witch hunt or the blood libel on Jews.

Witchcraft, including Wicca and Druidry, is entertainingly described. Even though these revivals may be seen as wholly modern creations, they are in fact native British religions, in that they originated on that island.

There is a vast array of weird and inventive traditions on display here. Two of my favourites in terms of sheer bizarre, tripped-out whackiness are: the Church of All worlds, which uses sci-fi elements, particularly from the novels of Robert Heinlein, and has a website described by Barrett as "a real-life online version of J.K. Rowling's fictional Hogwarts" (p.313) and the Aetherius Society of His Eminence Sir George King. King channelled an entity known as Mars Sector 6 and travelled astrally in spaceships. Members charge Spiritual Energy Batteries by chanting mantas and prayers. The energy in these storehouses may be then released later to help humanity during times of global crisis.

There isn't much here on the Gnostic revival outside of the chapter on Independent Apostolic Churches, which devotes a page to Jules Doinel and his legacy. This reflects a the British focus, in which Gnostic groups are not very evident. The section on Gurdjieff is fair enough, but the point of view of Barrett's main source is very obviously that of the Gurdjieff Society.

This is an exhilarating tour of the variety of new religious movements, and doubles as a reference book. Highly recommended for anyone who needs to differentiate between Druidcraft and the Druid Clan of Tara, or jog one's memory as the identity of Ruddlawm ap Gawr, Oberan Zell-Ravenheart or Kveldulfr Gundarsson.

Andrew Phillip Smith

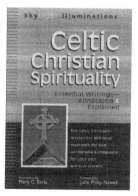

Celtic Christian Spirituality: Essential Writings—Annotated & Explained. Mary C. Earle. Skylight Paths. Paperback. 176pp. $16.99.

The Celtic countries, which are generally taken to be Wales, Ireland, Scotland, Brittany and Cornwall (though the latter two do not appear in this collection) developed a form of Christianity which, although Catholic, had a distinct complexion. The native Christian literature exudes a sense of wholeness and celebration, full of the appreciation of nature. Though life must have been hard in those poor, wet and often chilly areas, the questioning and angst of the Gnostics was not for them.

Here we find prayers, poems and hymns that are deeply Christian yet are filled with hedges, blackbirds, sea, moor and headlands.

One prayer requests the help of the trinity and lists the parts of the body in great detail, including septum, epiglottis and (the poet is female) cervix. Another blesses the udders of a cow as it is being milked.

Medieval prayers are complemented by excerpts from such writers as St Patrick (probably Welsh but famous for his work in Ireland) Pelagius, also of Welsh origin but one of the most notorious heresiarchs due to his rejection of original sin, and John Scotus Eriugena, the ninth-century philosopher-theologian influenced by Christian Neoplatonism. Each of these exhibits some of the distinctively Celtic Christian characteristics.

I was particularly pleased to see a scattering of Welsh poets, from Dafydd ap Gwilym's "The Mass in the Grove," in which he sees all the elements of the sacrament in a grove of trees in a valley (though in another poem spends his time when he is actually in church ogling the girls), plus extracts from the poems of twentieth-century mystic Waldo Williams and Church in Wales vicar Euros (pronounced *Ay-ross*, not like the currency Euro) Bowen's "Eulogy on his Refrigerator".

As this is in the Annotated & Explained series there is a facing page commentary. I glanced at this occasionally for factual detail, but in general the poems and prayers speak for themselves.

Perhaps no poem expresses the odd enjambment of Christianity and nature as well as the following from the Carmina Gadelica (p.91),

Help me to avoid every sin,
And the source of every sin to forsake;
And as the mist scatters on the crest of the hills,
May each ill haze clear from my soul, O God.

Andrew Phillip Smith

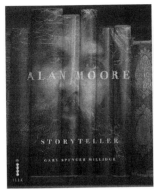

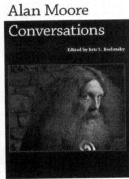

Alan Moore: Storyteller

Alan Moore: Conversations

Alan Moore: Comics as Performance, Fiction As Scalpel

A major and revolutionary figure in comics since the 1980s, Alan Moore's status has been elevated to that of a hugely significant figure in popular culture. Yet he has clung to his roots, living in a terraced house in Northampton, ordinary on the outside, apart from a carved head above the front door, but inwardly transformed into an Aladdin's Cave of occult decoration, complete with a cavernous ritual space in his cellar. His general fame is largely due to the Hollywood movie adaptations of his comics, yet he despises these and, since the production of V For Vendetta, has declined all income from them, passing his share of the money on to the artists who collaborated with him.

These three books are the most recent in a succession of books about the writer, being, respectively, a visual biography, a collection of interviews and a work of literary criticism. Previous books on Moore have included a summary of his life and works by Lance Parkin in the Pocket Essentials series, the texts of two interviews by Brian Baker, two separate collections for his fiftieth birthday, one focusing on tributes, the other consisting of extensive interviews accompanied by rare illustrations, and Jess Nevins' series of annotations on *The League of Extraordinary Gentlemen*.

Here I should state my own involvement. In addition to interviewing Alan for issue 1 of *The Gnostic*, and receiving permission to include his essay "Fossil Angels" in issue 4, I have been working on an unauthorised biography of Alan Moore for a few years. It was therefore with a sinking heart that I read that Gary Spencer Millidge—a talented comic creator in his own right (read his brilliant but unfinished *Strangehaven* series)--was putting together a biography of Moore with the full cooperation of the man himself, and access to the writer's personal archives.

While this is a wonderful book it falls well short of being a thorough biography, much to my relief. It is a great slab of a hardcover, heavily illustrated, with superb design and some elaborate production values, which include fold-outs and Moore's thumbnail sketches for comics pages reproduced on the endpapers. Though it is 350 pages long, the wealth of visual illustration takes up about three-quarters of the book with only what must be about 30,000 words of text.

The first chapters cover, of course, Moore's early life in a generally chronological sequence. Once Millidge reaches the stage where Moore has become a jobbing comics writer the narrative disintegrates into a series of informed summaries of his works, generally arranged in double-page spreads, with occasional articles and cut-outs on other aspects of his life and works. This is a problem intrinsic to the material, and one that I have come across while writing my own biography of Moore, but after a while the book ceases to be a biography proper and is rather an overview of Moore's work.

The book's semi-authorised status appears to have limited Millidge's coverage of some of the more difficult aspects of Moore's life and character. For instance, though his dislike of corporations is noted, there is no mention of Moore's deteriorating relationships with his previous collaborators (of which he has spoken publicly) nor of his tendency to exile friends and associates when he feels that his trust has been broken. Though Grant Morrison's name appears in the index, his public feud with Moore (instigated and prolonged, it must be said, by Morrison's public digs at Moore) Morrison is mentioned only as one of a list of writers who has been influenced by Moore. Nor is there any reference to Moore's ill-considered attacks on contemporary comics, few of which he seems to have read. My guess is that having been given so much help from Moore, Millidge simply didn't have the heart (or perhaps the word count) to address these aspects of Moore's life.

Alan Moore: Storyteller is very accessible to those who may only have read Watchmen and a couple of Moore's most popular comics, but it has plenty of goodies for the dedicated fan. These include the script for an unpublished episode of *V For Vendetta*, rejected with good reason by series artist David Lloyd, the massive chart that plots out the character development for each issue of the incomplete *Big Numbers* project (though the edges of the chart are cut off and a magnifying glass is essential to read it properly), thumbnail sketches used by Moore to design pages prior to producing typewritten scripts, and a host of other fascinating material and personal photographs.

Over the years Moore has written and performed music. This ranges from just enjoying himself performing semi-comic songs on stage with the Sinister Ducks and the Emperors of Ice Cream to a series of brilliant multimedia performances marrying the spoken word with music, visuals and dancing, such as *The Birth Caul*, *Snakes and Ladders* and *Angel Passage*, his meditation on William Blake, an extract of which appeared in *The Gnostic* 1. An extensive selection of his musical work is included on the CD which accompanies the book. It's a wonderful volume for Moore fans but fortunately leaves plenty of room for the more thorough biography that I still intend to complete.

Alan is a superb interviewee. As he once said, just give him a keyword and he'll ramble on about it for half an hour. *Alan Moore: Conversations* collects representative interviews from the full span of his professional life, beginning with a rare 1981 interview for the Society of Strip Illustrators. There are important interviews missing from this book, for instance Gary Groth's mammoth 1991 interview, Eddie Campbell's interview on Magic, included in *A Disease of Language*, the Blather interview available online, Pádraig Ó Méalóid's recent series of interviews and, I suppose, my own interview with him. Still, these interviews— which, as a number of wags have pointed out, are hardly conversations as Alan dominates the text so much—are full of colour and contain edifying and entertaining insights on everything from the creation of comics and other stories, to the nature of fiction itself,. To anarchism and pornography. Moore has a distinctive voice in both the literal and metaphorical senses, and his English Midlands rumble is always audible.

Comics as Performance is a more specialised publication, drawing on Moore's entire career to contextualise and analyse his work. Since I grew up with his comics from *2000AD* onwards and inhabited Thatcher's Britain (*V*, *Halo Jones*) and endured the cold war (*Watchmen*) and broadly shared the same cultural sphere with many of my musical and literary tastes overlapping with Moore's, plus the interest in occultism, there is much here that is obvious to me, but it may not be so for others, particularly those who are not of an age or nationality to understand the cultural backdrop. The academic lit-crit speak can be a little wearying, but it is not excessive, and overall the book provides an interesting perspective on aspects of Moore's work. The four chapters look at Moore's formal aspects of his work, at his approach to time and space in his stories, at his relationship to and reflection of changing English identity and an entire chapter on Moore's pornographic *Lost Girls*.

Moore himself was initially hostile to

academic study of his work, but has since read some of the studies and come around, to the extent of feeling that he has been shown aspects of his work of which he was unaware.

Each of these books is recommended to anyone who wishes to explore Moore's work in depth.

Andrew Phillip Smith

Biocentrism: How Life and Consciousness are the Keys to Understanding the True Nature of the Universe. **Robert Lanza and Bob Berman. Benbella Books. 200pp. $14.95.**

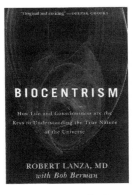

Many New Age writers (let's just use this as a term of convenience) have proposed that consciousness is central to the universe, drawing on the role of the observer or of measurement in quantum-level experimentation physics and the neurological discoveries that our perceptions of what appears to be the physical world are formed in the brain.

It is all the more impressive to discover that the author of this book is a widely-respected biologist who is a leader in his field. Lanza builds up seven principles to show that it is biology that is primary to existence, not physics. Though it may seem self-evident, there is no scientific experiment or observation that can take place without consciousness, simply because it is we humans who are doing the experiments. Though we commonly imagine otherwise, there is no objective universe out there because any perception of it involves a subject as perceiver. It is indeed blindingly obvious, but like the rest of us, the whole of physics, even perhaps the whole of science, excepting quantum physics, fails to notice most of the time.

Along with various observations on quantum physics he brings in the Goldilocks principle— why the universe is just right, not too hot, not too cold, for biological (let alone human) life. In fact he gives two pages of physical constants which are fine-tuned for the development of life. If any of these is minutely altered the resulting physics could not produce a universe that could support life.

The science is gently explained at a primer level, though Lanza is very careful to delineate all the objections to the double slit experiment and shows how elaborations of the basic experiment have answered and clarified these objections.

Interspersed with his central argument are anecdotes of Lanza's origins in an ill-educated and poor family and his ascent through the scientific world. These, and the folksy jokes that are sprinkled throughout the book, weren't quite to my taste, but they, and Lanza and Berman's facility for simple exposition, make for a light read.

The book merely sets up the principles of Biocentrism and doesn't indicate what might really be done with the theory and approach, but this is a stimulating and bold thesis.

Arthur Craddock

Austin Osman Spare: The Life and Legend of London's Lost Artist. Phil Baker. Strange Attractor Press. Hardcover. 272pp. £25.

In contrast to Aleister Crowley, who remains infamous in the popular imagination for his outrageous persona, questionable practices and arguably destructive influence on those who know him, yet is celebrated by occultists of many stripes, Austin Osman Spare remains on the margins, unknown to popular culture, wilding a quiet influence in occultism, largely through the adoption of his sigil technique by chaos magicians.

Phil Baker's is the first biography that utilises truly critical scholarship. Baker assesses the truthfulness and reliability of the many anecdotes about Spare, a substantial number of which were transmitted by Kenneth Grant in a long series of books and articles. While he does his best to pass sober judgement over difficult materials somehow the myth of Spare still survives. Careful scholarship and consideration is not caustic enough to scour away a good story.

The book's subtitle demonstrates that Baker is keen to reclaim Spare as an artist. Despite his creative approach to magic and his opaque writings it seems clear that visual art took the lion's share of his time and a central place in his inner life.

Born in 1886, Spare had an ordinary working-class childhood, neither really impoverished nor privileged, until his facility in drawing and painting led him to art college.

After a series of successful gallery exhibitions he retreated from the art world. Spare lived a life of genuine poverty. In 1941 during the blitz a bomb destroyed his studio, including all the paintings he had been working on. He had been out on duty as a fire warden and was therefore saved from death. He was homeless for a while, then found a cramped basement in which he could work. Having no bed he slept on two chairs pushed together. Baker shows that Spare's poverty was certainly no legend.

Spare acquired a reputation for boundless sexual appetite, satisfied mainly by congress with legions of worn out old washerwomen who were happy to oblige. He certainly sketched nudes of older women who, according to conventional taste, were ugly or undesirable. But Baker feels that most of Spare's sexual congress was achieved by means of the member with which he held his paint brush.

Certainly his invention of the technique of sigil magic, using the letters of a sentence that expresses a magical desire to form an original design which is then "charged" by the magician on entering an intense state of consciousness, typically through orgasm—referred to as gnosis—shows that he was not unfamiliar with masturbation. Chaos magic has made this into his most significant contribution to occult practice.

This is a superb biography, full of careful detail expressed in balanced prose. The design and production values are superb, as is typical of the publisher, Strange Attractor Press. It is clearly a huge step forward in assessing the life of Austin Osman Spare. I can't say that I felt that I understood who Spare was, or what he was expressing in his strange images and baroque prose. Having to spoken to a couple of people more familiar with his work than I am, this seems to be by no means unusual. As Baker writes (p.150), "Biography can only follow its subject so far, especially a character like Spare, whose real life was internal."

Andrew Phillip Smith

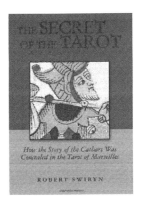

The Secret of the Tarot: How the Story of the Cathars Was Concealed in the Tarot of Marseilles

Robert Swiryn. Paperback. Createspace. 274pp. $13.95.

Thee beautiful and mysterious imagery of the major arcana of the Tarot has inspired countless interpretations and explanations. Drawing on hints from others, Robert Swiryn sees the Tarot--or, at least the Marseilles Tarot--as originating as a memorial to the specific teachings and tragic history of the Cathars of southern France. He recognises that, at the earliest, the Tarot of Marseilles is a good 200 years after the fall of the Cathars, and admits that there are problems with the tarot containing survivals of Catharism but suggests that the teachings and memories of the Cathars may have survived underground for this time.

The first third of the book looks at the history oft he Cathars and general issues regarding the tarot, while the bulk of the book treats each trump card individually. There are reproductions of each card and additional images, but the resolution is poor, which is a pity because the author has obviously taken some trouble in licensing the rights and obtaining permissions.

He draw on what might seem like incidental detail in the images, for instance, the two figures kneeling before the pontiff in card V, the Pope, are seen as the papal legates, who travelled in pairs. The Pope is taken to be Innocent III, the two legates the Cistercian brothers Rainer and Guy who went to the Languedoc to oppose the heresy, or as the Inquisitors sent to the Toulouse. Or as Ralph and Peter of Castelnau. The latter's murder when he was just returning to Rome sparked off the Albigensian Crusade. Swiryn comes up with other possibilities, which is intellectually honest but diminishes the possibility of any definitive identification. There are simply too many possibilities for each card to make the case convincing.

Not every card is interpreted historically. For instance, the Wheel of Fortune is seen as teaching the Cathar doctrine of transmigration. He sees a Chi-rho in the spokes of the wheel in the particular Marseilles Tarot.

The Hanged Man was a medieval symbol of a traitor, hence the card could depict any number of traitors or turncoats who joined the Crusaders--and there are a good many to select from.

The Tower could represent montségur or any number of towers which destroyed in the Languedoc in the course of siege warfare.

Andrew Phillip Smith

The Inner Lives of Medieval Inquisitors. Karen Sullivan. Hardcover. University of Chicago Press. 312pp. $45.

Popular culture has a pretty powerful image of the Inquisition, all dungeons and pointy hoods, so extreme as to be comical—think Monty Python. It's as unassailable a belief as the glimmerless darkness of the Dark Ages, no amount of historical revisionism seems able to shift it. Modern sympathy will so obviously be for the heretics, Inquisitors figure as the "baddies", as psychotic sadists. Karen Sullivan is doing her bit to offer a different view.

She sets about trying to examine what we can ascertain about the worldview and rationalisation of the orthodox side of things from the lives or rather- as much as possible- the words of Bernard of Clairvaux (1090-1153), Dominic Guzman ("St Dominic", 1170-1221), Conrad of Marburg (1180-1233), Peter of Verona ("St Peter Martyr", 1203-1252), Bernard Gui (1261/2-1331), Bernard Délicieux (1260-1319) and Nicholas Eymerich (c1320-99). Granted, it's not that easy to probe into the inner worlds of people from so long ago, but sometimes it's very dry going. As someone laconically said in an online review of another of her books, it's not "exactly a page- turner" but if you persist past the introduction and the first chapter, it does get better! The Introduction has the tone of an apologetic wink from one academic to others assuming perhaps that the general readership will skip it. Her prose is often a little turgid. There is also a lack of a declared point of view; she resists clearly stating where she stands on a point again and again, I had the feeling that there was a hidden sympathy but not declaring it seems like a false attempt to appear neutral. Surely it's not unnatural for a writer to have their own beliefs; if they are declared upfront then the reader can weigh them as part of the writing.

The lives, then, that are studied cover a three hundred year period and are understandably different. But as a selection it documents a period which was decisive for western European culture, leading, on the one hand to the cruel murder of the burgeoning alternative (heretical) Christianities which developed at the time and on the other to the development of a new rigidity in orthodox Christianity which paved the way for the horrors of the Spanish Inquisition, among other things and closed off the church from many possible developments. The new social structures of the Middle Ages led to a greater openness in society. The greater freedom of the common people; exchange brought about by travel on the crusades, all led to increased criticism of the established church and new ways of thinking-heresies- became more widespread. Catharism in particular, having achieved widespread acceptance among the landowners of the Languedoc, had become established enough to be seen as a great threat. It wasn't until well into the thirteenth century that inquisition became institutionalized, in 1231 death penalty for unrepentant heretics, in 1252 torture was allowed. In these writings we see different ways that orthodoxy viewed heretics. Are these misled souls who can be rescued or devious representatives of evil who must at all costs be expunged? Bernard of Clairvaux was not involved in inquisitorial trials but he spoke out against Abelard and others and he saw the heretic as an embodiment of evil trying to destroy the faith hence, although the cleric should do what he can to persuade him of the error of his ways, he should not enter into discussion since it is unlikely to succeed due to their essential wickedness. At the time neither he nor the church actively advocated violence, yet they tacitly approved of the violence which happened.

We see a change over time, though not a straight line progression, from the mindset of Bernard of Clairvaux who saw heretics as wolves and serpents, to Dominic who went out among them and saw them as misled and rescuable,

Conrad saw them as worshipping evil itself. Peter of Verona, from an heretical family, staunch inquisitor whose martyrdom at the hands of the heretics (which he embraced) served to rigidify the catholic attitude. Finally, Nicholas Eymerich who wrote the Directorium inquisitorum, while he may not have done much himself, nonetheless set the pattern for the ensuing years of the Spanish Inquisition, a frankly barbaric and duplicitous torturing technique that essentially sees any accused as guilty and the main point being to wring confession out of them. Fascinating to see how unperturbed he is by the idea of killing an innocent man- it was a different relationship to the idea of dying for it was seen as offering the innocent man a chance of glory. She treats Bernard Délicieux as an example of someone who could easily have been on the side of the inquisitors and used a lot of the same sort of reasoning against them and yet also had something modern: the ability to see that the inquisitors were actively forcing others into an antagonistic role.

Finally, in the conclusion, she lays some of her cards on the table in an evident analogy to current times. What defines the outsider? If they belong to a different, alien creed which seems to threaten our existence, are we not justified in torturing to protect our own? If we believe him incapable of humanity, do we still have to be humane? The sort of self justifications that were used in the Middle Ages is illustrated by the progression of responses seen in this book. She leaves then the open question; what kind of self justifications are used now?

Tessa Finn

Stealing Fire From Heaven: The Rise of Modern Western Magic. **Neville Drury. OUP. 376pp. $29.95/£18.99.**

Over the decades there have been many histories of western esotericism and occultism, both from an insider's point of view and from a scholarly perspective. In the former category we have such extravagant classics as Eliphas Levi's History of Occultism and Manly P Hall's Secret teachings of All the Ages, in the latter works such as James Webb's The Occult Establishment and The Occult Underground, on to recent works such as Nicholas Goodrick-Clarke's The Western Esoteric Traditions.

Stealing Fire From Heaven manages to straddle the two categories, though it functions as, and is published as, an academic work. Neville Drury has written books such as *Don Juan, Mescalito and Modern Magic*, which suggests similarities between Castaneda's work and western esotericsm and proposes the Golden Dawn system as being more suitable for westerners, and straightforward esoterica such as The Tarot Workbook. Drury's doctrinal studies have also involved him in academic work on the magical tradition. Thus Stealing Fire From Heaven has an unusually sympathetic tone. Drury has met some of the figures he discusses, including artist H.R. Giger, witch and artist Rosaleen Norton and various characters involved in the neo-shamanic tradition.

Arthur Craddock

The Cook, the Rat and the Heretic by **Hugo Soskin.**

Summerdale. £7.99.315pp.

Hugo Soskin is the son of Henry Lincoln, famous for his co-authorship of *The Holy Blood and the Holy Grail* and other works that cover the Rennes-le-chateau mystery. Soskin makes much of his dislike of being called by his father's nom-de-plume Lincoln, and much of this book gives the impression of a fun-loving son eager to shrug off the esoteric obsessions of his famous father.

Soskin and his partner decide to travel down the Languedoc in their camper van. They end up staying at a restaurant and campsite near Rennes-le-chateau run by another Englishman, initially helping him to recover from a bad flood, but eventually establishing themselves and chef and helper.

The tone is blokeish throughout, full of slightly laboured funny stories, much drinking of local wine and a few spliffs. Soskin is unimpressed by his first visit to the village since his childhood and has never believed that there is anything significant to the mystery.

The steady stream of enthusiasts who arrive are called by him Rennies, referring to the anti-indigestion tablets. Despite his best efforts he gets drawn into the world of the Rennies, who include Rat Scabies, former drummer for the punk group the Damned. In one of those odd coincidences, the current keyboard player of The Damned, Monty Oxymoron, is a dedicated reader of *The Gnostic*!

In the final pages Soskin discourses on his take on the mystery. He sees it all as a series of unrelated coincidences assembled by the Priory of Sion which just happen to appeal to a post-religious western world.

It's an insubstantial memoir, which is entertaining enough but tries a bit too hard to be funny. To be fair it's categorised by the publisher under "Travel" and belongs more with the sub-genre of Englishmen having boozy fun in the south of France.

Biographies

Nicholas Baker-Brian is Lecturer in Theology at Cardiff University. He is an expert on the Religions of Late Antiquity, especially Manichaeism, and is the author of *Manichaeism in the Later Roman Empire: A Study of Augustine's Contra Adimantum* and *Manichaeism: An Ancient Faith Rediscovered.*

Jordan Bloom is associate editor of *The American Conservative* and a music reviewer at Tiny Mix Tapes, where this essay first appeared. He resides in Arlington, Virginia, a stone's throw from Babylon, and occasionally plays rock and roll.

Miguel Conner is the author of the novel *Stargazer* and host of the Internet radio show *Aeon Byte*, formerly *Coffee, Cigarettes and Gnosis. Voices of Gnosticism*, a selection of his interviews with scholars of Gnosticism is available from Bardic Press.

Arthur Craddock is having an existential crisis, but a good nap should sort him out. He has assembled the review copies he receives from *The Gnostic* into a small bungalow which serves to keep off the mid-Wales rain.

Stevan Davies is Professor of Religious Studies at Misericordia University. He has studied the non-canonical gospels and acts for over thirty years. Among his books are *The Gospel of Thomas and Christian Wisdom* (Bardic Press) *The Gospel of Thomas: Annotated and Explained,* *The Secret Book of John: Annotated and Explained* (both SkyLight Paths) and T*he Revolt of the Widows: The Social World of the Apocryphal Acts* (Bardic Press, 2012). He has also published *New Testament Fundamentals* and *Jesus the Healer: Possession, Trance and the Origins of Christianity,* to be republished by Bardic Press. His website (www.misericordia.edu/users/davies/thomas/thomas.htm) is a leading Internet resource on the Gospel of Thomas.

Sorita d'Este is an esoteric researcher, author and an initiatory Priestess of the Mysteries who manifests her knowledge and passion for knowledge and understanding through her work. She is best known for her research and work related to the Goddess Hekate, as well as for her ability to push at the boundaries of esoteric research and practice through her workshops, lectures and writing.

Scott Finch received his BFA from Louisiana State University in 1994 and his MFA from the Tyler School of Art at Temple University in 1996. Finch has exhibited at galleries across the United States and in Europe. He has been featured by the Critic's Choice Exhibition at the Dallas Visual Art Center, the Fleisher Art Challenge at the Fleisher Art Memorial in Philadelphia, and the Gulf South Regional Artists Exhibition at Bridge For Contemporary Art in New Orleans.

A Little World Made Cunningly is available digitally from http://graphicly.com/a-little-world/a-little-world-made-cunningly/gn

Tessa Finn graduated from University College Dublin in Biochemistry and Industrial Microbiology whilst writing poetry and being published in Dublin poetry magazines, always feeling that the best education is the one you give yourself by following your interests. When she's not just staring into space, her interests have led to work in cancer research, catering and winemaking and passionate dabbling in a broad range of things such as history, drama, esotericism, sculpting in bronze and baking.

Patrick Harpur is the author of *The Philosophers' Secret Fire: A History Of The Imagination*, *Daimonic Reality: A Field Guide to the Otherworld*, *A Complete Guide to the Soul* (UK)/ *The Secret Tradition of the Soul* (USA) and three novels including *Mercurius: The Marriage Of Heaven and Earth*.

Jeffrey S. Kupperman has studied hermetics, Kabbalah and the Western Mystery Tradition for the last fifteen years. He has degrees in psychology, graphic designs and religious studies, where his emphasis was in Western mythology as well as mystical and occult practices. He is the publisher and designer of the *Journal of the Western Mystery Tradition*.

Gary Lachman is the author of several books on the link between consciousness, culture, and alternative thought. His books include *Turn Off Your Mind: The Mystic Sixties and the Dark Side of the Age of Aquarius*; *A Secret History of Consciousness*; *In Search of P.D. Ouspensky*; *A Dark Muse*; *Rudolf Steiner: An Introduction to His Life and Thought*; *Politics and the Occult: The Left, the Right, and the Radically Unseen*, and *The Quest for Hermes Trismegistus*. As Gary Valentine he was a founding member of the rock group Blondie.

Sean Martin is a writer and filmmaker. His books include *The Knights Templar. The Cathars*, *Andrei Tarkovsky*, *The Gnostics: The First*

Christian Heretics, *Alchemy and Alchemists* and *The Black Death*. Among his films are *Mystery Play* (2001), and *The Notebooks of Cornelius Crow* (2005).

Petra Mundik currently holds the prestigious Prescott Postgraduate Scholarship in the School of Social and Cultural Studies at the University of Western Australia. She has published extensively on Cormac McCarthy.

Andrew Phillip Smith is the editor of *The Gnostic*, co-editor of *Foreskin Magazine* and editor emeritus of the Unification Church's twice-daily newsletter *Moonie!* His illegal investment of the millions accrued through his Gnostic pyramid-selling scam led to his arrest as a figure at the root of the Irish financial crisis. He is currently under what is to all intents and purposes house arrest as Occupy Dublin are constantly camped outside his front door.

Dean F. Wilson is an author, journalist, Gnostic and ceremonial magician. He was born in Dublin, Ireland and is a member of the Dublin Temple of the Magical Order of Aurora Aurea, a modern Golden Dawn group. His first non-fiction book, *Enochian Magic In Theory*, was published in February, 2012. See www.deanfwilson.com for more info.

Food for Thought

History is the endless repetition of the wrong way of living, and it'll start again tomorrow.

Lawrence Durrell

We are all hunting for rational reasons for believing in the absurd.

Lawrence Durrell

The Devil is a dualist. He's forever trying to make two out of one.

C.G. Jung

And I was in the mouths of lions. And the plan which they devised about me to release their Error and their senselessness - I did not succumb to them as they had planned. But I was not afflicted at all.

Second Treatise of the Great Seth

The entire system of salvation offered in Gnostic documents is at odds with that found in numerous New Testament texts. Gnosticism emphasizes esoteric knowledge and matter-spirit dualism. The focus of the New Testament is on the historical life, death, and resurrection of Jesus, not on some esoteric knowledge that Jesus revealed to the elite after Easter. And it is precisely the life, death, and resurrection of Jesus that is said to be the means of our salvation.

Ben Witherington III

"I call it [Gnosticism] the Gospel of Narcissism."
Ben Witherington III

The rulers of this most insecure of all worlds are rulers by accident. Inept, frightened pilots at the controls of a vast machine they cannot understand, calling in experts to tell them which buttons to push.

William S. Burroughs

He is not a man like me that I might answer him, that we might confront each other in court. If only there were someone to arbitrate between us, to lay his hand upon us both, someone to remove God's rod from me, so that his terror would frighten me no more. Then I would speak up without fear of him, but as it now stands with me, I cannot.

Book of Job 9:32-35

A separate issue is the return of ancient Gnostic ideas under the guise of the so-called New Age. We cannot delude ourselves that this will lead toward a renewal of religion. It is only a new way of practicing Gnosticism — that attitude of the spirit that, in the name of a profound knowledge of God, results in distorting his word and replacing it with purely human words. Gnosticism never completely abandoned the realm of Christianity. Instead, it has always existed side by side with Christianity, sometimes taking the shape of philosophical movement, but more often assuming the characteristics of a religion or para-religion in distinct, if not declared, conflict with all that is essentially Christian.

Pope John Paul II

Applying specific images from foreign traditions or assigning human features to her profundity causes one to miss the True Gnosis of Barbelo.

Barbelo can be anthropomorphized but not pictured, because our relationship to Barbelo is the relationship of a beloved infant to its loving Mother while still in the womb. She is warmth, light, nourishment. She is a Presence who is One with the Father, for how is an infant in the womb able to differentiate between the Mother in which he rests and the Father's presence which he senses as well? She is comfort and peace and the first Restriction, as the Womb is the first limitation experienced by the ensouled child.

Jeremy Puma

The world is a bell that is cracked: it clatters, but does not ring out clearly.

Johann Wolfgang von Goethe

What is required of us is that we love the difficult and learn to deal with it. In the difficult are the friendly forces, the hands that work on us. Right in the difficult we must have our joys, our happiness, our dreams: there against the depth of this background, they stand out, there for the first time we see how beautiful they are.

Rainer Maria Rilke

Civilization is the agreement to have gaps between wars.

Jeff Lint.

Everything that is squint-eyed, doddering and grotesque is summed up for me in this one word, God.

André Breton

The Outcast

Sometimes when alone
At the dark close of day,
Men meet an outlawed majesty
And hurry away.

They come to the lighted house;
They talk to their dear;
They crucify the mystery
With words of good cheer.

When love and life are over,
And flights at an end,
On the outcast majesty
They lean as a friend.

AE (George Russell)

From the Weekly World News 25th May 1985

Also Available from Bardic Press

The Gnostic 1 & The Gnostic 2 & The Gnostic 3 & The Gnostic 4

Voices of Gnosticism
Miguel Conner

Boyhood With Gurdjieff; Gurdjieff Remembered; Balanced Man
by Fritz Peters (not available in the USA)

New Nightingale, New Rose: Poems From the Divan of Hafiz
translated by Richard Le Gallienne

The Quatrains of Omar Khayyam:
Three Translations of the Rubaiyat
translated by Edward Fitzgerald, Justin McCarthy
and Richard Le Gallienne

Door of the Beloved: Ghazals of Hafiz
translated by Justin McCarthy

The Gospel of Thomas and Christian Wisdom
Stevan Davies

The Four Branches of the Mabinogi
Will Parker

Christ In Islam
James Robson

Don't Forget: P.D. Ouspensky's Life of Self-Remembering
Bob Hunter

Songs of Sorrow and Joy
Ashford Brown

Planetary Types: The Science of Celestial Influence
Tony Cartledge

Visit our website at www.bardic-press.com
email us at info@bardic-press.com

Made in the USA
Lexington, KY
21 September 2012